Cultural Diversity, Worship, and Australian Baptist Church Life

New Wineskins Volume 2

National Library of Australia Cataloguing-in-Publication entry:
Title: Cultural Diversity, Worship, and Australian Baptist Church Life
editors: Darrell Jackson, Darren Cronshaw.

ISBN: 9780992275532 (paperback)

Series: New Wineskins; Vol. 2.

Subjects: Baptists--Australia--Religious life.
 Cultural pluralism--Religious aspects--Baptists.

Other Creators/Contributors:
Jackson, Darrell Richard, editor.
Cronshaw, Darren, editor.

Dewey Number: 286.194

Cultural Diversity, Worship, and Australian Baptist Church Life

New Wineskins Volume 2

Edited by
Darrell Jackson & Darren Cronshaw

Morling Press
First Published 2016
122 Herring Rd Macquarie Park NSW 2113 Australia
Phone: +61 2 9878 0201
Email: enquiries@morling.edu.au
www.morlingcollege.com

© **Morling Press 2016**

This publication is copyright. Other than for the purposes of study and subject to the conditions of the Copyright Act, no part of it in any form or by any means (electronic, mechanical, micro-copying, photocopying or otherwise) may be reproduced, stored in a retrieval system or transmitted without the permission of the publisher.

Scripture quotations are from The Holy Bible, English Standard Version® (ESV®), copyright© 2001 by Crossway Bibles, a publishing ministry of Good News Publishers. Used by permission. All rights reserved.

ISBN: 978-0-9922755-3-2

Designed by Brugel Images and Design **www.brugel.com.au**
Cover designed by Beni Creative **www.benicreative.com.au**

Contents

Foreword
Tim Costello . . . . *vii*

Part A:
Cultural Diversity and Australia's Baptist Churches 1

Australian Baptist Churches and the Marginalisation of Ethnicity
Darrell Jackson *3*

Ministry in Urban Aboriginal Communities
Billy Williams *19*

Baptists Responding to Cultural Diversity
Ian Duncum and Ruth Powell *31*

Being the Church without Four Walls
Marc Chan *49*

Strengthening Intercultural Ministry in Local Congregations
Sue Holdsworth and Julian Holdsworth *59*

Drinking New Wine Together
Stephen Chatelier *77*

Welcoming the Stranger
Gordon Stewart *87*

Part B:
Transforming the Worship and Life of Australia's Baptist Churches 99

New Parishes for Anglicans and Baptists?
Gordon Preece *101*

Contemporary Spirituality and Mission
Philip Hughes *119*

Two Streams Converging
Beth Barnett *133*

Transforming Expectations
Frank D. Rees *143*

Re: Baptism: A Case for Removing the Requirements of Rebaptism for Membership in Baptist Churches in NSW and ACT
Ben Rodgers. *155*

The Lord's Supper as Meaning-Full Sacrament
Anne Klose *169*

The Liturgical Participation of Children in Small Churches
Alison Sampson and Nathan Nettleton *181*

Growing the Seeds of Emergence
Darren Cronshaw and Stacey Wilson *195*

The Trinity and the Ontology of Worship
Jeff Pugh. *209*

Improvising a Renewed Story at AuburnLife
Darren Cronshaw. *225*

Conclusion
Darren Cronshaw and Darrell Jackson *241*

Endnotes
All Contributors *245*

Foreword

Tim Costello

Christianity is a universal faith and so by necessity it must encompass both unity and diversity. Australian society has always encompassed diversity and, although historically this has often been problematised, in recent decades it has also become the focus for celebration and for many a defining element in national identity.

I think it is true that in Australia "multiculturalism" has not been mainly a principle of policy, but more a descriptive term. It has not entirely escaped the ideological mauling of the "culture wars" but at the same time I do not think it has excited the same degree of fear, hostility, and political backlash that has been experienced in some other countries. Even in the context of confusion and disharmony about the nature and place of Islam in relation to Western culture, public support for diversity and the belief that diversity is good for Australia remain strong.

Australia has long been, and will long remain, a country of immigration, and the importance of building community across cultures is hard to overstate.

For all Christian churches, cultural diversity brings both opportunities and challenges within the church and in our interactions and relationships with people "outside", including Christians of other traditions, and people of other faiths or none.

For Baptists in particular, some of the distinctive characteristics of our churches are very relevant to how we might understand and respond to diversity. For example, the historical Baptist aversion to state religion or uniformity of religious practice remains important as a foundation for appreciating pluralism. Also, the tradition of congregational church government allows for innovation, adaptation, and for organic change at the local level.

But most important is a theological aspect. Any specifically Baptist understanding of diversity must start with an appreciation of the significance and impact of believer's baptism. As Karen Armstrong has discussed in her stimulating book, *Paul: The Misunderstood Apostle*, in baptism everything changes. Among those who emerge spiritually reborn from the waters of baptism, there is neither Jew nor Greek, male nor female, slave or free. It is baptism that completes the gap and resolves the paradox of diversity and unity.

The papers which make up this volume are not just about diversity, they are themselves extremely varied in their framing ideas, their methods, and their conclusions. They do not contain definitive answers so much as vital and varied insights, and they form part of a necessary and enriching conversation.

Reformation is not something which happened once in history, but a process of rethinking and renewing the ways we practise faith in community that needs to keep happening over and over again. A living church must not become a predictable and static institution. A thriving church will always be one where there is a certain amount of ferment and exploration.

These papers are a sign of good health, of churches that are alive and are doing the important intellectual and spiritual work of renewal.

Congratulations to all who have contributed to this work, and I earnestly pray that it will be well read, messages taken to heart, and played out in ever more lively and inclusive communities of faith across our country.

Reverend Tim Costello AO
Chief Executive Officer
World Vision Australia

Part A:
Cultural Diversity and Australia's Baptist Churches

Australian Baptist Churches and the Marginalisation of Ethnicity

Darrell Jackson

In this chapter I introduce the need for a theology of ethnicity and ethnic diversity that is biblical and contextually engaged. I intend to demonstrate its relevance to the search for Australian ecclesial practices that are sensitive to issues of identity, integration, power, and the embrace of ethnic particularity.

"You're not ethnic, you look like us!"

I arrived as an economic migrant in Australia on the 18th January 2012, arriving here on a 457 temporary residents' visa. I'd travelled from the UK with the three other members of my family; all of them dual nationals. As a newly appointed member of faculty at the Baptist Theological College in NSW I rapidly settled in to the rhythm of teaching as the new semester got underway.

In the August of 2012, the annual gathering of Baptists in NSW and the ACT, "*Revive*", was a great chance to get to meet new friends and colleagues from across the State. The workshop programme was typically varied and I picked one or two to fit around my coffee shop programme. A workshop on "Inclusivity" was on my list. In the workshop I discovered that Baptist churches were making great efforts to include females, young people, and the disabled and that this was also true of "many of the ethnic churches". During the Q&A I queried this use of the term "ethnic church", suggesting that we were all ethnic, that to use it solely of others was possibly a form of exclusion, and that actually it was very hard to imagine what a "*non*-ethnic church" would look like.

At the end of the workshop, feeling like I'd rained on the parade ground, an elderly lady approached me and told me that she understood what I was trying to say but that I was not ethnic because, "Well, you look like us!"

I was subsequently asked to preach at the annual Assembly of NSW/ACT in 2013 and took the opportunity to address ethnic diversity and gender equality. Some described it afterwards as "brave"; I simply saw it as an opportunity to say one or two obvious things that I believe are vital to the health of our Baptist movement.

Ethnic alterity: The ethnic "other"

The trend towards identifying some churches in Sydney as "ethnic" is the characteristic way of describing those Baptist churches which draw a majority of their members from particular ethnic backgrounds that are distinct from the white Australian majority (and presumably also seen by the same white Australian majority as distinct from the indigenous, Aboriginal Australian minority).

This usage is what social scientists label "alterity" (or "otherness"). In other words, ethnicity is something used to describe people who are "other" than ourselves. If "ethnic" always means somebody else, it means that they are not necessarily *my* responsibility and the "ethnic issue" will always remain somebody else's problem; something that *they* have to learn to deal with.

Marginalising the experience of ethnicity

After my presentation at the annual 2013 Assembly I spoke with the white pastor of a Chinese Baptist Church in Sydney. Their story was fascinating and in a Facebook response to something I posted, they subsequently wrote,

> Having worked in a Chinese Church for over 10 years, I was sometimes given the distinct impression by some Anglo-Christians that I had a less prestigious, second-class pastoral position, which would not have given me as valuable ministry experience as more "mainstream" churches. So-called ethnic churches in Australia are often looked down on as outside of whatever is happening in the "proper" churches.[1]

The distress this causes me is probably shared by many other Baptists in NSW and the attitudes that generate these kinds of dismissive attitudes are familiar across the denominations. In 1996, Pope John-Paul II's *World Migration Day Message* took the opportunity to remind Roman Catholics that such attitudes were unwelcome, for "in the Church no one is a stranger, and the Church is not foreign to anyone, anywhere".

The consequences of marginalising ethnicity

Persisting with the usage of the category "ethnic church" has a number of unfortunate consequences. In particular, I'm convinced that,

- It will hinder the ability of Australian Baptist Churches to speak with clarity about our common Christian identity.
- We will continue to miss out on the mutually transformative process of integrating Baptists who are living in Australia as second- or third-generation migrants from non-Caucasian ethnic backgrounds.
- The existence and experience of the "ethnic church" will continue to be seen as marginal to the life of the various State Baptist Unions and, therefore, less valuable.
- The status of the "ethnic churches" will remain firmly in the category "foreign", "transitional", and "exotic".

Of course it's possible to build a case arguing that integrating ethnic diversity has many pragmatic advantages, but it also requires a theological response.

The first thing which must then be said is that theology has not simply been a distracting activity for academics and priests down through the centuries. It has been used to authenticate and validate a range of social policies and social institutions, from dictatorship to democracy, from monarchy to republicanism, from free-market capitalism to social democracy, from slavery to emancipation, as well as from apartheid to multiculturalism.

That's why it's so important to understand how and why theological positions have been adopted by theologians at various points in history. Christendom has its "shadow side" when it comes to its treatment of ethnic and cultural difference; so too does the Reformation.

In the context of our discussion it's important to remain sensitive to the question of majority–minority relationships, especially to the discriminatory abuse of privilege, power, and authority when dealing with minority ethnic and cultural groups.

Oliver Buswell argues that racial [sic] discrimination is not simply an issue of skin colour but is a question of the determination of one group of people to dominate and subdue another.[2] This requires a theological diagnosis and prognosis for the desire to dominate and subdue is fundamentally an issue of flawed and broken human nature. In short, it is an all-too-human sin.

Established majority cultures protect institutional norms

The use of certain forms of language can be a way of reinforcing norms. Referring to "Australian Baptist Churches and the Ethnic Churches" implies a mainstream and a margin. Power always resides with the mainstream and preserving the status quo is the price of this particular form of idolatry. In contrast, renewal and innovation are typically characteristic of the margins.

I want my students at Morling College to understand that "culture" (and there are a myriad of definitions) is a product of ideas, artefacts, and *institutions*. Most analyses of culture focus only on the first two. The institution as a guardian of cultural norms has to be acknowledged if cultural and ethnic power and privilege are to be adequately taken into account.

As I have been pondering this question in the context of our own Association of Baptist Churches in NSW/ACT I've tried to reflect on what the Baptist "institution" in NSW/ACT has at stake in this issue. I'm still searching for an answer but, as a theological educator, I understand the need to recognise the new global realities. In the Morling classroom, I work hard to deal intentionally with our own ethnic diversity and multiculturalism. In this, I've taken a cue from others who are recognising that

> practical theologians, ethicists, historians, and other scholars of religion have all commented on the need for classrooms that honor [*sic*] multicultural perspectives (Kitano 1997). Most scholars today understand the value of a culturally sensitive classroom and may well devise syllabi that reflect the perspectives of different racial ethnic minority groups (Green and Stortz 2006).[5]

I'd be the first to acknowledge that there's a level of institutional self-preservation involved here. This simply recognises that theological institutions in today's world cannot continue to act as if they were islands of Caucasian privilege. My archaically titled "EM308 Cross-cultural communication" classes are, I hope, laboratories involving inter-cultural participation and dialogue, rather than lectures describing the transfer of information by the representatives of one cultural group to the recipients of another.

Daniel Aleshire writes,

> If theological schools don't learn how to be effective educational institutions for racially and culturally diverse students and effective theological institutions for the communities they will serve, they will simply waste away as viable institutions by the end of this century.[4]

Does God have a stake in ethnicity?

If my encounter with an ethnically blind workshop participant at *Revive* was the primary stimulus for this ongoing journey in theological reflection, the second stimulus was the following quote, stumbled across at an early stage of the journey.

> ...few missiologists are developing a theology of "ethnicity" itself. This task is becoming increasingly urgent because the demands of ethnicity will probably dominate the world's agenda at least in the opening decades of the new millennium.[5]

A biblical theology of ethnicity portrays it as the pinnacle of God's creative acts (Gen 10:32), laments the consequent rebellion and hubris (Gen 11:4), declares it to lie within the scope of God's missionary purposes (Gen 12:2-3), incorporates it into the body of Christ (Rev 7:9), and concludes with the eschatological worship of God, enriched by the contributions of ethnically diverse participants (Rev 19:15). Ambiguously, it's possible to read the biblical narrative of ethnic diversity as both a consequence of human pride and as a consequence of divine creation. For example, we can note the following:

Ethnic and cultural diversity are a consequence of human rebellion

- In Genesis 11, the diversity imposed upon the nations is described as a judgement of God upon the peoples of Babel.

- In Exodus 1:1ff. Pharaoh "plays on the prejudices and fears of his own people to justify his own racist attitudes... the story of the exodus presents a classical example of racial conflict. It shows how racial prejudices lead to persecution and oppression, coupled with economic exploitation, and thus to forced migration".[6]

- Pentecost reverses the curse of diversity, overcoming mutual incomprehension and suspicion, and proleptically demonstrates the nature of God's reign.

Ethnic and cultural diversity are a consequence of creation

- In Genesis 1 the command "Be fruitful and multiply" results in diversity among the nations and is seen as a consequence of God's intention to bless the inhabitants of the earth.

- Karl Barth understood the "Table of Nations" in Genesis 10 as the pinnacle of God's creative acts. It's possible to understand the nations as an aspect of God's renewed promise to Noah's children and grandchildren after the Flood.

- In Ruth 1:1ff. Ruth demonstrates the ethnic diversity that can exist within the nation of Israel. The book of Ruth portrays its central character as a non-Israelite who is prepared to embrace the religious convictions and customs of her mother-in-law, Naomi. A Moabite can find a place among the Semitic Jews — presumably we can imagine God smiling. Ruth's story points to potential complexities, however. How does her religious conversion impact her sense of ethnic and cultural identity? The honest reader is left with the distinct feeling that intercultural integration sets the parameters for Ruth's decision. Assimilation is neither sought nor urged. This is the free decision of a young Moabitess.

- Pentecost is an affirmation of ethnic and cultural diversity, relativising it in the light of the unifying Spirit of Pentecost. The reference to Pentecost is impossible to avoid in the context of relations between the different Christian traditions. In the account of Acts 2, the miraculous work of the Spirit enables each person present to hear the word of the apostles in their own mother tongue. The miracle can be understood to have affected either the speakers or the listeners. Either the apostles speak several languages at the same time or each person present hears the word of the apostles in their mother tongue.

- When a migrant arrives in a second country, he or she may decide to learn the language which is spoken there. At a certain point they manage to think in the language of the country, finally to dream in the new language. The language of faith is hidden deep inside in the ethnic identity of each person. In his Epistles, Paul is twice filled with wonder at being able to call God *Abba*, an expression of a similar form of spiritual and cultural intimacy.

- Eric Barreto makes the startlingly insightful comment that the gift of tongues in Acts 2 is not merely an act of divine simultaneous interpretation.

> The fact that simultaneous interpretation requires expert knowledge of the cultural assumptions and norms which shape language requires the work of the Holy Spirit to be a work of simultaneous and multiple inculturations: "the Holy Spirit accommodates and lives into the multiplicity of human language and culture".[7]

- The Pentecost narratives of Acts 2 contain the message that this diversity of language is not detrimental to communion within the church. In Acts 2 we can imagine the Spirit announcing "Here and now, the church is the gathering of women and men who hear the gospel each in their own mother tongue". We can extend this image to the relationship between our churches and pray for the Spirit to equip us to live in fraternal communion while allowing each of us a special place for the language, spirituality, theology, and cultural assumptions which enable us most to draw close to God in worship. It is not enough to confess that we believe in the universal church — it is necessary for us to live what we confess.

Concluding his discussion of the nations, Chris Wright notes that

> The Bible does not imply that ethnic or national diversity is in itself sinful or the product of the Fall... God's rule over the nations is simply a function of the fact that He created them in the first place.[8]

Why is it important to frame ethnic diversity faithfully?

As a missiologist, I work at the intersection of theology and the social or human sciences in order to better understand the manner in which the church lovingly initiates people into the community of Jesus the Messiah.

I am, for this reason, an applied theologian and am acutely sensitive to the cash-value of theology. To put it another way, theologies have legs. Theology has the capacity, in the hands of the powerful or influential, to mobilise collective and individual action in the name of Christ. The ends towards which theological energy is directed might include the call to volunteer for service in Christian mission or ministry, mobilising a voting public in democratic elections, driving the Christian contribution to public debate, and buttressing populist views that, on careful inspection, might be considered to have been far from Christian in their response to ethnic diversity. One of these immediately comes to mind.

Theologies of creation and apartheid versions of ethnic diversity

In 1829 the Presbytery of Cape Town of the Dutch Reformed Church (in South Africa) considered a question from its Somerset West congregation. They discussed whether persons of "colour" should be allowed to take Communion together with "born again Christians" (white people), or whether these people should take Communion separately.

The 1857 Synod of the Dutch Reformed Church (DRC) resolved that,

> The Synod considers it desirable and according to the Holy Scripture that our heathen members (non-whites) be accepted and initiated into our congregations wherever it is possible; but where this measure, as result of the weakness of some, would stand in the way of promoting the work of Christ among the heathen people, then congregations set up among the heathen, or still to be set up, should enjoy their Christian privileges in a separate building or institution.[9]

Such debates and decisions paved the way for the establishment by the DRC in 1881 of the first racially separated church in South Africa, the Dutch Reformed Mission Church (DRMC) for "coloured" people. Next the DRC established the Dutch Reformed Church in Africa (DRCA) for black people and then the Reformed Church in Africa (RCA) for Indian people. In 1948 the National Party was elected on a platform of apartheid. Following the election, the DRC announced in its newspaper *Kerkbode*, "Apartheid is a Church Policy".

A retrospective investigation of the apartheid theology of the DRC argues that the divisions were construed along openly ethnic lines, not theological ones. The DRC saw ethnic boundaries as creation ordinances that were considered immutable and required careful policing. The Dutch Calvinist Abraham Kuyper's political theology of "spheres" of sovereignty/authority was appealed to (he would probably have rejected this use of his theology) as a way of underlining separate development of the "nations".

> Apartheid theology was essentially about ethnicity and as such provided an example of the first typical relationship of religion and ethnicity, namely religion as constraining primordial force.[10]

Anti-apartheid theology emphasised Christology and ecclesiology as integrating theological motifs which broke down unbiblical and sinful efforts at raising ethnic boundaries. Later multicultural statements, adding to these insights, have gone on to stress the diverse character of God's kingdom, mission to all nations (Matt 28:19), hospitality (Rom 12:13; Matt 25:31–46), and reconciliation (2 Cor 5:16–20), among others.

However, it's equally important to note the existence of forms of theology that have moved the discussion of ethnic diversity in a different direction to that listed above (and, we might add, to the earlier theological justifications of slavery).

Trinitarian theologies and intercultural versions of ethnic diversity

In 2007 the language and practice of "intercultural dialogue" was introduced into the European vocabulary. It heralded a route beyond the multicultural impasse. European theologians and church leaders responded with a vision of integration that went beyond coercion, assimilation, and cultural imperialism. An increasingly common theological discussion has centred on an emphasis upon the Trinitarian nature of God. Trinitarian theology offers a potential roadmap towards an integrated view of culture and ethnicity. For example,

> The human experience of God as three-in-one suggests that unity in diversity is fundamental to reality and that the mission of God as Creator, redeeming Son and Holy Spirit is a multicultural mission: It is the loving dance of difference in unity, not a monoculture, that God seeks (Gen 1:26, Matt 28:19).[11]

My own theological contribution has been to bring this discussion to bear on the human experience of migration, overlying the human experience of ethnic alterity.

> Our missiological starting point begins with the trinitarian God who self-reveals, supremely in Jesus Christ, and who extends self-giving love towards the whole of creation, desiring and working towards its salvation and liberation from the corruption of sin and death. In this sense we understand God to be a missionary God, from where we derive an understanding of the *missio Dei*. This enables us to imagine a migrant God who wanders through the wilderness with his people. This is the same God who experiences exile, social marginalisation, and a sense of rootlessness in and through the incarnate life of Jesus. [...] God's nature, demonstrated in the movement between Father, Son, and Holy Spirit, points to a level of [diversity and] integration within God's own self that does not obscure essential differences. The

Son is not the Father, but the love of the Son that leads to the Cross is the same love that the Father extends to the whole of creation.

The extension of God's self-giving love towards the whole of creation implies that the *missio Dei* and the unity of humankind are indelibly linked together (Gen 1:26,27; 1 Cor 15:28; Col 1:19–20) and any discrimination between human beings is a violation of God's own dignity.[12]

Contextual theologies and the re-framing of ethnic diversity

After the 2005 Cronulla riots the Evangelical Alliance in Australia issued *Christ and Multiculturalism* which began with, "In the light of the community tensions exposed by the Cronulla experience there is one simple reason for re-affirming multiculturalism: it is an essential part of the gospel".[13] Brian Edgar's paper argued for multicultural approaches on the basis of ecclesiology, creation, soteriology, Christology, baptism, pneumatology, and the kingdom of God. In other words, "One Lord, one faith, one Spirit, one baptism". Edgar posed the contextual question for Australia, "Tolerance or active love?" and went on to insist that a multicultural vision involved an absence of cultural coercion or attitudes of ethnic superiority. Positively, it implied the presence of religious freedom, a willingness to work to enhance life for all people, and to celebrate the value located in each culture.

Liberationist theologies

Liberation theologies arose in response to political and military oppression and dictatorship in Latin America. These theologians stressed God's "preferential option for the poor", demonstrated most clearly in the example of Jesus. In some places this struggle has taken on an ethnic character: for example, *mestizo* Indians in Latin America dispossessed of land or property rights, first nation Americans, the Roma of Central Europe, the indigenous Sami people of Norway, the Inuit of Canada, and the Aboriginal people of Australia.

It follows that the only groups with which the church is obliged to establish a *working alliance* are the poor and the oppressed (in complete contrast with the usual church-state alliances found across the world). This may include the ethnically oppressed and those who are impoverished because they are ethnically discriminated against.

Post-colonial theologies

Post-colonial theologians read Scripture and address power relationships within the church and society from the perspective of the "subaltern". Dalit theology from India and Diaspora theologies are good examples of post-colonial theologies.

Post-colonial theologians talk of freeing ethnic groups from colonial subjugation, including the colonisation of the mind (by which an ethnic group might come to believe the mythology or rhetoric of a more powerful group that its language or customs are "less civilised" or "heathen", for example).

Local theologies

"Local" theologians reject the tendency of Western theologians to assume that their theology is universally true, irrespective of their Western context. Western theologians, in writing about theology being written elsewhere, have typically labelled it as "African", "Asian", or "Indigenous" theology. They have never applied this to their own writing, for example: "The Institutes of *French* Christian Religion" by Jean Calvin or "*Swiss* Church Dogmatics" by Karl Barth. Local theologians argue that all theology is contextual and therefore a reflection of/response to prevailing cultural factors. Some of them talk about the "priesthood of all cultures".[14]

Local theologians prefer to talk about "global" theology but they understand this to be the product of a dialogue of historically received universal theologies and currently emerging local theologies.

> Christianity is a universalism which affirms the particular, unlike modernity (a universalism which denies the particular) and post-modernity (a set of particularisms which do not attain universality). …Evangelicalism's combination of universalism and particularity may be uniquely powerful in creating global community.[15]

Whose Lunar New Year is it?

At a more mundane level, getting ethnic diversity right is important. I worship at Epping Baptist Church, along with people from 29 different nationalities. Every year the church hosts a New Year dinner for over 300 church members, their families, and friends. It is *not* a Chinese New Year Dinner, it is our *lunar* New Year dinner. These things matter and our Chinese members are quick to resist any appearance of colonising a celebration shared, among others, with our Japanese, Malaysian, Thai, Vietnamese, and Korean church members.

Steps forward: Renewing Australian ecclesial practices from the margins

In the stumbling attempt to suggest the kinds of practical and concrete steps that our Baptist community can take, here are some suggestions for addressing the question of ethnic diversity in a more satisfactory way.

Begin the hard work of understanding and describing ethnicity

Dewi Hughes defines an "*ethne*" (in its French noun form) as a community with six common characteristics:

- It reflects a common proper name.
- It implies a myth of common ancestry.
- It evokes memories of a common history.
- It contains elements of a common culture.
- It provides a link with a common homeland.
- It suggests a sense of solidarity.

Secondly, Hughes suggests that "Ethnic groups that for various reasons, such as migration, are dispersed in a state that is remote from their homeland are called 'ethnic minorities'".

Thirdly, "a 'nation' is a territorially concentrated ethnic group. Where nations have been oppressed or marginalized in their ancestral territory they are called 'national minorities' or 'Indigenous peoples.'" In light of this, Hughes argues that the majority of nation-states have a plurality of *ethnes*.[16]

Commit to understanding ethnic diversity in contemporary Australian Baptist identity

In attempting to try to understand the various forms that ethnic diversity takes in Australia, I want to suggest that there remains the need to more clearly define and illustrate at least the following five categories (there may be more):

a. Societal inter-ethnic diversity (where society is composed of more than one ethnic community)
b. Societal intra-ethnic diversity (where society is composed of multiple and hybrid ethnic communities)
c. Communal intra-ethnic diversity (where the ethnic community is composed of multiple and hybrid ethnicities)
d. Familial inter-ethnic diversity (where the family includes individuals from more than one ethnic community)
e. Personal intra-ethnic diversity (where a family member has parents — or claimed ancestry — from more than one ethnic community).

A key question currently facing Australian Baptist Churches is the question, "When will today's ecclesial ethnic diversity become a commonplace part of tomorrow's ecclesial ethnic unity?" In other words, when and how will mainstream Baptist life be understood as ethnically diverse and when will it be possible to acknowledge that, "We're all Australian Baptist Churches now"? There are certainly authentic African, Korean, and Chinese spiritual traditions, just as there is an Australian spiritual tradition. However, none of those traditions is fixed and intercultural experience and engagement leave none of them untouched.

Throughout this section I have been talking about "us". This is a necessarily and collectively autobiographical conversation. In discussing ethnic diversity I am not describing some constructed "other". However, I recognise that this necessarily exists in something of a tension with the missionary idea of "The Church's missionary calling of being other-centered rather than being self-centered… as the theological foundation for a conciliatory existence".[17]

The church has to move beyond being mere community and learn the discursive practices of dialogue and debate. The language of integration can only be a source of renewal if the community into which it is introduced is a discursive community. This implies mutuality and the potential transformation of all parties in the dialogue. If the community is not thoroughly discursive, the language of integration will never move beyond the practice of mere assimilation.

Commit to embracing ethnic diversity within contemporary Australian Baptist experience

The church in Antioch is a powerful reminder that, before Paul was able to articulate the egalitarian sentiment of Galatians 6:23, he had to experience ecclesial and missional practices that witnessed to the essential unity of the human race in Christ. The missional innovation of Acts 11:19–30 is clear enough: Africans and Cypriots witness to Greeks. The ecclesial innovation is equally clear: the church and its leadership are ethnically diverse. The Paul of Acts 11 is clearly a long way from the Paul of Galatians 6:23 and the transformation of his own missional understanding and practice is his experience of learning from anonymous missionaries who saw the non-determinative nature of ethnic particularity.

In Acts 11, ethnic particularity is embraced and a new era of Christian mission unfolds in the life of the early church (Acts 11:29–30 and Acts 13:2–3).

John Toews simply assumes Jewish ethic identity and legitimates this by reference to the historical reality of Jewish ethnicity: "Ethnic identity is function of history".[18] He concedes that "'In Christ' Jews remain Jews and Gentiles remain Gentiles" yet posits the church as a "third race", the "body of Christ" in which "ethnic identity is a legitimate historical and sociological reality".[19]

The majority of contemporary scholars are critical of the idea of a universalising "non-ethnic" ethos in the New Testament, seeing this as an unhelpful avoidance of the fixity and fluidity that fails to take us far beyond the Greek–Jew–Roman triad of the Acts of the Apostles. For example, Barreto argues that,

> Luke does not imagine the creation of a new ethnicity of Christians; instead, he projects an interstitial ethnic space between the competing and overlapping ethnic claims of Jews, Romans, Greeks, and the other peoples that populate the pages of Acts. Luke does not erase ethnic difference but employs the flexible bounds of ethnicity in order to illustrate the wide reach of the early church movement.[20]

Barreto concludes with a vision of an ethnically diverse church that is disarmingly honest about the human tendency towards exercising "leverage" over others.

Both Christianity and Judaism in antiquity traded on the cultural leverage that ethnic discourse provides. Moreover, both recognized that the negotiation of our ethnic differences is an irreplaceable component of our social fabric.[21]

He continues by advocating for four basic principles that might guide our theological reflection around these important but difficult issues:

1. race and ethnicity are unavoidable;
2. race and ethnicity are indispensable;
3. race and ethnicity are a gift from God;
4. race and ethnicity shape profoundly our reading of Scripture.[22]

The purpose for including this material here is to provide a point of biblical and theological reflection that reminds us that we cannot bypass discussions of our ethnic identities and our ethnic diversity by simply pretending that they do not exist or that it does not matter now that we are "all one in Christ".

The renewal of ecclesial identity from the marginal experience of ethnic alterity

The margins can only transform the mainstream where Australian Baptists have become discursive communities, allowing space for diversity and dialogue.

Several simultaneous acknowledgements are required:

- The adjective "Australian" must be used of all churches on this continent.
- The adjective "Ethnic" must be used of all churches on this continent. Our churches must own both of these labels if we are to more adequately address the issue of our ethnic diversity. Until we do so, ethnicity will always be somebody else's problem — usually those who are of darker skin.
- That we, until we arrive at a more comfortable accommodation of Australian Baptist identity to our ethnic diversity, follow Hughes and use the more statistically accurate "ethnic minority churches".[23]
- We develop ways of talking about ethnicity within the Christian community that are eschatologically shaped — perhaps "fulfilled ethnicity", "transformed ethnicity", or "eschatological ethnicity" — and work towards filling out these categories with theologically and pragmatically rich meaning and experience.

Ethnic diversity can become a casualty of narrowly conceived, nationalist communities precisely because it is not allowed to participate in the mainstream discourse. Only a thorough-going dialogical process that disavows the use of certain mythical narratives and discourse, which includes ethnically diverse participants, and which reflects ethnic diversity at all levels of Baptist life, will enable us to move beyond the current unhappy state of referring to our "Australian Baptist Churches" and our "Chinese Baptist Churches". What the apostle Paul discovered in the church at Antioch (Acts 11:19–30) and then went on to articulate in writing to the churches in Galatia (Gal 6:22–23) remains a pertinent point of theological reflection on our shared life together in the community of Jesus' disciples.

Rev. Dr Darrell Jackson is the Senior Lecturer in Missiology at Morling College, Sydney, NSW.

Ministry in Urban Aboriginal Communities
New Perspectives for a New Era

Billy Williams

This chapter addresses a key concern for the church amongst urban Aboriginal communities. Understanding how a more effective evangelism can take place in these contexts is essential. This chapter asserts that two simple yet profoundly important strategies are the way forward for an urban Aboriginal ministry. Firstly, there must be a contextualisation of the true gospel; in doing this the key concept is that of belonging to the family of God. Secondly, there must be living out of that true gospel by Aboriginal Christians, so as to give a clear demonstration of the kingdom of God. These strategies are established by looking at the impact on Aboriginal people of social, political, and evangelistic activities through Australia's history; considering the social-scientific findings related to conversion; and, importantly, drawing upon a theology of evangelism.

Introduction

This chapter will assert two very simple, yet profoundly important, strategies to be more effective in reaching urban Aboriginal people and communities. These strategies are, firstly, the need for contextualisation of the true gospel; and secondly, the living out of that true gospel by Aboriginal Christians who profess to be connected to it. The author's theology of evangelism insists on a broader understanding of and influence by the concept of the kingdom of God in order to be more biblically sound and practically effective. Therefore, these two strategies can be directly linked to the need to understand better what it means to belong to the family of God, and what it means to truly demonstrate the kingdom of God.

To do this the chapter will briefly discuss the context of the author's ministry. It will then provide a selected consideration of the impact on Aboriginal people by various social, political, and evangelistic activities associated with European colonisation. From there the two strategies will be discussed, drawing upon a theology of evangelism and the social-scientific findings related to conversion. These two strategies will be viewed practically for the author's ministry, trying to highlight any potential deficiencies or considerations.

The author's ministry targets urban Aboriginal communities in Brisbane, Queensland. The church is supported by a larger Baptist church and was originally planted in a more missional mode. Three years ago it was moved into the current Baptist church precinct on a Saturday evening and draws people from various cultural, geographical, generational, and denominational identities.

The impact of European colonisation

Social/Political history

In terms of the social/political history there are incredibly significant events which have influenced and continue to influence the lives of Indigenous Australians: from the "invasion of the first boat people",[1] through the policies of segregation, protection, assimilation, reconciliation, and now "intervention". The line between social impact and political intrusion has been blurred. Dr Rosalind Kidd comments, "for almost a century Queensland governments controlled almost every aspect of Aboriginal lives by designating thousands of people wards of the State in the name of 'protecting' their interests".[2] Such sustained and cumbersome interference has created many concerns and much distrust from numbers of Indigenous Australians towards political and, by association, missional approaches.[3]

Not only has the Indigenous community built up significant perceptions from this history, but so too has the broader Australian society. There is a distinct lack of information which has led to many negative perceptions from broader Australians towards Indigenous people. This has often been fuelled by uninformed and unbalanced media portrayals and reporting. There is a strong need for concerted efforts to build a bridge between Indigenous and non-Indigenous Australians. Some of the personal effects of the implications of this issue have been explored in the cultural considerations outlined in this chapter.

For some Indigenous people the experience of forced removal from their families is a reality — considered to be between one in three and one in ten Indigenous children.[4] The treatment of children in these situations, of course, varied but the vast majority of the children were ill-treated and were subjected to humiliation, especially in terms of their understanding of their identity. In many instances where the Aboriginal children were in such homes they were encouraged to forget their Aboriginal background and to "live white, think white".[5] The impact of this on a person is almost incalculable.

It is true that "a person's Aboriginality has never been a matter of genetics. Culture and identification with a group are learned, not inherited".[6] We must recognise that "Aboriginality no longer resides only in some notional 'tribe'; but that the concept of identity has multiple and multiplying sites".[7] This chapter does not have the scope to enter into the vast details of the social/political history with regards to Indigenous Australians; however, what it does is identify the complexity and significance of issues that lie at the heart of Indigenous experience. Of course, those Indigenous people who live in urban environments often face added layers and difficulties in terms of their identity and their cultural understanding, and their expressions of this.[8]

Evangelistic history

Unfortunately many evangelistic practices have had a long-lasting and negative impact on Aboriginal Australians. At times some of the Western missionaries have had an "Acts 15" attitude — "if you don't become like us, you can't become a true Christian".[9] This, of course, was not always intentional; however, it does closely reflect the dispute leading to the Council of Jerusalem which, as Diab states, "was not doctrinal but cultural".[10] This passage should become an important signpost for evangelistic activities by considering, historically, how the cultural packaging of the gospel has undermined the message, because "'Christian' had become synonymous with 'Western', and had naturally been rejected".[11]

Of course, there have been wonderful stories of God's grace, both to the missionaries and to Indigenous people themselves. The Torres Strait Islanders celebrate "The Coming of the Light Festival", "which marks the day the London Missionary Society first arrived in Torres Strait".[12] The missionaries landed at Erub Island on 1 July 1871, introducing Christianity to the region. In many Aboriginal communities, significant leaders and opportunities have risen from the Christian ranks.[13] Yet, in many ways these activities have locked Indigenous people into ways of being and seeing Christianity that are millstones and have led to a great number "falling away from the faith" (if indeed they were ever brought into it in the first place).

The subtle and, at times, overt fact that the "Church has continually forgotten the lesson of Acts 15"[14] has led to difficulties that linger today. Paulson portrays this in his statement that "the popular notion of Aboriginal Christianity, from Fingal and from other urban situations in which I have been, was that they copied the lifestyle of the missionary". He explains the outworking of this, stating:

> Aboriginal people come from an oral tradition and, in order to remember those stories, the mythology of their creation and their whole world view is set into song and dance and into ceremonial observance… And yet here was a new mythology, here was a Christian story, and the only way that the Aboriginal people could lock it into place as they had been used to locking stories into place, was to copy the ceremony in which it had been handed down. And so Aboriginal people then, instead of sitting in a circle, entering into a ceremony that was mostly celebratory and participatory, were taught to sit in chairs in straight lines and look the one direction and have one person conduct the whole service, and not be able to participate in the manner in which they had been accustomed over many, many centuries.[15]

One can still visit urban and more remote Indigenous communities and see the preservation of the 1960s missionaries' church service complete with red hymn book and "Sunday best" (despite 30+°C heat!). Once again, this chapter does not have the scope to fully explore the history of missions within the Indigenous Australian context; however, the impact cannot be underestimated in terms of the perception of Christianity and the practice of evangelism.

A new strategy

Evangelism is best understood in terms of the kingdom of God.[16] Within this, two key aspects for this chapter arise (that is, effective evangelism strategies for the urban Aboriginal context). They are the need for contextualisation of the true gospel (belonging to the family of God); and the living out of that true gospel by Aboriginal Christians (demonstration of the kingdom of God).

Contextualisation of the true gospel (belonging to the family of God)

The concept of belonging and the pursuit to belong are fundamental. Maslow identifies this as such.[17] Belonging has long been a central cultural and spiritual principle for Aboriginal people and therefore remains the greatest single evangelistic strategy to effectively engage with Aboriginal people. The Bible's kinship language is the "language of belonging", imparting a sense of identity.[18] Paul often uses terms such as "father", "child", "children", and especially "brother"/"brethren". Understanding the people of God as a family explicitly demands an emphasis on relationships. This is important because God is unavoidably relational, the Trinitarian God: Father, Son, and Holy Spirit in perfect relationship.

The descriptions of the early church in Acts 2 and 4 picture a family who are so devoted to the needs of one another that they willingly and sacrificially give of their resources, their time, and themselves. It is little wonder that so many entered the kingdom. Unfortunately Western society's individualistic tendencies have crept into the church and we find, despite the biblical imperative, more a loose connection than a true sense of belonging. In Aboriginal society, relationship is everything. You belong to place and to people — you understand yourself only in relationship. Therefore evangelism suffers when the people being evangelised actually have, existing within their own ways of being, deeper levels of belonging and commitment than those proclaiming to be representatives of a special family that God has brought to be.

The effectiveness of evangelism often depends on the ability to "adapt ourselves and our presentation of God's message to the culture of the receiving people".[19] Yet, as discussed, this has not always been the case and now, more and more, outreach into Aboriginal communities is calling for contextualisation.

In urban Aboriginal communities this is, of course, not always easy. Difficulty arises when the practice is insufficient in its scope, as Paulson asserts:

> In the past, the process of theologising in Indigenous contexts was primarily a matter of taking theological principles — already shaped with western denominational enculturation — and then asking what they mean for Indigenous people.[20]

Cann states that, "there is a desperate need for churches to which it is easy to 'belong'".[21] Therefore, we must "set aside ways, habits and customs which are intimidating, exclusive and threatening". People living in communities are expressing their identity[22] and in order to reach them we must understand their "self-definitions".[23] In the urban Indigenous communities this means respecting and adhering to gospel-complementary cultural protocols. This avoids syncretism but also initiates incarnational ministry which shows Aboriginal people that "Jesus is 'of' their community".[24] The difficulty in this can be that for many Aboriginal Christians they themselves have been so culturally disconnected and/or theologically persuaded that they are merely mirroring what they have lacked or have been indoctrinated by, in terms of narrow views on culture, salvation, and faith.

In order to counteract these historical factors which have potentially undermined Aboriginal people's notion of self, culture, and spirituality there needs to be a strong injection of the principles and practices of contextualisation. This is often associated with overseas mission endeavours but it is fast becoming a louder call in terms of local ministry to urban Aboriginal people and communities. Kraft gives a wonderful analogy to explain the contextualisation practitioner's position:

> Christianity is not supposed to be like a tree that was nourished and grew in one society and then was transplanted to a new cultural environment… the gospel is to be planted as a seed… what sprouts… may look different… but… the roots are to be the same… the essential message will be the same.[25]

In much the same way, merely translating theological books into another language does not mean that the theological thought of the book contains the correct theological concepts.[26] As Jordan[27] suggests, in order to present the gospel amongst a people it is essential to "contextualise the theology of the book". For this reason many Aboriginal Christians and those with a heart for effective ministry have made an emphatic push to keep leadership training local and Indigenous.[28] In recent years, some missiologists have expressed the opinion that third world theologians are unlikely to think their theology through in a truly indigenous way if their initial theological thinking is done in a Western form.[29] This raises significant issues for Aboriginal ministry especially around leadership development and training.

Contextualisation then, as a key strategy for more effective evangelism amongst urban Aboriginal people, is first and foremost a reorientation about what it means to belong to the family of God. The Bible illustrates the power of the faith movement along social/relational lines, amongst households (Acts 16:31), and through communities (John 4:28–42). Stark and Bainbridge have identified that the need to belong is often a more compelling factor than the need to believe in the process of conversion.[30] Social Influence theory suggests "social relationships have the strongest effect on religious involvement".[31] In fact, Australian research identifies the critical importance of a strong sense of community, identifying church attendance of friends or a spouse as a key determinate of church attendance.[32] Furthermore, National Church Life Survey (NCLS) research suggests that a strong and growing sense of belonging among attenders is correlated to a high percentage of newcomers.[33]

Aboriginal people have a strong sense of family, and the cultural principles which are fundamental to identity revolve around relationships. In order to remain true to the true gospel, and in order to be more effective in evangelism to urban Aboriginal communities, a refocussing on the reality of what it means to belong to the family of God is essential. The gospel is an offer to be brought into right relationship with the heavenly Father through the life, death, and resurrection of the Son. This is a gift that makes people sons and daughters of the living God, brothers and sisters to Christ, and gives them eternal connection and identity. Understanding the gospel this way makes the approach to urban Aboriginal people less of a task to be undertaken and more a joy to share. God has already prepared, within the cultural elements of Australian Aboriginal society, fundamental connections to his gospel.

Living out the true gospel (demonstration of the kingdom of God)

The hoped-for outcome of contextualisation of the gospel is that it affirms, encourages, and enlivens the current Aboriginal Christian. For too long the Aboriginal church has limped along with very little in it to demonstrate the powerful and wonderful transforming work of the gospel. In part this was due to the cultural restraints of Western Christianity and also the inherited, theologically narrow, concept of salvation. I wholeheartedly believe that "the best hermeneutic of the gospel is a community of Christians living it out".[34] In fact, "If the church is to impart to the world a message of hope and love, of faith and justice, something of this should become visible, audible, and tangible in the church itself" — as Bosch asserts.[35]

The NCLS research shows that about two-thirds of newcomers became engaged because someone invited them to church.[36] Yet there is no point inviting people to a place where people aren't living out the true gospel. Nichols states:

> The church's message will be more credible in the community as a result of the church caring for people in need and actively pursuing public policies which affect the welfare of all Australians.[37]

Due to the culturally restricted nature of the gospel message in historical evangelistic efforts in Aboriginal Australia, converts have to some degree become twice as much a child of hell (Matthew 23:15) as those who evangelised them. Harris[38] captures the prevailing attitude of early evangelistic endeavours to Aboriginal people, stating of one missionary from the mid 1800s:

> He so entangled the gospel with European culture that he was unable or unwilling to see spiritual development, demanding to see total, absolute changes of lifestyle as evidence of conversion, which meant denying virtually all Aboriginality and becoming European.

Yet if the prevailing attitude remains that you have to stop being Aboriginal to be Christian, then there is a serious issue for evangelism. It is true that "there is nothing more impacting than congregations hearing stories of changed lives".[39] Yet the change is surely spiritual and not necessarily cultural. McLuhan asserts that "the medium is the message"[40] and what the urban Aboriginal community desperately needs is to encounter the true gospel lived out in Aboriginal people's lives; a proper demonstration of the kingdom of God in an Aboriginal life and community. Sarbin and Adler have identified that the most common element in transformation is the importance of the relationship between the convert and the teacher, mentor, or guide who provides a model for the new way of life.[41] This dynamic is needed for more effective evangelism amongst urban Aboriginal people: Aboriginal Christians who are living as salt and light.

By means of a more contextual and complete expression of faith, urban Aboriginal people will experience the kingdom, a key aspect of Jesus' ministry. Aboriginal people will enter this kingdom because "evangelism is only possible when the community that evangelizes — the church — is a radiant manifestation of the Christian faith and has a winsome lifestyle".[42] The church needs to be the missional Jesus community that "submerges itself into the culture it is reaching"[43] because this community has often suffered a Christianity that said what it never did.[44] It must be asserted that "faith is best expressed through action",[45] and this is certainly the faith required to impact urban Aboriginal people. The proclamation of the kingdom is not only words, but actions.

It is vital that urban Aboriginal people must be able to "see" the gospel. They have heard it many times before. Rational choice really requires tangible evidence. Rational Choice Theory suggests that people make decisions about religious involvement by weighing up the costs and benefits, just as they do in many other aspects of life.[46] Furthermore, Rambo's[47] model of conversion and Sarbin and Adler's study of significant change both show how the influence of other people is vital in the process of conversion.[48] In urban Aboriginal communities we need authentic and holistic expressions of what it means to follow Jesus because "we are called to be worshippers as a lifestyle, not just in meetings".[49] The challenge faced is that of all missionaries, "to link the always-relevant Jesus event of twenty centuries ago to the future of the promised reign of God for the sake of meaningful initiatives in the present".[50]

Churches seeking to reach urban Aboriginals must understand that "one of the most important questions of evangelism is whether we have the willingness to share our lives with others and to share in the lives of others".[51] This costs believers, but surely that is part of the true demonstration of the true gospel.

As part of this strategy a key concept is the development of Aboriginal Christian leaders who can lead Aboriginal churches and ministries. Christian leadership is an enormous burden in any context but, as Harris asserts, for Aboriginal Christian leaders the pressure is great.[52] The development of effective leaders is required. It is clear from biblical evidence that, "for Jesus, the job isn't simply to achieve a task, but also to develop people".[53] Yet as Malphurs and Mancini state, "the existing leadership doesn't have the training to equip other leaders"[54] and it is certainly true, especially in the Aboriginal context, that "most churches are strapped for good leadership and have no intentional strategy for developing leaders".[55] In order to move forward, urban Aboriginal ministry requires leadership development which understands the issues affecting evangelism and provides adequate reflections and applications to address them.

Potential limitations and practical implications

The existing structures within the Aboriginal ministry context are, in so many instances, imitations of what has been given by missionaries and the Western church, as Paulson laments:

> In general, Aboriginal people have been obliged to adopt western

styles of worship and church leadership. There has been very little theological reflection that begins from an Indigenous mindset and engages more directly with biblical theologies and practices.[56]

Therefore the challenge to be more effective in evangelism requires changes to theology and ecclesiology. Yet the changes must take place whilst still in the inherited structures and thinking that have contributed to the difficulties. A common issue in Aboriginal communities is that belief and behaviour become very locked in, and this is never truer than in the Aboriginal Christian community. Therefore, courage, grace, and wisdom are key requirements to try to bring about necessary changes. This is further complicated by notions of respect for elders and history that add more layers and potential limitations to the efforts.

The sheer energy and attention thus required for the successful implementation of these strategies can be overwhelming. Indeed, history would tend to indicate this as a key blockage. Many Aboriginal Christians throughout history have made attempts to contextualise the gospel in order to bring an effective witness in our communities. Yet that history is also, sadly, littered with shattered dreams, broken lives, lost faith, and lonely (and often lost) ministries. Yet, as always with the gospel, we must ask ourselves about the alternative. Now more than ever the urban Aboriginal context requires a generation who will take up their cross, amidst the chaos and confusion, in order to see the family of God grow as the demonstration of his kingdom is experienced.

A warning in regards to these strategies is also warranted. Whilst evangelism is essentially about those outside the body of Christ, it must be observed that the strategies put forward in this chapter are inwardly focussed. Throughout history the argument can be made that the reason evangelism has been ineffective is due to the inward-looking nature of those in the church, so by extension these strategies are in danger of perpetuating this. Yet the convictions put forward by the author hopefully show that the end result of these inward strategies is a more effective outward activity.

Conclusion

John Harris identifies the issue before us in terms of the urban Aboriginal context by stating that:

> Those who made a conscious rejection of Christianity mainly rejected its relevance to them as Aboriginals. They did not regard the Christian God as false. They saw God, rather, as the God of the white people.[57]

In order to more effectively engage in ministry to urban Aboriginals, churches should consider two very basic but fundamental strategies. Firstly, there must be a contextualisation of the true gospel. In doing this the key concept is that of *belonging to the family of God*. Secondly, there must be living out of that true gospel by Aboriginal Christians, so as to give a clear *demonstration of the kingdom of God*. This not only addresses historical issues, it aligns with social-scientific findings related to conversion, and most importantly, follows sound principles of a theology of evangelism.

Billy Williams ministers among urban Aboriginal communities in Brisbane, Queensland.

Baptists Responding to Cultural Diversity

Ian Duncum and Ruth Powell

Churches can potentially offer a sense of belonging and friendships for migrants and practical and pastoral support in settling into a new community. Yet the challenges posed by cultural diversity to individuals and churches are real and multi-faceted. This chapter draws from the 2011 National Census and the 2011 National Church Life Survey. A randomly selected, representative group of Baptist attenders provides an insight into individuals' views about cultural diversity. In addition, participating Baptist churches describe their activities. The study explores the views of individual attenders of Baptist churches to migration, how Baptist churches are involved in ministry to migrants, and the scope to which local Baptist churches engage and assist churches comprised of those from non-English-speaking backgrounds. It is clear from the results that Baptist attenders and churches are grappling with the issues and the opportunities brought by increased migration and greater cultural diversity. It is hoped this will give Baptist denominational staff, consultants, pastors, and other church leaders the opportunity to celebrate successes and identify areas for increased multicultural engagement.

Introduction

Migration — and the involvement by Australian churches in ministry to migrants — is a significant factor in the shaping of both Australian society and the Australian churches.

Many Australians have been directly impacted by the migrant experience. Some 5.3 million people, or 25 percent of Australia's population in 2011, indicated that they were born overseas, and 43 percent of all Australians in 2011 indicated that they had at least one parent born overseas. So almost half of Australia's population were either born overseas or have a migrant parent, according to the 2011 Census of Population and Housing.[1]

Some 1.8 million people have arrived in Australia between 2001 and 2011, indicating high levels of recent migration. Migration patterns have also shifted in recent years. The proportion of the overseas-born population originating from Europe has been in decline in recent years, from 52 percent in 2001 to 40 percent in 2011, while the proportion of migrants born in Asia increased from 24 percent of the overseas-born population in 2001 to 33 percent in 2011. The proportion of the overseas-born population arriving from countries outside Europe and Asia has also increased.[2] The top countries of birth in 2011 for Australia's overseas-born population were United Kingdom (21%), New Zealand (9%), China (6%), India (6%), and Italy (4%).[3]

This backdrop of migration has provided the opportunities for Australian churches, including Baptist churches, which are the focus of this research. While debate has swirled around various aspects of migration in the wider Australian society over recent decades, churches in Australia have seen and embraced migration as an opportunity for both hospitality and evangelism. Churches can potentially offer a sense of belonging and friendship for migrants who may be feeling displaced or struggling with their ability to communicate; an opportunity to explore or strengthen faith in Christ; and practical and pastoral support in settling into a new country and local community. In the face of community apathy or even hostility to migration, churches and individual Christians can provide a leadership role in expressing their attitudes and views about migrants in public and private discourse, as well as through their welcoming and hospitable actions.

Yet the challenges posed by cultural diversity to individuals and churches are real, multi-faceted, and can be difficult to overcome. This research will explore the views of individual attenders of Baptist churches to migration, the ways and extent to which Baptist churches are involved in ministry to migrants, and the scope to which local Baptist churches engage and assist churches comprised of those from non-English-speaking backgrounds. It is hoped this will give Baptist denominational staff, consultants, pastors, and other church leaders the opportunity to reflect on these areas: celebrating successes and identifying areas for increased multicultural engagement.

About this study of migration and Baptist churches

This project draws from two main sources. The first source is the 2011 National Census collected by the Australian Bureau of Statistics.

The second source is based on data collected through the Australian National Church Life Surveys (NCLS), perhaps the largest database on church life in the world. These five-yearly national surveys have been the result of collaboration across more than 20 Protestant and Catholic denominations. Each survey wave has collected responses from hundreds of thousands of individual church attenders in thousands of local churches.

In 2011, some 23 denominations took part in the Australian National Church Life Survey (2011 NCLS). Around 20 different forms of the questionnaire were distributed to all church attenders in participating congregations. There were core survey items that all respondents received, including demographics (such as country of birth for both individuals and their parents), and information about attendance background. Also, a series of polls were conducted on random samples of attenders. One of these surveys, 'Attender Sample Survey N'[4] contained questions about attitudes to migrants, and was completed by around 1,800 attenders, including a random sample of 106 Baptists from churches across Australia. Further, an audit of local church programs and activities is available for participating churches (2011 NCLS Operations Survey).[5] Some 199 Baptist churches provided information through the Operations Survey. Regional/denominational weights are applied to approximate the Australian church-going population as closely as possible.[6] In addition, a survey of local church leaders adds a further dimension; however, this data has not been used in this project.

A note of caution needs to be made about the representativeness of the sample. Although the 2011 NCLS was available in eight languages, there was a lower rate of participation of non-English-speaking background (NESB) churches.

Migrants with Baptist affiliation

The role of immigration in the growth of Baptists parallels the significance of immigration in many other Christian denominations.[7] Of the 1.8 million migrants arriving between 2001 and 2011, 767,000 were Christian. This is more than the 514,000 migrants of other faiths and more than migrants of "no religion".

The 2011 Census reveals that 29 percent of Baptists were born overseas and another 17 percent had one or both parents born overseas.[8] While this mirrors the place of birth of the wider Australian population, three points stand out regarding migrants to Australia with Baptist affiliation.[9] Firstly, there has been an increase in Baptist migration in recent years. Secondly, compared to other major denominations where there has been a decrease, the proportion of migrants with a Baptist affiliation has increased over the ten years to 2011. And thirdly, much of the growth in Baptist churches is likely to be through migration.

Increase in the number of recent Baptist migrants

An increasing proportion of Australians who identify as Baptists were born overseas — from 26 percent in 2006 to 29 percent in 2011. Of those who specified their year of arrival, 44 percent of those identifying as Baptist arrived after 2000. In other words, there has been a dramatic increase in the number of Baptist migrants arriving in Australia over the past ten years.

Between 2001 and 2011, 42,000 Baptist immigrants arrived in Australia.[10] Source countries that feature highly for Baptist immigrants are China/Hong Kong, England, South Africa, New Zealand, and Myanmar, all countries where there is a significant Baptist presence, and many of which are English speaking.

Increases in recent migrant Baptist affiliation are in contrast to other denominations

Recent arrivals shown in *Figure 1* are those who arrived in Australia over the period 2007 to Census Night (9 August) 2011. While the overall percentage is small, it shows an increase in the proportion of those with Baptist affiliation when compared with longer-standing migrants over that time period, while recent proportions of Catholic, Anglican, Presbyterian and Reformed, and Uniting migrants declined when compared with longer-standing migrants over that time frame. This is against the backdrop of increases in recent migrants identifying with no religion, Hinduism, Islam, and Buddhism.

Figure 1: Selected religions — longer-standing and recently arrived migrants (a)

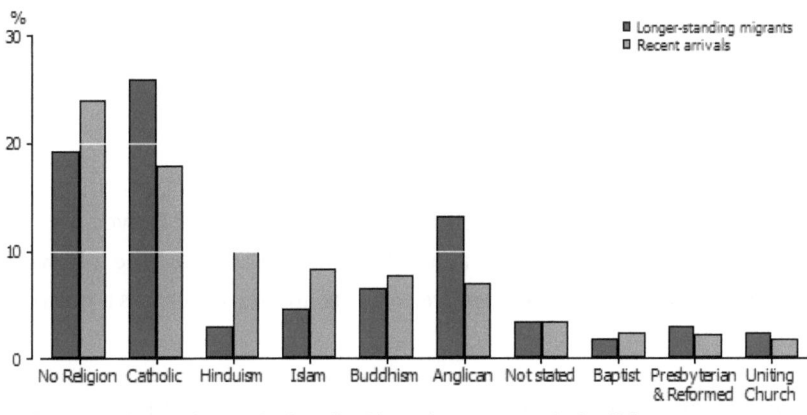

(a) Total includes inadequately described (supplementary codes) religions.

Source: *http://www.abs.gov.au/ausstats/abs@.nsf/Lookup/2071.0main+features902012-2013*

Almost all growth in the Baptist population has been through migration

Hughes and Cronshaw calculate that migration accounts for the vast majority of growth in Baptist affiliation between 2001 and 2011.[11] Migrants are also likely to influence the levels of church involvement, since they tend to attend worship more frequently than Australian-born people. The Australian Survey of Social Attitudes (2009) showed that 26 percent of immigrants said they attend religious services at least once a month, compared with 14 percent of people born in Australia.[12]

Therefore migration has brought additional people and new life to Baptist churches, as individuals and churches have reached out to and integrated those from culturally and linguistically diverse (CALD) backgrounds. The various state Baptist Unions have increasingly provided theological education (sometimes in other languages) and staff to oversee the development of CALD faith communities.

Baptist attenders' views of immigrants

As debate in wider Australian society has intensified around issues of migration and asylum seekers, how has this been reflected in churches? Around two thirds of Australians think that migration from a diverse range of countries makes Australia stronger.[13] So are these attitudes held by the broader Australian public mirrored by those attending Baptist churches, which are sometimes noted for a more conservative stance?

How do Baptist church attenders view immigrants and their impact on Australian society? In late 2011 as a part of the 2011 National Church Life Survey, a sample of Catholic, Anglican, and Protestant church attenders was asked the following questions. One was posed using negative wording and the other was a positive statement:

How much do you agree or disagree with each of the following statements? (Mark one on EACH line)

- Immigrants increase crime rates
- Immigrants improve Australian society by bringing in new ideas and cultures

Figures 2 and *3* display the results of Baptist attenders for these questions, compared with all attenders across 23 Australian denominations.

"Immigrants increase crime rates": When asked if "immigrants increase crime rates", the largest proportion of attenders indicated they were "neutral/unsure" about the statement (38%). This is perhaps because the question had an objective quality despite also measuring an attitude, and these attenders did not know the answer. However, among the remaining group, more Baptist attenders disagreed than agreed with the statement (36% vs. 26%).

Differences between the views of Baptist attenders and attenders from other denominations who answered this question were not significant. Further, there were no significant differences for age and gender. That is, on average, the responses of both young and old attenders, and males and females were similar.

In contrast, a person's level of education was related to negative views about immigrants. Attenders with lower levels of education were more negative. Those with schooling as their highest level of education were the most likely to agree that immigrants increase crime rates (36%) compared to only 17 percent of those with a university education.

Figure 2: Attenders' level of agreement that immigrants increase crime rates: Baptist vs all attenders

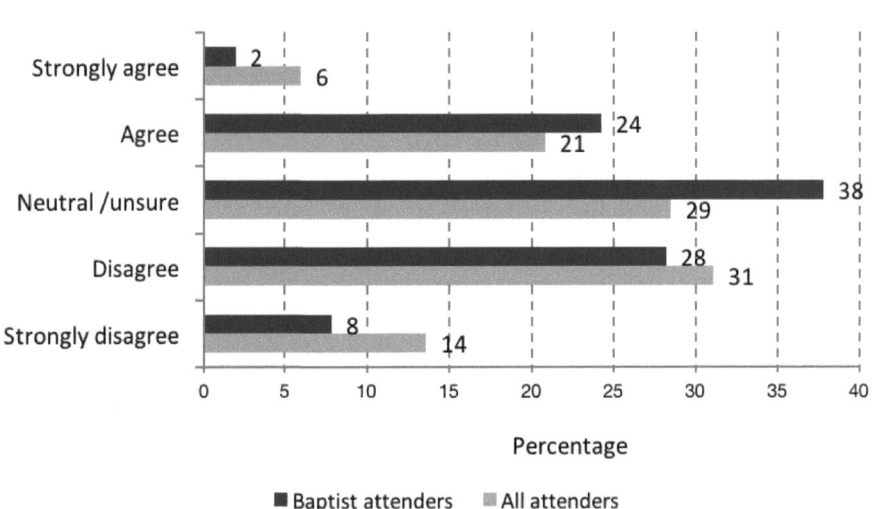

Source: 2011 NCLS Attender Sample Survey Nv2, Baptist attenders (n=106); all attenders (n=1,408).

"Immigrants improve society": For most Baptist attenders, the underlying attitude towards immigrants is a positive one. The majority (65%) of Baptist attenders agreed or strongly agreed that immigrants improve Australian society (see *Figure 3*). This is similar to 2011 surveys results for the wider Australian community, where 64 percent agreed or strongly agreed that 'Accepting immigrants from many different countries makes Australia stronger'. Although the proportion of Baptist attenders who were neutral/unsure was again large, those who disagreed (12%) or strongly disagreed (2%) were clearly in the minority. These results stand in strong contrast to the wider community where, in 2011, only 9 percent were either neutral or unsure and some 26 percent disagreed or strongly disagreed. Demographic characteristics, such as age, gender, or even education, made no significant difference to the levels of agreement on whether immigrants improve Australian society.

Figure 3: Attenders' level of agreement that immigrants improve Australian society: Baptist vs all attenders

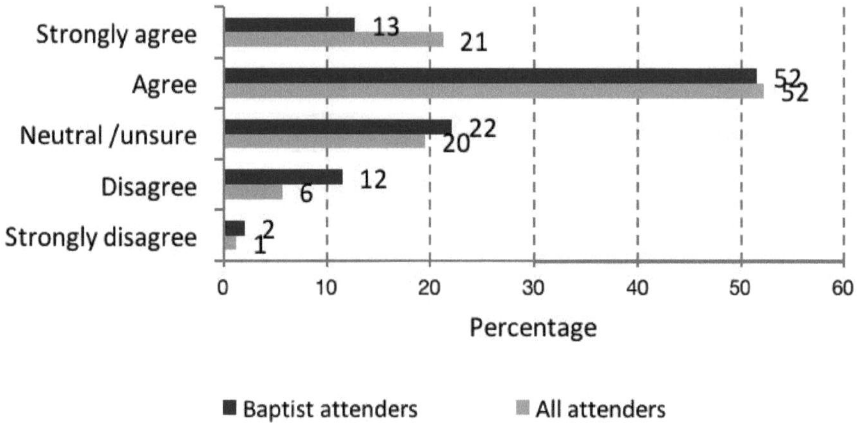

Response	Baptist attenders	All attenders
Strongly agree	13	21
Agree	52	52
Neutral/unsure	20	22
Disagree	12	6
Strongly disagree	2	1

Source: 2011 NCLS Attender Sample Survey Nv2, Baptist attenders (n=105); all attenders (n=1,408).

Baptist attenders did differ significantly from the overall attender sample in their views regarding this statement. Compared with other denominations, Baptist attenders had the highest proportion which disagreed or strongly disagreed that immigrants improve society (14%): this is double the proportion found in Australian churches overall. (See *Table 1*).

Table 1: Immigrants improve society by denomination

	Anglican	Baptist	Catholic	Lutheran	Pentecostal	Uniting	Other Protestant	Total
Strongly agree	25%	13%	23%	15%	26%	14%	10%	21%
Agree	49%	52%	55%	51%	49%	48%	52%	52%
Neutral/unsure	19%	22%	16%	22%	20%	30%	28%	20%
Disagree	5%	12%	6%	12%	2%	8%	9%	6%
Strongly disagree	2%	2%	1%	0%	3%	0%	0%	1%

Source: 2011 NCLS Attender Sample Survey N v2 (n=1,408)

Baptist church involvement in migrant ministry

Churches can potentially offer connection and a sense of belonging for migrants who may be feeling displaced, as well as practical and pastoral support in settling into a new country and local community. While there is a wide variety of ministries to and with migrants, the cultural and practical learning that must take place to enable migrants to function effectively in a new country is often a focus. Elizabeth Vreugdenhil explores the importance of building migrant capacity through "a strengths based model of helping based on an equal partnership between the two groups who each brought their knowledge and expertise to the situation" of settling Sudanese refugees in Australia.[14] More broadly, intentionality, a strong focus on "the dynamics of relationship and hospitality",[15] and the equipping of pastors who can in turn equip leaders and attenders with "cultural intelligence", are important ingredients enabling effective work in cross-cultural situations.[16]

Across all denominations, the 2011 NCLS revealed that churches have engaged with and responded to the multicultural context of their community in a range of ways, including ministry to migrants in the church and the community, supporting/partnering with monocultural churches from CALD backgrounds, and partnering with migrants in international/multicultural churches. Over one fifth (21%) of Australian churches in 2011 reported having a relationship with a non-English-speaking congregation, through either sharing property (9%), sharing small groups (6%) or worship services (2%), or through some other way (4%).[17]

How involved are local Australian Baptist churches in intentional ministry towards migrants? In the 2011 National Church Life Survey, a representative from each participating church was asked:

To what extent is this congregation involved in ministry towards migrants?

- Heavily involved
- We are taking first steps
- We would like to be involved but do not have the resources
- We are not involved for other reasons
- It is not a priority in our area

As shown in *Figure 4*, 40 percent of Baptist churches said they were involved in migrant ministry, with 16 percent heavily involved, and 24 percent taking first steps. This was a slightly higher level of involvement than that found among all Australian churches (35%).

Eight percent of Baptist churches reported having insufficient resources to be involved in migrant ministry, and six percent were not involved for other reasons. Almost half of all churches (45%) claimed ministry towards migrants was not a priority in their area.

Figure 4: Local Baptist church involvement in ministry towards migrants

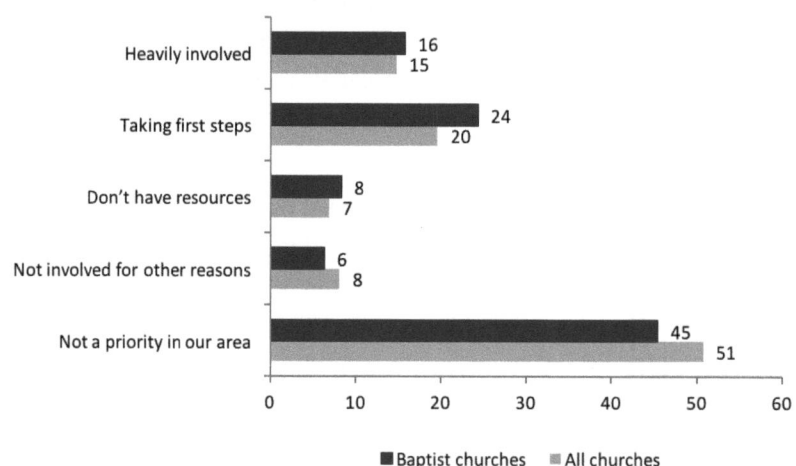

Source: 2011 NCLS Operations Survey, Baptist churches (n=199); all churches (n=2,347)

Locality: Baptist churches in rural areas (69%) were more likely than urban (30%) and regional churches (52%) to say that multicultural ministry is not a priority in their area. This makes sense, as most migrants live in urban areas.[18] The likelihood of churches being involved in migrant ministry was highest in urban areas (54%), followed by regional areas (39%). Only 16 percent of rural churches indicated they were involved in this form of ministry.

Denominational Differences: How does Baptist involvement in migrant ministry compare with involvement by churches of other denominations? As shown in *Table 2*, Baptist churches fell somewhere in the middle — showing higher levels of involvement than some denominations, but lower involvement than others.

Anglican and Lutheran churches had the lowest involvement in migrant ministry (26% and 23% respectively), although this may partly be related to the stronger rural presence of these denominations. Lutheran churches were most likely to indicate that ministry to migrants was not a priority in their area (65%). Pentecostal churches had the highest level of involvement, with almost half (48%) either heavily involved or taking first steps.

Table 2: Migrant ministry by denomination

	Anglican	Baptist	Catholic	Lutheran	Pentecostal	Uniting	Other Protestant	Total
Heavily involved	12%	16%	14%	9%	21%	13%	16%	15%
First steps	14%	24%	17%	14%	27%	19%	24%	20%
Don't have resources	7%	8%	7%	4%	7%	5%	9%	7%
Other reasons	8%	6%	10%	7%	6%	9%	9%	8%
Not a priority	59%	45%	52%	65%	39%	54%	42%	51%

Source: 2011 NCLS Operations Survey (n=2, 347)

Compared with Australian churches overall, Baptist churches appeared to have a slightly higher level of involvement in ministry towards migrants (40% vs. 35%), but otherwise had a similar distribution of results (see *Table 2*).

Changes in involvement over time: There has been an increase over time in the proportion of local Baptist churches who claim to be involved in migrant ministry, from 25 percent of local churches in the 2001 NCLS to 37 percent in 2006, and 40 percent in 2011.[19] This resembles the change seen for Australian churches overall. However, results may not be entirely comparable due to a wording change from 'ethnic ministry' in 2001 and 2006 to 'migrant ministry' in 2011. This is an encouraging sign that churches are engaging with an increasingly multicultural Australia and taking up the opportunities afforded by Australia being one of the most multicultural nations in the world.[20]

Local Baptist church engagement with non-English-speaking churches

There are 70 Baptist congregations in Victoria which worship in "Languages Other Than English" (LOTE), representing around a third of all Baptist churches in that state. The two largest language groups in Victoria are Chin and Karen from Myanmar (the third largest Baptist country after USA and India), forming some 52 new Baptist congregations across Australia, including 24 in Victoria, six in New South Wales, nine in Western Australia, and 13 in Queensland.[21] NSW/ACT has approximately 40 Baptist churches who worship in LOTE, as well as churches comprised of particular cultural groups who worship in English, and churches who have significant proportions of attenders from a wide variety of cultural backgrounds. These levels vary from state to state with net migration inflows, and with the overall engagement of State Baptist Unions and local Baptist churches with NESB churches.

What was the level of engagement of Baptist churches with NESB congregations in 2011? In the 2011 National Church Life Survey, church leaders were asked:

Are there any non-English-speaking congregations meeting for worship here? If so, which of the following would best describe your relationship? (Mark ONE only)

- We share the same property, but have no shared ministry
- We share the same church worship service, but have separate language small groups or other activities
- We have separate language church services, but share small groups or other activities
- No non-English-speaking congregations meet for worship here
- Other

Figure 5 shows the type of relationships that participating local Baptist churches have with NESB congregations.

Figure 5: Local Baptist church engagement with NESB churches

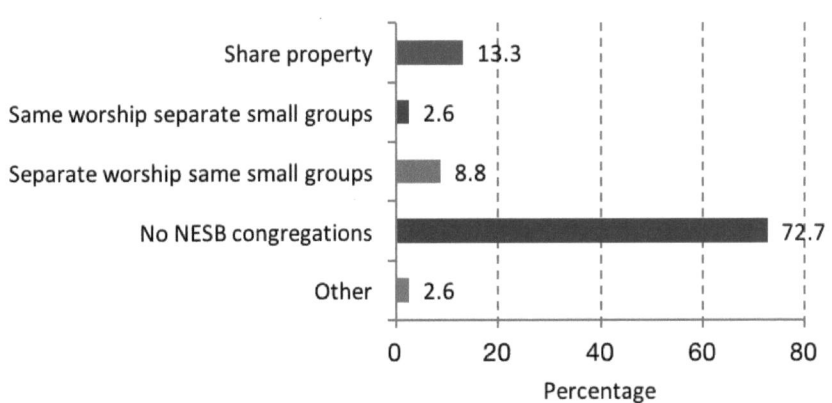

Source: 2011 NCLS Operations Survey, Baptist only (n=190)

A quarter of Baptist churches participating in the 2011 NCLS have a relationship with a NESB congregation. Most commonly, this centres on sharing property (13%), but this is nearly matched by sharing ministry, whether through small groups (9%), or worship (3%).

Some churches may think language is a barrier to a greater level of shared ministry between themselves and a NESB congregation. Australia's population is becoming increasingly multilingual, with more than half (53%) of those born overseas and migrating to Australia able to speak a language other than English (LOTE). However, only one tenth of migrants identified their ability to speak English as "not well or not at all" (*Figure 6*).[22]

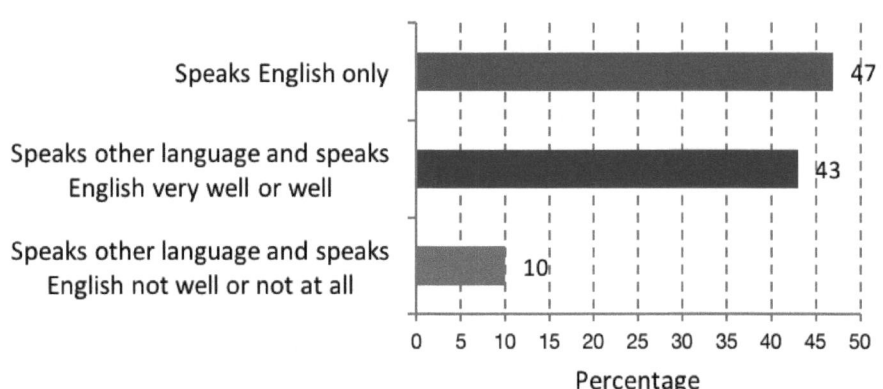

Figure 6: Proficiency in spoken English by migrants to Australia

Source: ABS (2011), table B11.

With 90 percent of migrants self-reporting that they speak English "very well or well", such barriers tend to lie more in other areas. In every cross-cultural situation, there are potential challenges which arise from communication and cultural differences, preferences, and understandings. These could include ethnic prejudices between groups, control of resources (e.g. property), and lack of willingness to share ministries and leadership.

Across Australia, those from NESBs tend to be located in urban centres. This pattern impacts church life, meaning that local church engagement with NESB congregations, or multicultural ministry generally, is much more likely to be relevant for churches in urban settings. This helps explain why 45 percent of participating Baptist churches responded: [ministry toward migrants] "is not a priority in our area".

Churches in regional and rural areas are more likely to say that multicultural ministry is not a priority. In smaller rural towns or areas (fewer than 2000 in population), this can be around twice as likely as for those in city suburbs.

Denominational differences are shown in *Table 3*.[23] Compared with Australian churches overall, Baptist churches were more likely to have some kind of relationship with NESB congregations (27% vs. 21%). This was particularly evident in the case of churches sharing property or small groups with NESB congregations.

Table 3: Relationships with NESB congregations by denomination

	Anglican	Baptist	Catholic	Lutheran	Pentecostal	Uniting	Other Protestant	Total
Share property	5%	13%	5%	8%	1%	16%	15%	9%
Share worship service	1%	3%	3%	2%	1%	1%	4%	2%
Share small groups	7%	9%	9%	2%	4%	4%	3%	5%
No NESB congregations	85%	73%	77%	86%	80%	78%	74%	79%
Other	2%	3%	6%	2%	14%	2%	3%	4%

Source: 2011 NCLS Operations Survey (n=2, 216)

Care should be taken in seeking to quantify the numbers of NESB churches from this data. This data only includes responses from churches participating in 2011 NCLS, rather than all Australian churches. As noted, although the 2011 NCLS was available in eight languages, a lower participation of NESB churches gives less information from their perspective about the relationship between NESB congregations with other congregations. In addition, the survey question only asks about NESB congregations that share property, services, or small groups, and not about congregations that are independent or have no relationship with another congregation.

Models of multicultural ministry

Drawing on the models of multicultural church described by Geoffrey Blackburn, Manuel Ortiz, and Jeannie Mok, Yang has specified four groupings that are a particularly helpful starting point for an Australian context, namely:

- Monocultural model,
- Friendship model,
- Partnership model, and
- Integrated model.[24]

Yang examines "the necessity for movement between the [cultural] models. That is, a church that represents a particular model needs to be aware of where it needs to move to next, in order to remain vital and viable. It cannot be presumed that any one model is an end point in itself."[25] This exploration of moving between cultural models of church is done in order to forge a more vital and healthy church.

The issues of young adult retention and wider local community outreach are consistently encountered by monocultural churches. In many ways second-generation migrants are similar to their Australian-born counterparts. This makes it more difficult for them to stay in churches that have many of the trappings of their non-English-speaking background culture. This presents monocultural churches with the challenge to provide a church environment that resonates with the needs and cultures of a younger generation.[26]

Conclusion

Baptist attenders are grappling with the issues and the opportunities brought by increased migration and greater cultural diversity.

As part of the 2011 National Church Life Survey, two questions were posed to examine attitudes of church attenders (including Baptist attenders) toward immigration. When asked whether immigrants increase crime rates, while there were some differences between the views of Baptist attenders and attenders from other denominations who answered this question, they were not significant. When asked whether immigrants improve Australian society by bringing in new ideas and cultures, 65 percent of attenders in Baptist churches either agreed or strongly agreed. This is a similar result to the survey of the wider community by Markus (2011), where 64 percent agreed or strongly agreed that immigration strengthened Australia. However, there are also significant differences concerning those who either disagreed or strongly disagreed with this statement: Markus's survey of the wider community (27%) and the NCLS Survey of Baptist attenders (14%).

Some 35 percent of Australian churches report being involved in ministry towards migrants, be it heavily involved or just taking first steps. About half of all churches claimed migrant ministry was not a priority in their area. Younger churches and urban churches were most likely to be involved in migrant ministry.

Baptist churches have enjoyed both higher levels of involvement in migrant ministry (40%) and a strong increase over time in the proportion of local Baptist churches who claim to be involved in migrant ministry, from 25 percent of local churches in the 2001 NCLS to 37 percent in 2006, and 40 percent in 2011.

It is encouraging that Baptist churches are engaging with and responding to the multicultural context of their community through forming relationships with non-English-speaking-background congregations. However, opportunities remain for many of the 73 percent of Baptist churches who have no association with a NESB congregation to engage in some way, particularly since only ten percent of migrants to Australia identified their proficiency in speaking English as "not well or not at all". For the churches who do have a relationship with a NESB congregation, the main connecting point is a shared use of property (13%), rather than any form of shared ministry, whether services (3%) or small groups (9%).

Baptist churches have engaged with and responded to the multicultural context of their community in a range of ways, including ministry to migrants in the church and the community, supporting/partnering with monocultural churches from CALD backgrounds, and partnering with migrants in international/multicultural churches. However, much more can be done to respond attitudinally, personally, and in ministry to the rapidly emerging mission field on our doorstep. As Connolly so eloquently states:

> The tendency in migration is for the hosts to think they have little to learn and don't have to change. However, exposure to other cultures can be an opportunity for profound personal learning, for a deeper insight into yourself and life, for learning greater tolerance, and for developing increased freedom and ability to love. Engagement with our migrant brothers and sisters will help us develop the ability to listen to minorities, cultural awareness and the ministerial cultural competence we need for mission in Australia today. It will also provide us with a link and exposure to the Third World church where the Holy Spirit is clearly saying something.[27]

Dr Ian Duncum has pastored a variety of Baptist churches, works as a consultant and trainer with many churches, and is an Associate Researcher with NCLS.

Dr Ruth Powell is Director of NCLS Research, responsible for the five-yearly National Church Life Surveys across 20+ denominations. She has co-authored publications on church health and other topics.

Being the Church without Four Walls

Marc Chan

When we mention the word "church", we immediately have an image of a building with an organised group of people running it. The change in the makeup of the Australian population has encouraged a phenomenon which is becoming more and more common — church without four walls. For many churches with mostly refugees, circumstances have caused them to become churches without buildings but passionately doing what church should be — caring for one another. This phenomenon is looked at in the context of refugee churches in Western Australia, especially those from a Burmese background. These refugees come from a traditional understanding that church is not church without a building. Most of them are now churches without buildings and growing at an incredible rate. Can we learn something from their experience?

In today's context, we usually consider church to be the gathering of God's people within a building. Even dictionaries connect the church to a building — thus, the four walls. However, with the rapid change in population diversity within Australia, there is a challenge to this concept of church being within four walls.

During my theological studies, I was particularly interested in the chapter on "The Doctrine of the Church" in Alister McGrath's book *Christian Theology: An Introduction*.[1] He describes the development of the church from Old Testament times through the New Testament up until the present times. He points out that, before Israel was ruled by a king, "Israel existed without a temple, priests, sages, or prophets. Its identity as a people was not defined by institutions, but by a common commitment to Israel's central story".[2]

With the establishment of the monarchy, this changed slightly. The kings were the secular leaders of the nation with a commitment to rule under the religious principles dictated by the temple and the priests. During the New Testament times, McGrath identifies five ways in which the church identified itself:

a. The church as the people of God

b. The church as a community of salvation

c. The church as the body of Christ

d. The church as a servant people

e. The church as the community of the Spirit[3]

Over the next few centuries, in the midst of persecution and controversies, the church was more focused on the role of its Bishops (in Rome, Alexandria, Antioch, and Jerusalem) as the spiritual leaders of the Christian world than on what the church was supposed to be doing. As time went on, the church became more and more institutionalised and the understanding that the church building is the church became common. This is just a very brief and simplified version of the way in which we have come to consider the four walls to be the church.

It is interesting to note that there have been several books and articles written to counter this understanding — even within the Roman Catholic denomination. For example, Professor Komonchak considered several ways in which the church has been referred to within the Roman Catholic denomination (including the document produced as a result of the Second Vatican Council) and argues that this definition of church is more appropriate:

> The phrase "community of disciples," then, approximates one of the oldest and most common terms for the Church, "congregatio (or convocatio) fidelium," the assembly of believers. I believe that this is more than a nominal definition of the Church, an identification of that to which the word refers. It approximates a real definition, that is, a statement of what constitutes and distinguishes the gathering of human beings known as the Church. It is a primary notion, both sociologically and theologically.
>
> This is, then, the referent of the word "Church" and of any images, symbols, models that may be employed in reference to the Church: they refer to the assembly or community of believers, whether gathered in particular places, or considered in their totality as the one worldwide Church.[4]

Malphurs firstly defines the church in terms of its nature, or its being, and then goes on to define it in terms of what its members do. He writes,

> I define a local church as a gathering of professing believers in Christ who, under leadership, have organized to observe the ordinances and obey Jesus' Great Commission. This definition has two basic ingredients: being and doing.[5]

Yet another definition of church:

> Church is more than just a worship center or a mini-seminary. Rather church is the visible and visceral expression of Jesus living among a people.[6]

Therefore, in recent years, there has been a significant move away from the church existing as four walls to being more people oriented. This is even more significant when we consider the challenges that come with the change in the makeup of the population in Australia, more specifically in Western Australia.

According to statistics published by the Western Australia State Government Office of Multicultural Interests, from the 2011 Census, Western Australia recorded the highest proportion of overseas-born residents (33%) in their population. If we consider that a bit above 16 percent out of the 33 percent were born in an English-speaking country, it means that almost 17 percent of the population in Western Australia was born in a non-English-speaking country. If we add to this figure those who were born here but with at least one parent born in a non-English-speaking country, the estimate is that roughly one out of four persons in Western Australia is either a first- or second-generation migrant and speaks another language — apart from English. As this proportion has kept on increasing over the past few decades, this has brought about a challenge to our understanding of what church is.

Migrants coming to this country, especially refugees, initially tend to stick more to their languages of the heart and congregate together through the establishment of monocultural non-English-speaking churches. This is largely due to the fact that many have found it difficult to join with established churches. There are several reasons why this is the case. Among them is the fact that most find it very difficult to understand and/or speak English. Most do have some knowledge of English but need time to be able to process what is being said and respond. Thus, to be able to continue worshipping, there has been a need to set up churches to meet their needs.

However, the big difference is that they meet either in buildings owned by established churches or use community centres/schools as worship places on

Sundays. This phenomenon has been mostly prevalent among churches planted in the last decade or so. Churches which have been established in the sixties and seventies have mostly bought their own buildings since their understanding was that the church was not really a church without a building. There is an absolute need to own a building for the organisation to be called a church. This attitude towards a building does not only apply for churches established in the sixties and seventies but also for more recently established churches consisting mostly of refugees. However, though the building was originally considered to be what determined the status of the church, things had to be different. With the enormous costs involved in the purchase of land and building, it has become very difficult for this to become reality for most churches consisting mainly of refugees. Having church services and fellowship in the language of the heart is more important than having a building to start with. This has, reluctantly in most cases, fostered the idea that a church has the possibility of existing even without a building — church can be church without a building.

In reality, these churches have not completely changed their idea of a church existing without a building. The dream of many is still that one day, in the very near future, they will have enough resources or they will be able to take a loan somewhere in order to get that elusive building. Many such churches, no matter what their membership is, have building funds already in place. Nevertheless, such is the rate at which the price of real estate is rising that, realistically, not many of these dreams will become reality.

So, this shift in mindset has occurred more as a result of circumstances than a shift in the understanding of what church is. Dreams and reality are most of the times quite the opposite of each other. Nevertheless, it has brought about a significant change in the way in which they do church — in fact, very different to the way in which church was done in their countries of origin. In a way, this can be used as a model of what the church in general can do to move beyond the four walls even if these four walls are still there. Many come to our shores as refugees — some have been in camps for years. Church, in the minds of these refugees, is nowhere near what we know it here.

Most of these refugee church congregations are meeting on the premises of established churches and many are already outnumbering their hosts. Apart from Sunday services, all of the other activities take place in homes because they are only allowed to meet at those premises on Sundays or the church hosting them has other activities going on and these rightfully have priority on the use of the building. Over time, they establish a workable solution around the premises which they are using and members' homes. Once this pattern is set, their concept of church is no longer that of an organisation with activities organised by it within the confines of their own building. It is now a case of what happens when they meet on a Sunday plus all the other activities that take place over the rest of the week at several locations. It is no longer focused on the building and what happens inside the building but what they do in order to be known as a church. This, for those communities, is a redefinition of what they have always understood and known church to be. It is a circumstance driving a significant change in their thinking.

We are then prompted to ask ourselves this question: is this not what the Greek word, *ekklesia*, normally translated as church, means? — a gathering of people for a common purpose, to worship God together, to study his word, to have fellowship together, to pray together, and to care for one another. This is very close to how the church in Acts 2 was described; and this is church as it is actually happening today in many churches consisting mostly of migrants and/or refugees.

To gain a better understanding of why those churches are the way they are, it is appropriate to briefly look at migration in general. There are surely many diverse reasons why people migrate to another country. Certainly, economic reasons play a major role in this. However, many of our churches with mostly refugees exist for reasons beyond just economic ones. Many of the members come from refugee camps and have lived there for many years. For some, even though they are in their twenties, this is the only life they have known before coming to Australia. They have been displaced from their homeland as a result of civil wars in their countries of origin.

As an example, we can look at the refugees originally from the Karen State in Myanmar (formerly called Burma). Since the end of World War II, the Karen people have been seeking their independence from the Burmese government in order to create their own country. The Burmese government has been trying to push out the Karen "rebels" from their territory and only allow those who agree to abide by the Burmese rulers to stay. A substantial proportion of the Karen crossed the border into Thailand in the late 1960s in order to escape persecution in their homeland. However, the Thai government also did not want to allow the Karen people to roam freely in their country for fear that they might also claim part of their territory as being Karen land. So, the Thai government built refugee camps along the border with Burma and those who managed to escape from Burma lived in those camps.

Most of those refugees who are living in Western Australia have been through these refugee camps. The distinction is quite noticeable — those who have not stayed in the camps for a long period of time generally speak good English. Those who have spent a long time in those camps speak mostly the Karen language and are more reluctant to adopt the way of life here and also to speak English.

Furthermore, there is currently a strong wish for some to support the struggle for land in their home country. They believe that their struggle is not over as long as the Burmese government is occupying their land. They are only a refugee here and will always be. They have an organisation in Western Australia which coordinates the fund-raising program and also the sending of these funds to carry on the fight in Myanmar. There is also another group of Karen who believes that there is not much point in sending money for the freedom fighters. So, their intention is to help those who are in refugee camps in Thailand to settle into other countries. A large proportion of those refugees have gone to the USA and a relatively smaller proportion has settled in Western Australia. The size of the Karen population in Western Australia is uncertain since there is no official figure yet, Karen not being officially recognised as an independent country. A rough estimate is that it is around the 4,000 mark. However, this has been disputed by others who say that the figure is much higher than this.

With the above brief history in mind, it is possible to see that the role of the church here has been to "not only cater to dislocated immigrants in their quest for truth or meaning through their religious orientation, but also offer them much needed practical guidance and support".[7] The church, in an effort to provide this to its members, sees itself having to be involved not only in religious activities but also in non-religious ones. These activities are essential to the church's relevance to the rapid changes facing these people on the one hand, while it continues to help people toward a meaningful life on the other hand.

After many years living in refugee camps, very close relationships develop and this is reflected in many of those communities. When they come to our shores, these bonds still exist and this is what keeps them going in spite of the hardship that they face when trying to settle down here. When employment becomes a problem, these communities have been very creative in helping the unemployed.

One of the Karen community leaders, also a member of one of the Karen Baptist churches, works at one of the government agencies providing support to migrants settling in Perth. He has a strong passion to see Karen people actively participating in the activities of the society and fully integrated into the Australian way of life.

He was saddened by the fact that people from his own community were finding it very difficult to find regular jobs due to their lack of reasonably good spoken English. In one of the meetings with employers willing to offer jobs to recently arrived migrants, he was talking to a manager of the abattoir in Katanning. He was told that the abattoir was looking for local people to work there. He encouraged a couple of unemployed people from the Karen church community, with reasonably good spoken English, to go with him to Katanning and see whether the work would be suitable for them.

Having seen the work required of them and also the opportunity to lead a decent life in Katanning, they decided to move down there with their families. They were good, hard workers and started to build up their reputation among the management at the abattoir. They rapidly got promoted to being supervisors. When that happened, it created a situation whereby the language barrier no longer existed. Management, through the supervisors, could provide instructions to the workers on what was required of them. This started something that is still going on today.

A few months later, two more families moved down there to join the first ones. Two and a half years down the track, the community numbers more than one hundred. The Karen community is now well established and has a strong reputation within the Katanning population. This has been enhanced by an incident whereby a girl from the Karen community saved the life of another girl from drowning in a swimming pool. At a thanksgiving service held a couple of years ago in Katanning, many locals came to show their support to the Karen community. Another indication of their wish to settle there is the purchase of real estate by more than fifteen families. Currently, members of the Katanning Karen Baptist Church are not only employed in the abattoir but in the hospital and the local supermarket as well. Some are even trying their hands in planting vegetables in order to sell to the locals. One lady is actually specialising in providing fresh chillies to a local restaurant. This is the variety of roles that they are playing in a small regional community and it is expected to grow and become more and more varied over the years — the result of the church leadership caring for its members in whatever is required for that congregation.

Yet another example of what church without four walls can be is that of a Chin church — affiliated with the Baptist Churches of Western Australia, the very first Chin church in existence in Perth. To understand the Chin community, it is helpful to briefly look at their background.

The Chin State is located in the west of Myanmar (Burma). The Chin community group makes up the majority of the state's 500,000 people. The capital of the state is Hakha. The state consists of many mountainous regions, with very few public transport facilities to link the regions. This has resulted in the area being sparsely populated and it remains one of the least developed areas of Myanmar.

The British gained control of the Chin Hills after the Third Anglo-Burmese War of 1885. The ensuing Chin resistance to the British was suppressed by 1890. American missionaries began arriving in the 1890s and by the middle of the twentieth century the vast majority of the Chin community had converted to Christianity.

The region also marked the limit of the advance of the Imperial Japanese Army which invaded in November 1943. After the war, the Chin leaders, along with other community leaders, participated in the Panglong Conference to discuss the future of an independent Union of Burma. Knowing that their region is economically heavily dependent on Burma, the Chin leaders, unlike the others, asked only for a "special administrative division" instead of a fully-fledged state. As a result, when the 1947 Constitution of Burma granted the right of secession to states following a period of ten years after independence, the Chin did not get their own state. (Ironically, the Karen who did not even participate in the conference received the state status, along with the right to secede.) On the 4th January 1974, it was officially given the status of state and became known as the Chin State.

Since 2000, the population of the Chin State has been decreasing quite rapidly due to migration. For more than twenty years now, a large number of Burmese soldiers have been moving into the Chin State despite the fact that there has not been any sign of rebellion against the military regime. It is estimated that more than twenty percent of the population has moved to the neighboring countries of India, Malaysia, and Thailand. From there, a substantial number have gone to other countries like Australia and New Zealand. It is also estimated that in Malaysia alone there are close to 40,000 UNHCR-recognised Chin refugees waiting to be settled in other countries.

How has the Chin community settled into Western Australia? Their experience is far from the experiences described by Swedish researcher, Elisabeth Gerle. She describes how the move to integrate migrants in Scandinavia had shifted the educational system from a situation where religion was being something taught to every child to one in which nobody dared to talk about it anymore. She says:

Schools were supposed to be similar all over the country and seen as a democratic project to bring children from different social backgrounds together. Equality was a key value. During that period religions were thought to gradually disappear from the public sphere. Hence, religions were taught about, not learned from. They were seen as part of a cultural heritage and as a way to understand foreign cultures, less as resources in a continuing interpretation of life to find meaning and direction.[8]

It could also be that theologians tend to be more interested in analysing small communities than the broader society. It seems closer to religion. So much of religious life is relegated to private arenas in late-modernity. Religious institutions are not at the centre of society any more.[9]

The Chin community believes in something completely different — the church is at the centre of their community. Everything revolves around the church; there is no difference between the Chin community and the church community, it is the same one. Whatever happens in church is the business of everyone. Since this is the case, the church community does whatever is practically possible to help new refugees to settle here.

As soon as they become aware of the arrival of a new family in Perth, the church executive committee decides on which family will be most appropriate to take care of them. The host family is contacted and given the details of the new arrivals. This new family will be met at the airport and provided with initial accommodation until they can sort something out for the long-term basis. The first Sunday, they are taken to church and introduced to the whole church community. Soon after, the church will officially visit the family and give them a "love gift" — some financial help which will allow them to obtain the basic necessities they need here.

Every month, the senior Pastor will pay a visit to each of the new families and he will lead a full service at their homes — including a full sermon. This demonstrates to the family that they are cared for and that the church will look after them. Subsequently, they will be picked up to go to church every Sunday in the church buses until they can organise their own transport. That church has a retention rate of more than ninety-five percent — and the flow of newcomers consists of attendees coming from as wide a range of backgrounds as Roman Catholicism and Pentecostalism. Yes, they have issues — and the most recent one they are having is: how can we cater for those who are arriving in so great numbers in such a short period of time? The Chin people's struggle to survive in their country of origin and then in refugee camps has made them into a stronger community here with the will and determination to care for one another. They do not have a building to take care of and their resources are being used to look after people in the church community. However, they have started a building fund recently and are looking to get a place of their own. It will be interesting to see what happens once they move into their new building — the elusive four walls.

This is church and it is happening without the four walls. While it is true that this is happening because of circumstances, we can learn so much about the church beyond the four walls from how those communities are doing church.

> To love our own kind of people, and to have a monocultural church: that is ordinary. To live and worship in a multicultural church, which reflects the crucified Christ: that is extraordinary, for God is extraordinary.[10]

Rev. Dr Marc Chan is the Multicultural Consultant, Baptist Union of Victoria after sixteen years (1998 – 2014) of involvement in the Cross Cultural and Indigenous Ministries at the Baptist Churches Western Australia.

Strengthening Intercultural Ministry in Local Congregations

Sue Holdsworth and Julian Holdsworth

In this chapter we will argue for a greater degree of active collaboration between church leaders, our theological academies, and mission agencies. This collaboration will aid the development of intercultural awareness amongst both church leaders and congregations. The result, we hope, will be an increasingly effective intercultural engagement by Australian churches within their local settings. We will argue that all three of these agencies are vital elements for maintaining effective intercultural initiatives, undertaken by Australian congregations. To do this, we discuss a case study of a multicultural church in Melbourne. We attribute the efficacy of this congregation to collaboration with a mission agency plus high levels of "cultural intelligence", a concept that is being integrated into the missional teaching at several theological colleges in Australia. We will look at some significant theological themes and some suggested praxis that anticipates a future of deeper and stronger collaboration between church, mission agencies, and the theological academy.

Introduction

First, we will discuss our general perception of the current situation amongst our churches, illustrated by examples of successful intercultural relating in Melbourne churches where mission agencies and congregations have worked together. These illustrate two helpful approaches to intercultural relating, which are offered by either mission agencies or theological academies. This will be followed by a brief theological exploration of the need for congregations to have an informed praxis of intercultural engagement. Finally, we will make some practical suggestions regarding the form this collaboration might take and what it might achieve.[1]

We believe that "being the church" amongst people of different ethnicities warrants special consideration in our discussions of church and mission.[2] Our reasons for this are outlined in the following discussion.

When we speak of pastors and churches in the following argument, we are referring to our experiences with people from any or no denomination. It is a given that Australia has many different cultures living within its borders. This is the context in which intercultural issues are addressed.

Local congregations

One of our roles within Wycliffe — the mission agency that we work with — is that of coming alongside local churches in order to help them interact in their intercultural context, within congregations and within the wider community. An ever increasing number of congregations are engaging interculturally, with varying degrees of enthusiasm and effectiveness. Sue has spent significant amounts of time with various congregations. During her sojourn with a particular congregation, she has often interviewed both pastors and members about their church's intercultural experiences. When reflecting together on these experiences, we have both felt sympathy for those pastors who say they see the need for a focused intercultural engagement within their congregations and in the community, but who have too many calls on their time to do this. Some pastors are troubled by the seeming indifference of their congregation to intercultural issues. Other pastors have invited input, but then been defensive when gentle suggestions to further cultural integration have been made. In some churches, efforts have been made to include those of different language backgrounds in the services. The reality is, however, that during the coffee time afterwards or when lay leaders are appointed, people of different language backgrounds often remain at the periphery of group life.

Overall, despite operating in some of the more multicultural municipalities in Australia, Sue has encountered relatively low levels of cross-cultural understanding amongst both congregations and pastors. Sue is yet to meet a pastor who is uninterested in relating interculturally, but the step from desire to the reality of congregations doing this, can seem, at times, overwhelming. The reality is, people don't know what they don't know due to many of us being constrained by an ethnocentric worldview.

While we've both promoted the message that everyone can form meaningful intercultural friendships, we have found that it has been an uphill task persuading church leaders and members of the necessity of intercultural training. Yet all of us have much to gain from interaction with other cultures. We acknowledge that some churches are making big efforts to engage meaningfully in this respect. The following examples of ways in which congregations have related interculturally in various contexts are encouraging.

A number of churches regularly have public prayers in more than one language, as representative of the different languages used amongst the congregation and as an acknowledgement that God communicates to each one of us in our "heart language". We have seen worship songs in languages other than English displayed using PowerPoint so that everyone can engage in meaningful worship. Another church hands out sermon notes in simplified English. A few churches have put in the considerable effort of simultaneously translating sermons into one or more languages, by the use of headphones. Most congregations with a number of members of a different ethnicity regularly enjoy mouth-watering international cuisine!

These are all helpful initiatives but we have sometimes felt that, in reality, they achieve little more than to scratch the surface of intercultural relating. A framework of reference is required so that congregations can assess progress and discern what needs doing as the next step in a congregation's intercultural journey.

An example of healthy intercultural relating

Canterbury Presbyterian Church, in Melbourne, has an inspiring story of what can result from cooperation between congregation and agency.

In 1990, a young missionary from "Mission to the World" was looking for a church in Melbourne where he could start a ministry to the Japanese diaspora in the city. He was invited to base himself at Canterbury Presbyterian Church. He soon started teaching English in a facility in the CBD to which young Japanese students, who were spending time in Melbourne, were invited. These young adults were then invited to attend a dinner, together with songs, games, and a brief Bible talk, every Friday evening, in the church building. The following year he started a Japanese congregation at the church on Sunday afternoons. A faithful group of women from the Anglo congregation, who were known for their prayerfulness, would come each week to serve afternoon tea to the Japanese. When the church at

Canterbury appointed a new senior pastor a few years later, he, together with the missionary, decided to run the Japanese service at the same time as the English service. Morning tea or a lunch together followed these parallel services together.

Around the same time, a few Korean young adults started attending the English lessons in the CBD. They were Christians and the missionary soon got them helping out at the Friday night dinner. They also started attending the English service on Sundays. The English lessons quickly attracted an equal mix of Japanese and Korean students, plus a few other nationalities. With a number of Koreans regularly attending the English services, the senior pastor realised the need to accommodate their language needs, to help them access the service content. Full sermon notes are translated into Korean every week, and Bible readings and songs are translated into Korean and projected using PowerPoint. This has proved to be a more popular approach than simultaneous translation, as it keeps the service moving along at a satisfying pace for all attendees.

After eight years, the missionary was moved on by "Mission to the World" but he strongly encouraged the church leadership to appoint a Japanese pastor with experience of living overseas. It's been a tall order to find someone who fits the bill over the years, but this has proved key to the health of the Japanese congregation. Likewise, a Korean pastor was also appointed for the joint English/Korean congregation. This congregation has decided to stay combined and now has many Korean and Aussie/Korean families attending. One significant advantage of this has been that the needs of second generation Aussie/Koreans are more readily met in a mixed congregation. Another advantage is that the Korean pastor will often advocate for Korean members when cross-cultural difficulties arise.

The English lessons have continued and are part of a staged outreach plan that starts with the English lessons and moves through to the Friday night dinner, attendance at church services, and own language Bible studies for those who are interested. This has resulted in a non-pressured situation, in which the students are valued at every level of involvement. This love and acceptance have been demonstrated by church members in other ways. For instance, many of the students have experienced exploitation by unscrupulous landlords and the senior pastor found himself regularly advocating for them. This resulted in the church renting and furnishing two houses, for the sole use of the students.

Initiatives to aid cultural integration over the years have included people from the English congregation helping at the Friday night dinners, a Korean/Aussie women's fellowship meeting monthly in order to learn about each other, and the

Japanese congregation holding regular joint services with the Aussie/Korean congregation. Korean/Aussie/Japanese men's fishing trips have also proved to be a popular activity while at the same time, own language needs are addressed through Korean Bible studies and a monthly weekday Korean-only service.

None of this would have happened without the trained and gifted missionary who was willing to take a risk, but who also wanted to become rooted in a local congregation. The senior pastor, who arrived a few years into this project, was also highly motivated to work with this significant, though demanding, opportunity for developing an intercultural congregation. The wider church leadership recognised the needs and also came on board fully. They dared to risk losing some of their Anglo-Aussie congregation who may not have been happy with the influx of Koreans and Japanese.

Secondly, this initiative wasn't driven by just a few people in the church. Although inevitably some were much more involved than others, enough people made a pro-active contribution to keep this initiative viable. Newcomers (including Anglo-Aussies) were then attracted to the congregations, because of their multicultural dynamic.

A third key element to success has been the motivation of love. Members from the English-speaking congregation have met practical needs of the students and those who volunteer to teach English lessons, or who help at the dinners, appear genuinely to enjoy the students' company.

A final key to effective cross-cultural relating, we believe, is seen in the congregation's willingness to stand in the shoes of others. For instance, numerous Anglo-Aussie members have learned either Korean or Japanese and church members frequently visit Japan and Korea. These visits are a chance to catch up with new friends who have previously spent time at the church and have now returned home. They are also an opportunity to learn more of their cultures.

This church is the best example we know of a congregation that has become truly multicultural. They can be said to have displayed high levels of cultural intelligence.

What the members of Canterbury Presbyterian achieved, partly by circumstance and partly by intention, can be achieved by any congregation, if an informed strategy is implemented.

Some people are more naturally gifted in cultural intelligence — for example, the English-speaking senior pastor of Canterbury Presbyterian — but all of us can develop cultural intelligence. It is also important to acknowledge that the missionary taught the pastor much that he didn't know about working with Koreans and Japanese.

What is cultural intelligence?

Cultural intelligence (CQ) is a construct of intelligence, created by Earley and Ang and based on the multiple-loci-of-intelligence theory of Detterman and Sternberg.[3] It was initially implemented within the world of global business relations. This model has been rigorously tested and is now widely taught in business and educational contexts. This model also has helpful implications for intercultural ministry.

The original model has been refined and now identifies four distinct dimensions to cultural intelligence. It is necessary for someone to employ all four dimensions in order to achieve successful, ongoing, cross-cultural relationships. The four dimensions of cultural intelligence are "metacognition" (mindfulness in cross-cultural planning and interactions), "cognition" (cultural knowledge), "behavioural" (a willingness to adapt behaviour), and "motivational" (a willingness and ability to persevere). Some aspects of cross-cultural intelligence come more naturally to some people than to others, but everyone can grow in their ability in each dimension.

The cultural intelligence model may explain why some congregations give an impression of having "something missing" in their cross-cultural relations, despite at times, considerable efforts to be inclusive.

Canterbury Presbyterian displayed metacognitive CQ in planning their outreach model. They realised that church life would need to be significantly adapted if they were to retain and effectively integrate those from overseas. Cognitive CQ (sometimes labelled "cultural knowledge") informed the leaders that East Asian people enjoy a different diet from Westerners. This cultural knowledge informed their behavioural CQ, as they realised that serving East Asian food at the youth group would communicate care more effectively than would the provision of only Aussie food. The fairly conservative nature of the congregation resulted in a calm, thoughtful approach to social interactions with the Asian students. This was a good match for students from cultures which are still somewhat more restrained than the comparatively boisterous Aussie youth culture. We observed the more extrovert members of the Anglo congregation adapting their behaviour around the Asian students' generally quieter approach to socialising. The congregation at Canterbury Presbyterian has clearly demonstrated motivational CQ, by persevering in its cross-cultural ministry over many years and through numerous challenges. It didn't stop at making just one or two adjustments to church life — it continues to adjust its cross-cultural ministry to fit whatever changing circumstances it encounters.

David Livermore[4] has adapted the CQ model for cross-cultural ministry. While not detracting from Early and Ang's model in any way, he has added the motivation of love as a driver for growing in each cultural dimension. He writes of God's incarnational love, shown through Jesus, as the model we are to emulate. Livermore is highly recommended reading.

Love has been key to the ministry at Canterbury Presbyterian. Understanding and responding to needs have resulted in the formation of new friendships and congregational initiatives, and have enabled perseverance when people have become weary or discouraged. Love has also resulted in the staged programme they have created, as described above, that maintains the gentle invitation to explore Christianity, without conveying a sense that friendship is conditional on participants displaying an interest in Christianity.

Of all the available tools, we believe that CQ is key to effective cross-cultural relating, within our congregations and into our wider communities.

"Operation Encounter"

A model which has proved of great benefit in enabling congregations to begin to relate inter-culturally, both within the congregation and in the wider community, is the "Operation Encounter" course. This programme, which was designed by staff of Wycliffe Australia, has been successfully implemented within congregations for a number of years now, including at Canterbury Presbyterian. This is an introductory, practical course in applied anthropology, designed for use in local churches. It is a non-threatening way of helping congregations build one-on-one, cross-cultural friendships, simply by spending time together and asking questions that enable the student to learn about the other person's worldview. This short course is ideally delivered over four to five weeks, in sessions lasting around two hours each. Participants are asked to find one person from their community, or amongst work colleagues, who is from a culture different to their own. "Homework" between sessions consists of spending time together with this person, asking questions that range from "Tell me about the food eaten in your culture" to "From your background, what are the four most important things in life and why are they so important?"

During the course, participants are asked not to attempt to convert their homework partner, as the emphasis is one of learning about the "other" and forming genuine friendships. This request is sometimes very hard for evangelicals to comply with!

Many lasting cross-cultural friendships have resulted from such homework assignments and not a few homework friends have sooner or later become Christians, as participants continued to share and listen together. However, the emphasis is firmly on learning to practise incarnational listening.

Julian once taught Operation Encounter (OE) in a congregation where one participant conducted her homework with a Sri Lankan couple. They soon built a firm friendship and at the end of the course they asked her if they could look at the Bible together with her — it's worth noting that many people from non-Western cultures find talking about spirituality easier than Westerners do. Several months later, one of the couple became a Christian, followed by their spouse a while later.

While not always happening quite so quickly and dramatically, this pattern has been repeated numerous times following participation in an OE course. Meeting just four times as part of a course won't cut it, but when these relationships are maintained they are proved to be genuine and trust is developed. We should not be aiming to "make converts", but rather to incarnate the love of Jesus unconditionally. Key aspects of the success of OE are the low-key relational nature of developing cross-cultural friendships and the willingness of participants to listen to what is important to their new friends.

In sum, the Operation Encounter course is an excellent example of a mission agency using their intercultural training and experience, to help local congregations become more interculturally effective.

Theological motifs

"Why don't we just focus our services around the existing Anglo-Aussie culture in order to create a common understanding amongst congregational members?" "If they want to do things their way, why don't people from other cultures start their own congregations?" "We know we ought to love our neighbour, why do we need all this training?" These are common questions asked by pastors and congregation members alike. We will address them below with reference to the theologically informed practices of a variety people.

This will not be a comprehensive summary, but rather will outline a cluster of theological motifs that, to us, create an imperative that we believe is at the heart of the Christian faith.[5] This theological imperative calls us to embrace the need for the "other". Although the concept of "other" has applications broader than the scope of this paper, it certainly includes those of different ethnicities to us.

There is often pressure on pastors to deliver a lively and attractive spiritual product. Of course, many pastors will choose to be free of the ambition of being judged by others as successful in terms of congregation size or other fleeting criteria. We recognise that this can be a hard road to walk, particularly when the leadership team has such criteria as the dominant or even sole benchmark of success. We would argue that pastors might rather choose to operate from a theology of the now and future kingdom of God; a theology that expresses itself practically in an energised commitment to unity between all personality types, people groups, and otherwise estranged individuals. Could this be closer to God's definition of healthy church life?

For example, Wright argues that the encouragement to the slave owner Philemon to welcome his returning slave and perhaps go further by treating him as "a brother" marks it as a letter suffused with Paul's wider theology of the in-breaking kingdom. Therefore, in this apparently simple discourse, we discover the practical outworking of Paul's commitment to a theology of integration and reconciliation.[6] This theology anticipates the coming new creation and is experienced within the reconciling community of all God's people; as it was for slaves and owners, so also it should be for relationships with different ethnicities (Col 3:11). The inaugurated eschatology of all *ethne*[7] worshipping around the throne of God is, we would argue, the ultimate vision to which all present praxis should be oriented. It serves as a more accurate image of the kingdom than a large monocultural congregation with contemporary Western style worship, yet which doesn't reflect the ethnic makeup of the local population. This style of church too easily marginalises the "other".

Here again we are challenged with a pastoral tension relating to how to maintain both unity and diversity at the same time. Those around the throne are "all one in Christ" (Gal 3:28) and yet identifiable as distinct tribes and *ethne* (Rev 7:9).

Christ has overcome the barriers between us without destroying our particular identities. As we wait for that day, the church is called to celebrate the distinctive and different voices and perspectives that come with embracing the other. As Volf points out, we must allow those voices to be heard.[8]

Bailey talks of how Jesus' hearers in Luke 4:16–30 need to hear the voice of the Gentiles in their own defining stories in the Old Testament. And more than just hear but, rather, welcome the Gentiles almost as teachers of the faith.[9] He writes, "'I am not asking you,' says Jesus, 'to accept them. I am asking you to learn from them. Don't drive them out! See them as your superiors, your teachers'". Bailey cites an unreferenced comment by D.T. Niles that "the gospel is not safe in any culture unless there is a witness to Jesus Christ in that culture from beyond itself" and argues that "All of us must have among us a witness to Jesus Christ who comes from beyond ourselves".[10] Bailey does not make this point when elsewhere he writes of the Good Samaritan,[11] but it seems to us that precisely this point could be extrapolated from that parable: that is, the voices of others, not of our cultural background, are vital for the health of the gospel and we need to proactively listen to them.[12]

A clear theology of power is also important for our praxis. The first half of Philippians 2 is a benchmark passage in this respect, guiding the church's attitude and demeanour in relation to one another (2:1–4) and as a response to the relinquishment of power by the Son (2:6–11). Paul calls the congregation to serve one another in genuine humility. Their union in Christ ought to result in certain behaviours (2:1–2). He points them to a unity that is rooted in and modelled by the example of Christ Jesus. "The Philippians are here faced with the greatest possible incentive to unity and humility in the picture of the Lord Himself..."[13] Thus Paul sees their oneness established through the incarnation, servant lifestyle, and Easter sacrifice of Christ. This is an important motif for framing responses to our multicultural context and, in our case study, Canterbury Presbyterian seems to have done just this when they appointed Korean and Japanese pastors.

Why do we often find it so hard to identify the leadership abilities of people from other ethnicities? Is it because our definition of leadership needs re-forming? Perhaps we can find fresh ways to approach what admittedly is a complex issue, by relinquishing the gatekeeper role in the manner exemplified in Philippians 2. This will entail a conscious commitment to shed assumed power in order to express incarnated love in the way that Jesus did. Our capacity to flex to the needs of others will be an important measure of our cross-cultural skillset. A method to achieve this might be the application of behavioural intelligence, according to the CQ model described above. This will entail some significant challenges. For example, the criteria used when choosing a leader will vary significantly from culture to culture even when operating within biblical parameters.

Van Gelder writes, "Missions enabled the rise of a hegemonic worldview and an assumption of being in control of the social order. The history of having cultural dominance has deeply shaped western Christianity for both Catholics and Protestants".[14] This observation of the rise of mission agencies parallels the unquestioned assumptions of positions of power by people of European descent which we have witnessed taking place in Anglo-Aussie churches. This is created by knowing the culture and "how things work round here" and simply by having the national language as a first language. Why, for example, do we speak of "ethnic churches"? Aren't we all "ethnic"?!

Volf writes that there is a very real risk of creating situations of exclusion by taking oneself out of the pattern of interdependence and placing oneself in a position of sovereign independence. The "other" then emerges either as an enemy who is pushed away from the self and driven out of that space, or as a non-entity, a superfluous being who can be disregarded or abandoned. This dynamic can often play out within our churches, when we dismiss the others' point of view as strange, ludicrous, or just missing the point, and therefore to be summarily dismissed. Volf continues by observing that the "other" then emerges as an inferior being who must either be assimilated and made like one's self or who must be subjugated to the self.

A further application of Philippians 2 in this respect gives us not only a theology of relinquishing power, but also one of embracing incarnation (or of contextualising to the "other"). For in this passage, the conscious choice by Jesus to let go of power is embraced in order to enter the cultural milieu of first-century Palestinian Judaism. Jesus "dwelt among us" (John 1:14). "Dwelling with" introduces a whole process of learning cultural norms and stories, and a deep embedding in the life of the particular people group. Canterbury Presbyterian did just this as they journeyed with "others" and made visits to their home countries. This is, of course, at the heart of both best missional and best pastoral practice. Jesus' journey from God's "culture" to a particular people group is therefore a key theological motif for cross-cultural, missional practice within Australia.

The practice of multicultural inclusion also benefits our own spiritual maturity. In this respect, the multicultural character of Australia is God's gift to us all. "The

Spirit of God wants to break us out of the self-enclosed worlds which we inhabit and create 'fissures' in us through which others can enter in."

Volf writes that, "In order to keep our allegiance to Jesus Christ pure, we need to nurture commitment to the multicultural community of Christian churches. We need to see ourselves and our own understanding of God's future with the eyes of Christians from other cultures, listen to voices of Christians from other cultures so as to make sure the voice of our culture has not drowned out the voice of Jesus Christ, 'the one Word of God'".

A few examples of learning from the other might be helpful here. Our Zimbabwean friend, Langton, has taught us many things about the nature of persevering prayer. Our Iranian, Christian, asylum seeker friends have taught us much about the commitment and perseverance necessary to survive at the margins of society. They have also taught us the value of abundant hospitality and openness to the stranger. Aussies like to perceive of themselves as relaxed and friendly, but in comparison with many cultures, we probably present as quite cold and remote. Friends from numerous countries have taught us that relating to others is sometimes more important than strict time keeping. And there is so much more that we could learn. The need to encounter the voice of the other is therefore crucial if we are also to hear the voice of Jesus.

Indeed, what might we be missing when we fail to connect with the stranger? The parable of the sheep and goats in Matthew 25 suggests that is possible to miss an encounter with Christ by our neglect in welcoming strangers and hearing their voices. The bewilderment of the goats is surely compounded by realising the simple actions of love they might have taken to avoid such a judgment. The gifts of water, food, and friendship are the instruments that lead to encounters with Christ. Jesus elsewhere says to Martha, "one thing is needed" and that was to sit at his feet and listen to him (Luke 10:42). It may be in activities of service that we encounter Jesus in the other or it may be in quietly listening to their story, but we are called to see and engage with those who may be vessels of Christ coming to us.

We will make a final point here about the nature of love. Love ought to be the driving motivation for all that we do. While we acknowledge the reality of our fallen-ness, we would wish to highlight the importance of nurturing attitudes of grace towards the other. Too often, our involvement with congregations has taught us that cross-cultural engagement within, and by, a local congregation, as with any other ministry, can be borne out of mixed motives. For example, we have known people operate out of pride, a dysfunctional desire to dominate others (both colleagues and people of other cultures), or a need for a sense of self-worth. An unchecked "spiritual" ambition has also resulted in the undervaluing, even sabotaging, of input from other outreach team members. Others might be primarily motivated by a desire for numerical church growth, or converts, rather than simply wanting to incarnate God's love to others. Sooner or later, these mixed motives cause damage.

One local church leader we knew spoke regularly of his desire to show the local council that the local churches engage with asylum seekers. Such comments were frequently backed up by invitations for council officers, MPs, the local press, and even national TV to visit, even though many asylum seekers were fearful of anyone who might appear to be making notes about them or of being caught on camera. We cannot know whether lasting damage to some asylum seekers may have resulted from these visits.

Another type of church seems quick to claim credit for being multicultural when, in effect, little is done to integrate those attending from different cultures. More often, we meet pastors who are motivated to see their congregations relating across cultures, but who struggle to inspire their congregations to step out of existing patterns of church life.

Thankfully, we have learned that God's grace is abundant, despite our mixed motivations. He still chooses to work through human shortcomings. However mixed motivations for ministry may have been, we have seen genuine love for the "other" grow in the hearts of congregational members. This in turn has led to acts of service and the spontaneous development of genuine cross-cultural friendships. We cannot manufacture godly love for one another — it is always a gift.

The role of mission agencies and the academy

How might some mission agencies and theological academies enable congregations to become more intercultural? Some returned missionaries have effectively interpreted their field experiences through lenses of both cultural anthropology and practical theology. This has the potential to bring wisdom to situations where a local congregation is seeking to engage with those from different cultures. This is, of course, dependent on the reflective practice and theological training of the missionary.

Dewerse refers to Jung Young Lee, who writes that people he terms "new marginal" are key in teaching the theological academy how to interact in an intercultural environment. These "new marginal" people he describes as being people who are either from another culture or who have lived and interacted in different cultures. Dewerse calls such people "liminal". This description might therefore also include migrant congregational members as well as trained missionaries. The important point here is that their cross-cultural experiences need to have been processed effectively.

Many international mission agencies have needed to work out what unity in diversity looks like, in very practical ways. We can illustrate this point with an example from our experience of working with a mission agency, operating here in Australia and worldwide. Numerous denominations are represented amongst our members, from Pentecostal to Presbyterian, from Baptist to Vineyard, and so on. We send from many different nations who have to collaborate together in teams on the field. We happily operate overseas with anyone who shares our common purpose — Catholics, Orthodox, and people of other religions and none. All these factors have taught us a great deal about practising unity in diversity. The need to create a "new culture", in which modes of relating are agreed together, becomes necessary in intercultural teams. In addition, most of our workers have trained theologically and have learned skills of contextualisation. Maybe a number of mission agencies can offer some helpful insights to churches regarding cross-cultural contextualisation.

Over the past decade, mission agencies that have traditionally sent workers overseas have begun to place workers (often those returning from overseas) into cross-cultural situations here in Australia. For instance, Interserve runs the "Culture Connect" ministry. Other missions such as OMF have had diaspora workers in Melbourne. Wycliffe has also sought to serve the local churches with its experience and expertise in cross-cultural work. These are some examples of agencies which value the local church and theological engagement. This is true of many mission agencies, though not all. In our view, pastors should seek to work with mission agencies which have a theologically informed view of the importance of the local church in God's mission.

Some theological colleges in Australia are now engaging in exciting teaching programmes that have the potential to equip future and current pastors to engage cross-culturally within their congregations and into the wider community. A common experience is for colleges to teach mission courses together with academic practitioners who are currently working in mission agencies. This has, at times, been as much a consequence of a shortage of missiologists on faculty, as

While postcolonial scholars, writing from within a range of different disciplines,[23] will inevitably emphasise different aspects of the postcolonial, the critique of Eurocentrism, the focus on the possibilities for the subaltern voice, and the theorising of difference and of pluralised notions of the subject and of knowledge tend to remain.

So then, in imagining postcolonial Baptist churches, we might begin with the following from feminist postcolonial theologian, Pui-lan Kwok. "Postcolonial imagination," she writes, "refers to a desire, a determination, and a process of disengagement from the whole colonial syndrome, which takes many forms and guises".[24] If what has been discussed in this section is going to apply to Baptist churches, I suggest, as a starting point, we need to acknowledge the way in which "colonialism might be the other side of the one coin that we call Christendom".[25] That is, we need to drop our defences and confess that we are, wittingly or not, implicated in reproducing a Christianity that functions according to the imperialistic logic of colonialism. Christianity in Australia — in terms of its doctrines, its assumptions, its governance, its practice, and its evangelistic impulse — is implicated in Western colonialism. Once we acknowledge this, we may begin to reconsider the gospel and the church according to other cultural expressions and understandings. Such a move, however, requires a willingness to have our former views regarding doctrinal truths and ecclesial structures transformed. While I think it is fair to say that some Baptists — wed as they are to social conservatism, personal piety, and biblicism — would not be open to such radical possibilities, Baptist histories seem to suggest that freedom, local church autonomy, and, therefore, diversity are continuities in an otherwise contested and heterogeneous narrative.

Why Baptists (should) make good postcolonialists

If there is one thing that Baptists seem to agree on, it is that their narrative — and therefore their identity, doctrine, and practice — is diffuse. Gourley writes that "Baptists are a river broad and deep, with diverse theological currents".[26] So too, Tew suggests that "Baptist groups are many and varied: American Baptists, Southern Baptists, Alliance of Baptists, Independent Baptists, General Baptists. We span the spectrum economically, socially, and ethnically. Baptists fight over whose understanding of theology is correct."[27] While scholars such as Hatch seem to think that theological diversity amongst Baptists ultimately amounts to incoherence,[28] others like Fiddes appear more content with the idea that "Baptists have always resisted the idea that there is a distinctively 'Baptist theology', at least in terms of there being a Baptist version of such basic doctrines as the Trinity, Christology, anthropology, and eschatology".[29] Whether or not one thinks all this diversity is a good thing, it nevertheless highlights that Baptist life and theology are more dynamic than they are static.[30] Indeed, Fiddes uses the metaphor of "tracks and traces" when investigating the Baptist tradition. This metaphor evokes both the image of multiple directions, but also some form of continuity. Further, the word "trace" also connotes impermanence.

Such dynamism, it would seem, is related to the kind of contexts in which Baptists emerged. For example, McBeth narrates the beginning of the English Baptists by locating the movement within the context of the political changes during the seventeenth century. In doing so, he identifies the historical link between the challenge to the power and authority of the monarchy and Baptists' own suspicion of institutionalised power. In reference to the return to monarchic rule in 1660, after the tumult of the English Revolution and Oliver Cromwell, McBeth writes, "though England continued to have a monarchy, real political power had passed to Parliament. The rise of various dissenting religions to challenge the Church of England was in some ways the religious equivalent of the undermining of monarchy by a strong Parliament."[31] The somewhat mundane, obvious, and yet significant point being made here is that changes within the church were not divorced from wider political, social, and economic contexts. Indeed, while the faithful sometimes like to think that their beliefs and practices are merely "biblical" and a-cultural, McBeth makes the point that religion will — at least in some way — reflect the broader context of the day. He writes, "clearly the Baptists fit the temperament of their times. Conditions were right for the emergence of more individualistic forms of religion, and the spate of new religious groups in England shows that they took full advantage of the day."[32] To suggest, then, that a church could in some way be "pure" is a fallacy. Just as with the postcolonial critique of anti-colonialist's nativist tendencies, the postcolonial church must be wary of fundamentalist cries for the pure church to be recovered. Part of the — I think, necessary — challenge that postcolonial theorising brings is the way it problematises such notions of stability and essence.[33] While there is something to be gained from the idea, as McBeth puts it, that knowing "... the origin of a movement or a group gives a head start to understanding its present identity and significance",[34] this should not be mistaken as meaning that in the beginning was the true, pure Baptist church and any issues the church currently faces should be addressed by recovering these distorted forms or lost treasures.

Moreover, just as we may acknowledge the political and cultural shaping of Baptists in the seventeenth century, so too might we take notice of today's context. Focused specifically on the contemporary global and pluralistic milieu, Johnson suggests that today's Baptists consist of myriad formally and informally interconnected independent entities from across the world. With such a loosely connected denomination "with no centralized defining authority", Johnson asks, "how does one decide what is and is not Baptist?" Even within the era of modernity, this question has been notoriously difficult for Baptists to answer. Now in a postmodern context, Johnson suggests, "some observers object that this is not even the correct question to be asking".[35] So again, if the postcolonial imagination theorises identity differently, focusing on the mutability of ideas and subjects through a process of mutual transformation for both the coloniser and the colonised[36] rather than the affirmation of ontological fixity, Baptist identity will shift and be retraced according to actual lived experiences of local churches. This way of *being* the church may well hint at the kind of theologising that could be considered "Baptist". To say that Baptists are not defined so much by a set of propositions (or confessions) that become fixed in time, but by the way they live and act as a community of faith provides a good basis for being a church that embraces change and contextualises its theology and practice. Indeed, rather than focus on the content of Baptist theology, Brian Haymes suggests that Baptist theological method is marked by "a continual re-making, an imaginative living in the biblical story, a generous pluralism, and a collegiality in which doing theology is shared by experts and those who simply live out their theology in a practical way".[37]

So Baptists tend to be willing to respond to culture in a mutually reciprocal way and this is, in part, an acknowledgement that the church lives and acts in particular contexts. So, too, Baptists tend to defend the right of each congregation to develop their own theologies. While the English Revolution created a distaste for centralised power, Baptists' reformational roots also ensured they became rooted in the person of Jesus and the Scriptures. While an image of zealous biblicist Jesus Freaks might be immediately evoked, such a relation to truth and the biblical text need not be the case. Johnson writes that, "Baptists speak of the Bible as being inspired, although the larger family of Baptists does not have a common view of how that inspiration is to be understood". In fact, he continues, "Baptists' general agreement on the Bible's revelatory sufficiency does not ensure singularity of views on the many issues they confront. Wide differences can and usually do exist amongst Baptists on any given issue because of differences in how the Bible should be interpreted relative to each one."[38]

However, it is true that there also exists a strong conservative strand in the Baptist tradition.[39] Manley details debates regarding inerrancy that took place amongst mainly Victorian Baptists through the late 1960s up until the mid-1990s.[40] There are clearly Baptist leaders and churches who read the Bible literally or at least hold to a strict inerrantist position.[41] Approaches to biblical interpretation which function to flatten the Bible and turn it into an instruction manual or systematic theology do not fit with a postcolonial approach. This is not to say that postcolonial biblical criticism lacks careful textual analysis or respect for the Bible's provenance, but it does bring into question the dominance of the historical-critical method.[42] Nevertheless, as Sugirtharajah acknowledges, "Postcolonialism is largely an intellectual and political pursuit and has unashamedly a committed stance. Unlike other theoretical categories, it is not too preoccupied with detachment and neutrality".[43] What is important in this quote is the honesty that comes with declaring a committed stance. Part of the epistemic violence committed by the colonial church during Christendom was its universalising of Western biblical interpretation. While many Baptists would acknowledge that there can be multiple interpretations of a biblical text, postcolonial Baptists will need to be willing to engage in different methodologies that are not beholden to Western Enlightenment rationality.

What will be important for Baptists when it comes to imagining the Bible afresh is to ensure that the seriousness and power of the Bible to form the Christian community is maintained.[44] With this commitment assured, there arises the possibility to allow for a dynamic and creative engagement with the Bible which allows for different and disruptive voices and interpretations. While this will not always be comfortable, Walsh argues that, "a sure sign of [repressive] ideology is when the Bible *only* functions as a text of orientation in our lives. If this text never disorients us, then it will never then have the resources to provide us with reorientation in changing and confusing cultural contexts".[45]

Conclusion

In today's globalised world where communities are increasingly multicultural and in an era which is seeing Christianity grow in the Global South and decline in the Global North, what kind of Baptist theology and what kind of Baptist church are needed? The argument in this chapter is that the way forward for Baptist churches in post-Christendom should not be either a simplistic renunciation of, or alternatively a tenacious clinging to, the Constantinian past. I have tried to suggest that the postcolonial condition which emerges from this colonial/Christendom past is one that is altogether more creative and constructive. After Christendom, the postcolonial invites us to explore the mutual transformations that take place both for the new and the old and to imagine a different future altogether. Developing a postcolonial Baptist imagination — to simultaneously resist, subvert, and embrace Baptist implications in Christendom within the context of today's pluralistic and global era — will be the effect of "new" and "old" listening, joining together, interpreting, critiquing, imagining, and stepping forward in the journey.

While I do not suggest that diversity or pluralism should be a doctrine or fundamental proposition to which Baptists adhere, I do think that an inclusive posture, marked by openness to the Spirit, is an important element of Baptist histories.[46] The history and (ambiguity of) distinctives of the Baptist church should actually see it well placed to embody and enact a postcolonial theological imagination. This imagination is one that seeks a dialogue with its past which involves both critique of its excesses and violence as well as utilising its resources to forge a new future of witness to the gospel. However, seeing (political) postcolonial resistance as part of the church's mission to invite consideration of the gospel (kerygmatics) is not without its dangers. Pentecostal theologian Amos Yong warns that "the shift from a politics of resistance to a kerygmatics of resistance risks transforming resistance into violence, prophetic criticism into coercive rhetoric, proclamation of the universal gospel into a universalizing of a Christian vernacular".[47] Whereas Yong locates the power to avoid the oppressive, universalising tendencies of the church in the "many tongues" of Pentecostalism, Baptists are able to appeal to their commitment to freedom from centralised and oppressive religious and state structures which manifests in local church autonomy and, subsequently, diversity. For this kind of diversity to be truly postcolonial and biblical, however, Baptists must insist that those on the margins always have an opportunity to speak and, crucially, to be heard by those in power.[48]

Finally, the challenges and opportunities facing the church call for, I suggest, not simply new wineskins, but also new wine. This is part of the challenge that postcolonialism brings. A transformation of the wineskins fails, I suggest, to adequately deal with colonialism's epistemological imperialism and cultural oppression. By only concerning itself with the wineskin, and not the wine itself, the church perpetuates the marginalisation and silencing of alternate voices. Thus, the opportunity for Baptists is to embrace a church life that includes, and engages in theological work alongside, both the formerly colonised (in geo-political, historical terms) and the currently colonised (in cultural, theological, economic terms). To move towards this, however, there is a need for further work — both "theological" and practical — that needs to be done to begin to construct and make known examples of postcolonial Baptist churches in action.

Stephen Chatelier is both the son and son-in-law of ordained Baptist church ministers. He is currently undertaking a PhD focusing on the challenge of postcolonial theories to humanism and education. Stephen and his wife, Anouchka, also manage the Kew Student Residence in Melbourne.

Welcoming the Stranger
Addressing Issues of Ethos and Praxis in Multicultural Church Communities

Gordon Stewart

In view of our almost universal tendency to be shaped by monocultural or ethnocentric perspectives, the desire for multicultural expressions of church raises significant challenges in a variety of areas, including anthropology, sociology, and theology. In this paper I contend that for centuries the predominant model of Christian congregating, shaped by a prevalent ethos and accompanying structure and praxis, has been and is antithetical to the development of cross-cultural communities and the harnessing of their missional capacities. This is especially true as descriptive of churches in Western contexts (and elsewhere where the model has been promulgated). Reflecting on biblical perspectives concerning culture and ethnicity, and drawing on insights gained from involvement in a multi-ethnic and multicultural ministry to international students in Auckland, I seek to identify a number of counter-cultural elements in the ethos and praxis of congregations and suggest more contextualised approaches with potential to overcome the impasse and provide pathways for more fruitful kingdom-focused outcomes within multicultural churches and beyond.

Introduction

The gospel's encounter with culture is necessarily context specific. My premise is that there is no possibility of a reception of the gospel's core apart from or beyond the culture of the recipients, just as the expression of that gospel by those communicating it is shaped by their culture. If it is affirmed that there is a non-negotiable gospel core, this should not be taken to mean that this gospel is something hermetically sealed, to be responded to by all peoples apart from their frames of mind, their cultural and worldview formations. These premises relate directly to our focus on what it means for the church to be multicultural. As a result of globalising influences, urban centres in our Australasian contexts (broadening the focus here to include Aotearoa New Zealand) are increasingly characterised by cultural and religious diversity, evident in a multiplicity of rites and rituals, and the assumptions which underpin them. In these settings, surface expressions of culture tend to be multiplex, while those deep assumptions of people's worldviews remain quite resistant to change. An explanatory comment regarding terminology is in order. While the terms *multi-ethnic* and *multicultural* are used somewhat interchangeably in the paper, this is not to ignore the fact that within a single ethnicity we are bound to encounter cultural differences, identifiable sub-cultures determined by differentials in terms of the age of people, and the extent to which people within an ethnicity in one setting have had exposure to and been influenced by other cultures. As the abstract suggests, the desire for multicultural expressions of church raises significant challenges, including the need to draw on sociology for an understanding of context, on anthropology for meaningful engagement of the gospel with culture, and on theology, in particular a theology of the church. As we focus on what it means for the church to be multicultural, we soon become aware of our almost universal proneness to monocultural or ethno-centric perspectives in human relationships and also of our limited appreciation of the gospel's scope and power to engage diverse cultures.

Sociological questions

This paper is framed by my experience in many different contexts, but more particularly by the challenges and opportunities found in Auckland where rapid demographic changes have been occurring over the past 15 to 20 years, a reality that I believe is familiar to many of us who are urban dwellers in the countries we represent. Involvement in a ministry to international students in Auckland's CBD has provided many challenges and significant learning opportunities. Some reference will be made to that particular experience. Some sociological analysis is needed if we are to find meaningful connection with the cultural diversity of the contexts in which we live and serve.

Auckland's population in the early twentieth century was almost entirely European, as was the case with other cities in Aotearoa New Zealand. The Maori population was located in rural New Zealand. In the case of New Zealand — and probably also Australia — the factor of urban drift of the indigenous peoples needs to be taken into account, especially as it relates to commitment to biculturalism. In New Zealand, between 1936 and 1986, the Maori population changed from being 83 percent rural to being 83 percent urban, but with a significant portion of that urban population often located in suburbs that eventually had a predominance of Maori.[1] The other significant demographic change in our larger cities is the increase of migrant populations. In 2013, more than 25 percent of people usually resident in New Zealand were *born overseas*, a proportion that has been steadily increasing over the past 15 to 20 years.[2] In terms of Auckland's population, almost 40 percent were born overseas.[3] It appears that it is a very similar scenario in a number of Australian cities: Adelaide 40.7 percent, Sydney 42.4 percent, and Melbourne 48.7 percent to name several. Over a period of approximately 20 years, there has been remarkable change in Auckland city's *ethnic diversity*, with the European proportion dropping from 75.1 to 52.3 percent , and the Asian percentage rising from 5.5 to 23.1 percent, alongside some increases in Pasifika proportions and the Maori population remaining steady.

Religious diversity is another aspect of demographic change of significance for the church as it addresses the challenge to be multicultural.[4] In *Australia* during the decade 2001–2011, a significant decline in the percentage of the population identifying with the Christian faith (from 68% to 61%), and an increase in the number not affiliating with a religion (from 15% to 22.3%) is set alongside a large increase in non-Christian religions (up from 4.9% to 7.2%, or 0.9 million to 1.54 million). During the period 2001–2013 in *New Zealand*, of those who stated a religious affiliation, people identifying with the Christian religion dropped from 62.8 percent to 48.9 percent (a drop of 13.9%). There was also a significant increase in the proportion of the population indicating they had no religion, from 31.0 percent to 41.9 percent.[5] At the beginning of the same period, a little over 6.1 percent of our population were followers of a non-Christian religion and by 2013 this had reached 9.2 percent, with much of the increase accounted for by migrants to the nation.[6] The migrant factor is a significant one in Auckland's marked increase in religious affiliation, in contrast to the decrease elsewhere in NZ cities. In addition to the church's need of awareness of the cultural diversity that exists and of major demographic trends in cities as a whole, there is also the need for analysis of the ethnic and cultural distinctives that characterise suburbs where the church is being planted.[7]

Specific ministry context

The congregation with which I've been involved for a little more than a decade is located in Auckland's CBD, and is known informally as "Global", and has as its focus the fostering of relationships with international students. It had its beginnings in a quite spontaneous way 14 years ago, not as an intentional plant from the Baptist Church to which it is linked but as a result of a few young mainland Chinese migrants asking a member of that church if she could help them understand what the Bible was about. From those initial conversations with a handful of enquirers over coffee has evolved the Kiwi-International Friendship Group (Global) comprising 20 nationalities, predominantly from countries in Asia but also from Latin America and the Middle East. People meet in various contexts through the week, although the time when most attend is Sunday mornings. Attendance at that service is around 150 people, with approximately 40 percent having no previous experience of Christian community. Since for the majority who attend English is their second language, elementary English is used in larger meetings. (Free classes are available several times a week for those learning English). In the Global model, relationships and hospitality are prioritised. The relational dynamic of the early days of this ministry has been sustained. Half a dozen people sit at each round table with a leader seeking to make people welcome, especially newcomers. The latter are individually welcomed to the Global family by the leader of the "service", each receiving a welcome pack. Following the ESOL talk, which is usually focused on a narrative from Scripture, there is opportunity in the table groups to discuss questions arising and to discern where people are at on their journey of understanding. Most of the people now volunteering in worship, dance, drama, and other teams are people who have come to faith since attending Global activities. The sharing of a communal meal at the end of every Sunday gathering is of crucial significance in the way it communicates the value of relationship-building. During the week, this priority on hospitality is often in evidence in people's living situations. The Friends of Friends Fellowship, an outreach to Muslims and Muslim-background believers spawned by the Global ministry, meets in a neutral location but also makes hospitality a priority, such as in a recent post-Ramadan feast attended by approximately fifty Muslims. While English is used in Global activities, it is recognised that the nurture of people on a journey of faith can most helpfully be enhanced by the opportunity to meet in other language groupings such as Chinese, Japanese, Korean, and Portuguese. While the leadership team of Global recognises many challenges for ongoing growth, there is a sense of deep appreciation for the way that the dynamics of relationship and hospitality foster the realisation of the ministry's missional purpose. It is also heartening to see that some whose discipleship journey began in the Global group are now involved missionally back in their home countries.

Theological reflections

We turn now to a brief, theological reflection on the nature of the church. In the present day, the predominant model of Christian congregating tends to be antithetical to the development of cross-cultural communities and the harnessing of their missional capacities. What are some of the models in the church's history which have shaped its ethos and praxis, and what can we learn for the here and now? In the initial centuries of the church's existence, communal relationships and hospitality were central for the marginalised and often persecuted faithful. Once the first-century believers — initially Jewish and eventually also Gentiles — found themselves excluded from the formal setting of synagogue meeting, their changed circumstances necessitated meeting in homes and households which fostered the development of a more relational model of coming together, resulting in a sustaining dynamic of mutual encouragement, nurture, instruction, and a much enhanced openness to the surrounding community. For a number of centuries, these practical changes and the resulting ethos shaped the church's life and witness. With the coming of Christendom, the re-orienting of the church's gathering to centralised, physical structures in Europe's towns and cities appears to have radically modified the ethos. Architecture now trumps relationality, formality suppresses informality, the giftedness of professionals subordinates that of the wider body of believers, and the focus on particular sacred places eclipses where God is present and at work in the spaces beyond. Praxis ends up shaping ethos, instead of ethos informing the praxis. In a post-Christendom world, the question needs to be asked: is the essential nature of the church, to a large extent, still held captive to age-old physical structures and strictures? Some current calls for the "reinvention" of the church amount to little more than rearrangements of the furniture. A genuine critique of structures and a desire for change are commendable but unless this is shaped by a grasp on the essential character of the church, its fundamental ethos, no real transformation can be expected.

My purpose here is not to expound in depth on ecclesiology *per se*. I take *relationality and community* as foundational to the nature of the church. This entails the affirmation, in a given setting, of what God's people hold in common as well as that which characterises their diversity. But relationality, understood as other-centredness, is descriptive not only of the church's inner life but also of its outward expression. This concern for "the other" is found throughout Scripture. Instructions to Israel reveal the vital importance of loving God and loving one's neighbour. The identity of the neighbours is clear from the repeated reminders to the Israelites that the foreigners within the community were to be treated as their native born: *"Love them as yourself, for you were foreigners in Egypt. I am the Lord your God".*[8] Biblical anthropology is grounded in the divine purpose to create humans in God's image. The unity and harmony in God are deeply rooted in the reciprocal, other-centred love of Father, Son, and Spirit. As divine image-bearers, humans are called to the same expression of unselfish love for the other. And this other — the neighbour — is clearly not simply one like us in ethnicity and culture, but even the foreigner among us: *"The community is to have the same rules for you and for **the alien** living among you… **You and the alien** shall be the same before the Lord".*[9] Similar reminders are plentiful in the New Testament. Jesus calls for a distinctive attitude of love for our enemies, and denigrates a love reserved only for those who love us.[10] One can imagine the challenge for his closest followers — all Jewish yet from such contrasting cultural backgrounds — of his injunction to "love one another". His parable of the Good Samaritan underscores the importance of love, demonstrated in merciful action toward one in need, where the only identity that matters is of another made in God's image. The naked, half-dead, and therefore unidentifiable man was shown compassion by the Samaritan regardless of the victim's ethnicity. It is not necessary here to enlarge on the expansive inclusiveness of Jesus' ministry among Jews and Gentiles, and the vision and task entrusted to his followers to go to the ends of the earth, crossing frontiers of culture, language, religion, and worldview.

The gospel's impact on Paul the Jew transformed his attitudes about Gentiles, his willingness to become as a Greek to the Greeks, as one not under the law to those not under the law, matching his willingness to become like a Jew to the Jews and as one under the law to those under the law.[11] Such radical changes in outlook result in a distinctive understanding of *ekklesia*: "the children of God through faith" are not ranked in terms of their identities of ethnicity, gender, or social class; for those who are "in Christ Jesus", these identities do not disappear but the hierarchies between them lose their validity.[12] The divisions once existing between

Jews and Gentiles are rendered null and void through Christ, whose purpose through his death was "to create one new humanity out of the two".[13] At the same time, as other contexts show, the unity cannot be separated from the affirmation of the diversity.[14] In Romans, for example, Paul repeatedly encourages both Jewish and Gentile believers in the Christian communities to acknowledge their need of the other, recognise their interdependence, and value the mutuality of their relationship.[15] Without the endorsement and pursuit of these foundational values, one cannot envisage a multicultural church in the truest sense. Also, where the values of inclusiveness, of embrace of the other are affirmed *within* the church, there is greater potential for openness to the other *beyond* the church.

Though assent may readily be given to these fundamental principles, in reality many churches continue to function according to an inadequate paradigm that belonged to an era in which communities were predominantly mono-ethnic and with minimal subcultural diversity. This "Christendom mode of engagement" is described by Alan Hirsch as "evangelistic-attractional" and is usually based on a homogenous principle, seeking to attract and win those "outside" the church who fit a similar demographic to those "inside".[16] This often used "outside"/"inside" language belies the enduring attachment to the Christendom focus on church as the physical structure, or at least the mindset which sees people primarily through an evangelistic lens, where the primary goal is for the unsaved to be saved. For the "attractional" church, there is no sense of the need to cross cultural boundaries, little awareness of the need to engage the vast diversity which exists in terms of race, language, and culture. This mode is also accompanied by an oversimplified communication of the gospel which ignores the potential barriers to its meaningful reception by people shaped by religion and worldview.

With the "evangelistic-attractional" model of church, the temptation is to make a priority of church growth, the expansion of the church in numerical terms, or even to think of church planting *per se* as the primary objective. Such an ecclesiocentric model of mission, in vogue in Christendom and in much of the modern era of mission, contrasts with the kingdom-oriented ethos of the "missional-incarnational" model. Hirsch writes:

> Many of the new Protestant church movements of recent years are simply variations of the old Christendom mode. Whether they place their emphasis on new worship styles, expressions of the Holy Spirit's power, evangelism to seekers, or Bible teaching, these so-called new movements still operate out of the fallacious assumption that the

church belongs firmly in the town square, that is, at the heart of Western culture. And if they begin with this mistaken belief about their position in Western society, all their church planting, all their reproduction will simply mirror this apprehension.[17]

The dualistic thinking which has shaped Western thought is rooted in the thought forms of the Graeco-Roman world and has been reinforced through the Enlightenment. In the era of modernity, the view of the world as divided into physical and spiritual, secular and sacred, has profoundly shaped understandings of church, evangelism, and mission. As Frost and Hirsch have pointed out, "… what is needed is the abandonment of the strict lines of demarcation between the sacred and profane spaces in our world and the recognition that people today are searching for relational communities that offer belonging, empowerment, and redemption".[18] Therefore, the call is for a different model, one which Hirsch describes as "a missional-incarnational impulse":

> The purpose in combining these two words is to link two practices that in essence form one and the same action…
>
> …unless we embrace this mode, we will in effect lock up the genius of the apostolic church, namely, to seed and embed the gospel in different groups, cultures and societies and to thus sow the seeds of rapid multiplication.[19]

The ecclesiology of the missional church is not attractional but incarnational, meaning that it is not about the creation of sacred places into which unbelievers must come to experience the gospel. Instead, "the missional church disassembles itself and seeps into the cracks and crevices of society in order to be Christ to those who don't yet know him".[20]

The church's ethos and praxis are to be premised on the *missio Dei* — the divine nature and purpose as fundamentally missional. It is not the case that because there is a church, there is a mission, but rather, that because God is missionary and has a mission purpose, there is the church. As David Bosch has stated, "Mission is seen as a movement from God to the world; the church is viewed as an instrument for that mission. There is church because there is mission, not vice versa."[21] Only when this is firmly understood and embraced will the church be free to move beyond the "evangelistic-attractional" model to an "incarnational-missional" one. In the Global group, given that we regularly have a significant proportion of people in our main gatherings with no experience of God, we constantly find ourselves on the edge of fresh missional challenges. In the traditional approach, mission is often thought of as something the church engages in beyond itself, with the goal of attracting people into the church and "winning" them. In the incarnational model, the focus is on being present, building relationships with people, helping the strangers to find a place to be at home, and joining them on the journey of discovery.

It is essential that the church in its local expressions in society's "cracks and crevices" seeks in-depth understanding of its context, the demography and the cultural dynamics at work. As we have seen, this *sociological* focus must be accompanied by a thorough *theological* critique of the church, in order more effectively to understand its true essence and missional character. This inevitably entails a searching evaluation of existing structures of the church to determine whether or not they harmonise with its missional purpose.

Anthropological insights

A focus on some insights from anthropology may also prove helpful in our understanding of the way the church can engage its multicultural context. Anthropologist Paul Hiebert and others[22] have drawn on mathematical set theory to illustrate the contrast between static and dynamic approaches to evangelism and discipleship, church and mission. The "evangelistic-attractional" model mentioned earlier corresponds to a bounded (or closed) set whereas the "incarnational-missional" model represents a centred set. In *bounded sets*, boundaries are important. People are identified in terms of their position inside or outside the established boundary. The category to which they belong is likely to be determined by a particular act or decision. For example, one's relationship to God's kingdom depends on whether or not a person has crossed the boundary from "out" to "in", whether the unsaved person has become saved. One either belongs or does not belong. In this somewhat static approach, an act is the all-important basis for one's inclusion in the bounded set of kingdom-belonging. In *centred sets*, the Centre is emphasised. In this more dynamic model, the emphasis is on the direction a person is going, whether there is movement toward or away from the Centre, Jesus. In this case, the difference is not based on boundary-crossing but on whether or not there is active relationship with and movement toward the Centre. In the bounded-set approach, a person understood as having crossed a boundary through a particular act or conversion experience may no longer be moving toward Christ but is nevertheless still thought of as "belonging" to the kingdom. In the centred-set approach, the main emphasis is on the dynamic of following Christ, and conversion is understood more as a process, which is likely to include a number of decisive acts. As Dave Andrews has put it,

> The essence of Closed Set Christianity is all about being a "Christian" — defining being a "Christ-ian", and defending being a "Christ-ian". The essence of Centred Set Christi-Anarchy is all about becoming "Christ-like"— and encouraging everyone to become "Christ-like", whether they become "Christ-ians", or not.[23]

In an approach which is focused more evangelistically than incarnationally, the emphasis is on communication of truths and of assisting an individual to reach a decision in affirmation of those truths; in other words looking for a transaction by which a boundary is crossed and the person becomes a Christian. In this bounded-set approach, the initial emphasis is not placed on following Christ in a radical new allegiance. Discipleship tends to be viewed as a phase which is subsequent to and consequent of an initial act of boundary crossing. Depicting this perspective as the "Centred Set in the Closed Set", Andrews comments that "...it shows a fundamental misunderstanding of the relationship between salvation and discipleship", assuming that "salvation is separate from discipleship, and comes prior to discipleship; whereas the Gospels show that salvation, being saved, depends on discipleship, choosing to follow in the footsteps of the Saviour".[24]

In the more dynamic, centred-set model, there is a recognition of process, of being on a journey of discovery and opening up to the possibilities of transformation, evident in multiple changes of perspective and decisive actions. Christ's call to those who wanted to be his followers was expressed in terms of denying themselves, taking up his cross, and following him.[25] In the modern era of mission, much emphasis has been placed on people "becoming Christians" and "becoming part of the church". The New Testament emphasis lies rather on discipleship, people responding to the call to become followers of Christ and seeking his kingdom. Such centring on the Person should not be taken to imply that no boundaries exist. Andrews comments:

> ...though there are no set boundaries in the Centred Set, there are still boundaries. And one crosses the boundary from "not being saved" to "being saved", by choosing to follow in the footsteps of the Saviour...

> The Gospels show that "being saved" depends on "choosing to follow in the footsteps of the Saviour," but that may mean different paths for different people, depending on where they are coming from. Christ called everyone to follow in his footsteps... His expectations were not set standards, but individual variations on a common theme.[26]

The choice of paradigm to guide our approach to ministry in a multicultural church is a vitally important one. For effective connection with people of different ethnicities and religions in our various contexts, I affirm here the "incarnational-missional" approach which focuses on relational dynamics, being with people, meeting them at their points of need, and recognising the central importance of the life journey toward the Centre — our own ongoing process as Christ's disciples as well as that of others we welcome onto the same pathway. Taking the life circumstances and felt needs of people as a starting-point for communication often proves more fruitful than an almost total reliance on a message expressed in a monologue. Gene Daniels writes about the way the narrative of *Acts* describes numerous events which become the occasion for speeches clarifying the meaning of those events.[27] This approach, which he names "Event-speech", is one he found to be more fruitful in his work among Muslims than its alternative, communicating in a speech and seeking an event (a decisive act).

A further anthropological question concerns the relationship between a church's dominant culture — frequently European — and other cultures represented. One aspect of these relationship dynamics has to do with culture-specific modes of decision-making. In contrast to the affirmation of the individual's autonomy in a Western mindset, most other cultures favour communal decision-making or honour the wisdom of the older over the younger, as in societies shaped by Confucianism. Gospel communication in the "evangelistic" mode focuses on encouraging people to make an individual decision to accept Christ. A person's failure to respond may not necessarily mean resistance to the gospel, but simply that personal freedom to make a decision of such magnitude is foreign within that person's culture. A further aspect relates to people's religious or worldview background. Most people from Asian or Middle Eastern contexts see their national identity and religious identity as inseparable. In general terms, to be Pakistani is to be Muslim, to be Thai is to be Buddhist, and so on. A focus on getting people to "become a Christian" may too easily be interpreted as a call to abandon their religion and adopt a new one, Christianity, when in reality our primary focus is on inviting people toward the person of Christ and seeking his loving and liberating kingship. None of this is to deny the necessity for critique of religion and worldview. The gospel's dual function of affirming and critiquing culture must be kept in mind. No culture is totally good; none is totally bad. As Andrew Walls has shown, two principles are at work in the gospel's interface with cultures — an indigenising principle and a pilgrim principle; the former affirming the inherent beauty and wisdom within the culture and the latter taking elements of that culture on a journey of transformation.[28] These principles apply, of course, as much to those of us involved in multicultural church ministry as they do those of other cultures encountering the faith for the first time. This evaluation of worldviews is part of the ongoing movement toward Christ.

The desire to keep gospel communication simple has often resulted in oversimplification of the message, a reduction of the good news to a tidy package, "a one-size-fits-all" approach. When relating to people of diverse religions and worldviews, it is important to have an awareness of the concept of cultural distance. Several authors, including Engel and Norton, have provided insights regarding cultural variables in intercultural communication.[29] The Engel scale covers a spectrum indicating different groups' readiness to respond to the gospel, illuminating the need to move from a source-centred communication to a receptor or "other-centered" approach.[30]

Conclusion

Fruitful ministry in cross-cultural churches depends on a wide range of issues, some of which have been the focus of this paper. The call to welcome the stranger stems from the character and purpose of the triune God in whose image we are made. This underscores the importance of relationality and hospitality. There is a need for the church to undergo radical conversion from reliance on programmes and practical strategies to a recovery of the church's true ethos, an abandoning of flawed ecclesiologies and mission concepts, and an embrace of the full implications of the *missio Dei*, a willingness to forgo reductionist understandings of the gospel and to embrace God's kingdom purposes. We are called to get to know the strangers among us, understand their worldview and felt needs, and to welcome them into the journey toward Christ.

Gordon Stewart is a former missionary and served as the Senior Lecturer in Mission at Laidlaw College, Auckland, New Zealand, until 2014.

Part B:
Transforming the Worship and Life of Australia's Baptist Churches

New Parishes for Anglicans and Baptists?
Missional Transitions in an Age of Economic and Ecological Crisis

Gordon Preece

Australia, like most Western nations, is slowly moving into a time of chronic economic crises. The post-World War II baby and resources boom we've taken for granted was a blip in our history and the world's history. French economist Thomas Picketty predicts a return to the business as usual of slow growth and massive, increasing inequality between the rapid compound growth of inherited and invested wealth versus relatively waning wages. Rapidly rising numbers of regional and younger people especially are unemployed or under-employed, even before looming robotisation. In addition to these threats to our economic and social ecology the threat of climate change looms large, already causing climate refugees as the world's poor bear the cost of the West's profligacy. In the midst of rapid economic and ecological transition, a transitional churches or parishes movement, along with a vow of stability, may provide ways forward.

Introduction

The world is in transition. The post-World War II rapid growth economy is pincered between slowing population-driven economic growth and the debt collector at the door demanding long deferred externalised ecological costs. French political economist Thomas Picketty's book *Capital* and neat U-shaped graphs depict a likely return to the historical pattern of the past two centuries and most likely two millennia. It is a pattern of slow growth accompanied by a growing gap between capital and invested, compound-interest-generating inheritance and the waning comparative value of wages. We are already returning to historic highs of inequality.[1] By 2016 the Occupy movement's infamous one percent, now numbering only 80 billionaires, will own 50 percent of the world's wealth.[2]

The luck of "the Lucky Country" is starting to run out. Australia has ridden the sheep's back for a century and then relied upon the Chinese panda's insatiable appetite for our minerals. However, China's growth has now slowed to 6.9 percent, its weakest in 25 years.[3] Our economic surpluses were frittered away on middle- to upper-class welfare benefits such as effectively tax-free unlimited superannuation for millionaires and billionaires. John Howard's Government forfeited $40 billion of tax revenue through populist long-term tax cuts for the wealthy based on a temporary boom.[4] The opportunity to invest in the educational and environmental infrastructure of the future was thrown away largely due to minerals industry lobbying and media campaigns.

Former Treasurer Joe Hockey's Australianised "lifters and leaners"[5] adapts Ayn Rand's (former Federal Reserve head Alan Greenspan's guru) division of the world into economic light and darkness. A Manichaean productive and non-productive dualism that is not intrinsic to the population is ideologically imposed upon it. For instance, in the Australian context the Brotherhood of St. Laurence has tracked and projected a rapid increase in rates of youth unemployment in particular pockets of poverty.[6] In the map below, 14 of 18 hotspots of youth unemployment are in the south-east quadrant of the country but the worst are in the far north and west.[7]

Figure 1: Mapping youth unemployment: the worst hotspots in each state

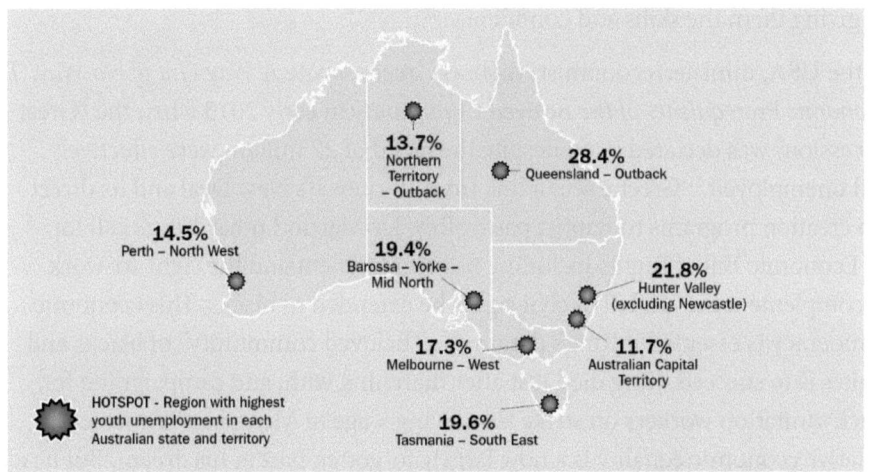

Around the world excessive educational expectations fostered by expensive universities have led to deep disillusionment among the young from the Middle East to India to the USA and Australia. There are just not enough of the jobs people are being trained for to go around and to enable transitions from education to first job, to stable jobs, to adulthood, and on to family formation.[8] Yet the rhetoric blames the victims and many find themselves saddled with mortgage-sized debts for their trouble.

In Australia, young males are more likely than young women to be unemployed (due to the decline in traditional working-class manufacturing jobs, trades, and apprenticeships). Young women are more likely to be under-employed.[9] There are particular problems for young men transitioning to work, adulthood, and family formation. Further, the effects of poor educational outcomes and high unemployment (including racial and religious prejudice) for young Muslims, especially men, in inner western Sydney and north-western Melbourne need investigation in relation to transitions to radicalisation and some ways in which transition to employment might perhaps reduce this.

Among churches, the recent UK Evangelical Alliance report *Working Faithfully* found that "Evangelicals care about unemployment, with 82 per cent saying that the government should... ensure... enough decent jobs for those wanting work. Seventy-five per cent define decent as including a 'living wage'". But more importantly, 40 percent of Evangelicals say their church offers practical support to local unemployed and many church agencies like Cardiff's Vocate and CAP Job

Clubs run innovative employment projects helping churches help people find jobs by giving them the skills and confidence.[10]

In the USA, minister/economist Michael Greene wrote *A Way Out of No Way: The Economic Prerequisites of the Beloved Community* in early 2013 when the "Great Recession" was declared over; despite the fact that 27 million were effectively still unemployed.[11] Greene sees a line from Roosevelt's New Deal and its direct job creation programs to Baptist pastor Rev. Dr Martin Luther King's call for an Economic Bill of Rights including full employment and the right-to-work to complement the US bill of civil rights he extended to blacks. This economic democracy is essential if King's dream of a "beloved community" of blacks and whites is to succeed. King died just after marching with, and campaigning for, black sanitation workers on strike for a living wage in Memphis, Tennessee. Relative economic equality is a now largely forgotten part of his dream. But he also had a nightmare:

> Looking toward the horizon, King sees, first of all, an economic tsunami that, if left unchecked, threatens to exacerbate existing joblessness and further destabilize the economic foundations... essential to a healthy community. More particularly, it is the uncontrolled whirlwinds of automation, deindustrialization, and economic restructuring that threaten to put millions of people in dire straits... He also contends that... American capitalism is plagued by a chronic jobs gap... between the number of jobs available and... persons in need of employment.[12]

King's nightmare of a technological tsunami has had various incarnations. The coming incarnation is that of robotisation. This tidal wave of technology taking out jobs is graphically described in *The Economist*.[13] It asks anxiously "can you ride it?" The answer appears to be "No!" if you're in easily replicable manual or mental jobs ripe for robotisation. However, economist R.J. Samuelson argues that, "Technology has profound effects on jobs, but changes occur over many years".[14] Panic is pointless, but for governments, civil society, and church agencies to prepare vulnerable communities for technological transition through pro-active school, university, and technical education is not. Fortunately, the new Labor Government in Victoria is committed to restoring previously decimated TAFEs and encouraging increased use of local apprentices on its infrastructure projects.

Climate change will also require preparedness and strategies to reverse it. Technology might be a critical factor in this but there will be no easy technological fixes. In such circumstances the role of the churches is critical, frequently found in the tension between the concerns of local and global communities. This forces decisions regarding under-employment, communities under-water or over-heating, communities facing permanent drought, and Pacific and Asian climate refugees. It is in this broad context that I now want to address the role of transitional churches.

Australian churches, schools, and agencies tackling unemployment

Can the local church or parish play any role in this transition process? Let me share some examples past and present. There are opportunities for government and church-based unemployment projects in Australia, sometimes under our noses. In the early 1980s, as an assistant Anglican minister in Sydney's Seaforth, I was looking for missional opportunities and walked across the road to the local TAFE. There I met a Uniting Church laywoman ironically called Laurel Dole who ran the Education Program for Unemployed Youth (EPUY). She invited me to do personal development work with EPUY. She and her students taught me more than I taught them, but it started a long journey. In one introductory game about favourites — foods, movies, music — I sat opposite a downcast young man marked by poverty and aggressive acne. I asked "what's your favourite food?" He mumbled "coco-pops". I said "for breakfast?" He replied, "No — breakfast, lunch, and tea". He was disempowered and despairing. Others were quick-witted enough to jokingly say "I work for the government" in answer to the inevitable question, "what do you do?" Now I ask people "how do you occupy yourself?" allowing for non-job answers.

Many churches have under-used property that could be turned into social enterprise and job training and creation projects.[15] Malabar Anglican Parish started doing this, in the1980s, before I arrived in 1985. Based on a peninsula, this parish bordered Sydney airport and some of Australia's dirty dozen industries. The area was undergoing major economic and ecological transition with traditional manufacturing like W.D. & H.O. Wills cigarette factory and General Motors Holden moving out along with the oil refinery closing.

La Perouse and its Mission was the local dumping ground for Aboriginals, lepers, and the first AIDS victims, who were treated at Prince Henry Hospital. Much of Sydney's sewage, half processed, poured onto our closed beach. When the offshore winds came in we'd say: "sewer's up". We lived "between the Devil and the deep brown sea". My wife, an asthmatic and mother of three asthmatics, ran asthma support groups from the minister's house. She was interviewed by local press regarding the sewer works and high asthma rates next door at our school. I joined CESS, Campaign to End Sewage Smells. I became the Anglican church expert on sewage![16] The parish facilitated ecological worship at the first Australian Ecumenical Ecology Conference in 1990.

On the employment front, the late social entrepreneur Steve Lawrence, Canon Edie Ashley, and others living in subsidised church housing and in Acts 2 and 4 style with shared purse, pooled their government salaries for computer training to create a social enterprise fund for WorkVentures. They took over half a disused church (apart from its Resale Shop) in Matraville and started job training and job creation projects using Christian community principles to develop the gifts, talents, and different intelligences (e.g. the great manual skills) of some ESL participants or illiterates. Three ex-Navy high-school drop-outs took early retirement and taught electronic repair and maintenance skills on ATM machines. This ITEC Centre, a model developed in the UK to be self-funding in the dire days of Maggie Thatcher, soon became a rich revenue stream giving relative independence from government funding. Baby business incubators were set up with mentoring, peer support, and pooling labour costs by having shared administration services as on-the-job training for those in computer courses. The normal 80 percent failure rate for first-time businesses was turned into an 80 percent success rate.[17] All this arose just from living alongside people, in the manner of Jeremiah 29, seeking and praying for shalom in a time of transition or "exile".

Introducing the concept of "Transition Parishes"

WorkVentures still operates from Surrey Hills, near Central Station, within reach of Malabar, but its start in Malabar Parish exemplifies what I call a Transition Parish, adapting Rob Hopkins' Transition Towns concept.[18] I've recently suggested this as a way for local parishes to transition towards tackling today's chronic ecological and economic challenges in sustained and sustainable ways.[19] Westerners tend to be better at dealing with crises than chronic issues because of our technological quick-fix mind-set, the limited attention spans of the media, and compassion fatigue. But quick-fixes for crises often produce crises elsewhere in the social and ecological system, not going to the roots of our relationship with God, humanity, and creation.

I've advocated the transition parish concept since the mid-1980s in Malabar; admittedly, its being on a peninsula made it better suited geographically to being a parish than many; my current parish is, for example, dissected by a freeway. Back then many church growth experts envisioned churches, particularly megachurches, as interest-based, not locality- or place-based. With the "homogeneous interest group principle", it was as if cars changed the character of church into some kind of vehicle for upward career and social mobility — thereby avoiding the need to cross cultural or class boundaries.[20]

While not upholding any exclusivity of the concept of parish or any biblical textual background for the exact concept, its grounding of the people of God in a particular locality holds together creation and redemption,[21] time and eternity, place/locality and the global/universal of the faith. I'll first draw upon Bishop Lesslie Newbigin's eschatological affirmation of the parish; secondly I'll reflect on Alison and John Milbank's Radical Orthodox praise of parishes as an alternative form of civil society movement to both state and market monopolies; and, finally, I'll examine the promising New Parish movement from the USA.

Firstly, Newbigin has an exciting eschatological and missional perspective on the parish in transition between old and new creation.

> The Church can be the first-fruit, sign and instrument of God's new creation planted firmly in the context of some segment of the old creation. "The world" is too vague a phrase to have any real meaning. Human life is lived not just in "the world" but in concrete and particular communities — this village, this factory, this school, this government office, this suburb, this trade union, this professional association. To speak of God's new creation means to speak also of God's will for these particular and specific communities... If the Church is to be in and for the world, it must be in and for these particular segments of the world. It must be the Church in and for this village, this factory, this suburb. In other words, the structures of the Church must be organically related to the structures of the secular world. *That is the enduring theological justification for the idea of the parish* [my italics]. There is no meaning in speaking of the Church as first-fruit, sign and instrument of God's reign in the world

if this does not apply specifically to this bit of the world where the Church is set.

Although originally writing for an Indian context in the 1970s, Newbigin is aware of changes to village and parish life in modern mobile cities. He asks:

> How, then, shall the parish be defined? In a small agricultural society such as that of medieval Europe, the village was a sufficient definition of the parish. It was a little world in which the ordinary man had his whole life's work, his recreation, his friendships. The Church could be organised as a network of geographically defined parishes, and with that structure could meet the real needs of society. In our modern world that is no longer the case. Most men in Madras city live in several worlds. There is the neighbourhood where their home is... the factory where the worker is... and the place where they spend their leisure or... go to church. In a world of this kind the parish cannot be defined in geographical terms alone. Certainly the place where a man lives, where his home is, has a fundamental claim to be regarded as primary. Therefore we are probably right if we continue to try to define our parishes geographically and encourage each congregation to take the responsibility for the people who live in its neighbourhood. But if we are serious in our mission we have also to develop other forms of congregational life related to other "worlds" — such as workers' groups in factories, student groups in colleges, and professional groups in... different segments of urban life. All of these have a rightful claim to be regarded as essential elements in the structure of the Church alongside of the traditional local congregation.[22]

Newbigin then uses three metaphors for the church's missional role, particularly focusing on the church's priestly role in relation to all the people in a particular parish, members or not, and presumably, given the previous paragraph, by extension going with the parish's people when they scatter in these various worlds of mission and everyday service and sustenance.

> How is the Church in each place to fulfil its role as first-fruit, sign and instrument of the reign of God? The congregation is to be: (a) the humble servant of Jesus for the sake of its neighbours... to help them in whatever need they are... (b) the witness to Jesus and his kingdom. It must point beyond itself to him. (c) The congregation is

> to be a priesthood on behalf of all its neighbours. As Jesus came to be the great High Priest for all mankind, so each congregation is to carry out his priesthood for its neighbours. Priesthood has a double character. It means bringing the truth and love and peace of God to worship, and... it is to offer up to God not only its own obedience and love; it is to act as the priestly people offering up to God the life of its whole neighbourhood that God's reign may truly become effective in the whole of its life... Many of the programmes in which we are engaged should be looked at in this perspective... It is easy to say that the Church is God's servant for the world. It only becomes realistic if we act concretely in relation to some segment of the world. That is the enduring validity of the parish.[23]

Newbigin here provides some answer to the stimulating articles by Glenn Hohnberg of City Bible Forum Brisbane, challenging a focus on local neighbourhood or parish mission given the evidence that most people's time is spent at work. For Hohnberg we are not witnessing if we are not primarily focused on reaching workers evangelistically.[24]

My own mission focus often emphasises the scattered roles of God's people at work.[25] But this is only one pole of God's people gathered on Sunday, scattered on Monday. It also seems to focus only on the second of Newbigin's biblical metaphors — witness — losing sight of the service and priesthood of God's people. This risks narrowly instrumentalising or turning the nature of God's people into a means towards an evangelistic end. However, it is priestly service and holistic, integral mission (1 Peter 3:15 or Colossians 4) which raise questions to which we can offer a hopeful answer. Hohnberg also risks instrumentalising our work as part of the creation commission (Gen 1:26–28, 2:15; Ps 8), which should be a sacrificial offering or an act of worship (Rom 12:1, 2). Further, he runs the risk of reducing our relationships, which are an integral part of the great commandment of love (Matt 22), to an evangelistic inducement. For me, the transitional parish model holds the theological tension together, despite the time-juggling, child-rearing, and commuting tensions of postmodern working life.

Secondly, Alison Milbank writes (with Andrew Davidson):

> In... *For the Parish*,[26] we... make a strong case that the parish is particularly adapted for mission today, offering a generous conception of responsibility to care for every person in its area. The parish is inclusive, public and a necessary mediating institution

between local and larger society. In a time in which society at large is learning the importance of locality in the drive for ecological sustainability, the Anglican Church is putting at risk the very structures that allow it to be a force for good.

Unlike the Homogenous Unit Principle [that like attracts like], the parish church is an inclusive and mixed community, and is present everywhere, not just in the suburbs but in public housing estate and village alike. The poor, we argue, are not mobile in the manner of the middle-classes, and stability for them is a positive quality.

We also point out that a great many so-called "Fresh Expressions" initiatives are the outreach of parish churches, and do not have an independent life of their own. In that way, they remain extra-liturgical outreaches and fit quite well with the hospitality of the parish idea. But bouncing castle and desert church — one Australian example — cannot be the whole worshipping experience of a mature faith.

Milbank's husband John sets parishes in the wider setting of debates about renewing civil or "Big Society".

Given that neither state nor market is able to supply various crucial local needs, we are seeing a natural return to mutual collaboration in order to make up for this lack — anything from voluntary-aided independent schools taking supposedly "impossible" students to cooperatives committed to keeping old bicycles in constant repair and renewed circulation.[27]

There are inherent limits to any system's attempts to dispense with the role of trust and reciprocal assistance. Central planning cannot assess people's various local and changing needs, while the pursuit of profit leaves many genuine needs and demands totally unmet.

In addition, we should welcome the rise of the third sector because it vastly increases the instance of genuine, spontaneous and participatory democracy in operation... Merely representative democracy has reduced the ordinary person's real decision-making power which can only come about through neighbourly collaboration.

> Fixation on the ballot-box means that governments are increasingly able to manipulate the choices of individuals in a vulgar Benthamite [utilitarian] manner that is supposed to increase their passive, consumerist "happiness". The population is in turn bought off with "welfare" which blinds them to the injustices of the workplace and releases them from any active thought as to what the pursuit of true education, true health and true care ... might really involve.
>
> [An]... equally crucial reason [is that] participatory democracy, in the realms both of welfare and of co-operative and stakeholder enterprise, was in the British past (as elsewhere...) almost entirely tied up with the practice of religion... [This parochial philanthropy] allowed intimate and collaborative relationships between donors and beneficiaries; it guarded against loneliness; it ensured an holistic union of body and spirit when it came to schooling and nursing; it rendered domestic labour communal and collaborative and it encouraged far more communication across class boundaries than pertains today. Moreover, it gave an enormous role to women.[28]

Thirdly, an outline of the US-based New Parish Coalition is in order. Lest you might think that parishes are just for Anglicans not Baptists let me introduce you to an ecumenical coalition of Seattle-based pastors and professors who co-lead www.parishcollective.org. In the face of US fragmentation, individualism, consumerism, and place-lessness, they urge the church to immerse itself *with* (missional church) and *in* (first-century church) a particular locale while collaborating there with others long-term.

> You and all your neighbours desire clean air to breathe, good schools for your children, livable vocations that serve the common good, justice for all, a voice in how things are governed, and so on. The locational limitation is liberating, forcing us "not to be church just for others like us, but for all our neighbours", "rooting deeply in the place God has planted you and expecting that your sense of community, your formation and your participation in God's renewing mission will integrate right where you live your everyday life".[29]

Further, they distinguish their new vision from the old Christendom or corporate corruptions. They expect ecclesial life to be centred in a neighbourhood or "new commons", not expensive drive-through worship entertainment extravaganzas or larger-than-life remote videoed pastors like Mark Driscoll, whose church has dissolved around him. As an Anglican I admit that the Cranmerian practice of Common Prayer lost some of its socially and even ecologically integrative power when the powers that be enclosed and privatised the Commons, land previously accessible to the poor.

New Parish churches seek to recapture something of this sense of neighbourhood commons in a non-denominationally specific or established church way. As Baptist Union of Victoria Mission Facilitator, Darren Cronshaw notes, "at their best, [they] take a local interest in education, civic leadership, economics and environmental care. Churches that really… take an interest in [neighbourhood] reconciliation and renewal, are… churches people want to join". Hence, incarnation and attraction are not opposed.

This local emphasis breaks down the false dichotomy of many missional models that distinguish between incarnation and attraction,[31] something that Scripture holds together (cf. Isa 2:1,2; Jer 29:4–9; Matt 5:13–16 with Matt 28:16–20). Rather than focusing on strategy and results, the parish model encourages people to focus on faces and places and to shift from the statistics of strategy to the stories of particularised humanity.

Thirdly, the practice of the new parish "begins with 'presencing' — through listening (in *Lectio Divina* style to Scripture, your own story and the story, needs and hopes of your own place)", discerning what "seems good to the Holy Spirit and to us" (Acts 15:28). "It also requires 'rooting' — growing stability in your place with personal and group practices; e.g., frequenting local cafés, exercising locally, and prioritising local community advocacy".[32]

This resistance to perpetually "moving on" in response to each successive postmodern whim taking us to the next consumer experience, involves learning to move at the patient pace of grace, that of "The Three Mile an Hour God".[33] It involves hi-touch human pace, not hi-tech inhumane pace, walking with people through "the hopes and fears of all the years". These are met in Christ as "O Little Town of Bethlehem" puts it poetically. Here the authenticity of genuine pastoral practice replaces the outmoded authority stance of Christendom. Christianity's authenticity as a religion for all seasons stands the test of time as opposed to fair weather religions and philosophies only for young hipsters and trendies.

"Transition Parishes", the need for roots, and the vow of stability

This need for roots is regarded as essential by the Jewish-Christian philosopher and French activist, Simone Weil, if we are to resist the fragmenting effects of modernity and the reactive threats of modern unitive totalitarianisms[34] of state and religion. Further, the poor are not middle-class cosmopolitans ever on the move, able to uproot when the going gets tough or the next creative project comes along. The secularisation and individualising of the Protestant vocational ethic into first a modern career with its sense of constant onward and upward motion and then morphing into a postmodern portfolio of creative projects have produced deep social erosion of families, local communities, and parishes.

Mark Sayers, a veteran of emerging churches, provides a penetrating cultural genealogy of the Romantic and literary movement and the influence of its organic values upon the creatives and postmodern de-constructors of the institutional church. He effectively critiques the critics and himself. People who were part of a café church without worship he once led were "fully wrapped around the organic values… We had created a space for Christians who had stopped going to church… happy to turn up twenty minutes late every few weeks. A liquid church in a liquid culture simply washes away".[35]

Such churches rarely last. An attitude of postmodern "whatever-ish" irony and critical detachment is ultimately better at destroying than creating, unmasking the misnomer of so-called "creatives". This is itself a cultural form of capitalism's so-called "creative destruction".[36] Sayers seeks and sees a movement in his Red Church "from destruction to devotion". He also cites pastor-sociologist Thomas Willer's perception of a rising new "generation of reconstructors" whose "'ground story'… was the self-sacrificial Harry Potter defeating the evil Voldemort and whose end point centers on restored family and the continuation of tradition… a grown Harry and his friends, now married and happy, sending their own children on the train to Hogwarts".[37]

Such remnants of stability still survive in many parishes. A recent ABC Radio show described how in New Orleans the impact of the 2005 Hurricane Katrina and the subsequent effect of the flooding were not effectively relieved by the "fly in and out" State agencies, nor their corporate replacements, but mainly the local, on the ground, congregations and parish-based groups and agencies. New Orleans' local government is also still based on the notion of parish.[38]

A parallel aspect of the commitment to Christian community expressed in the parish commitment to place is the Benedictine vow of stability, to stay put, hold on, and persevere through the roller-coaster of Christian community. Some recent experiments in new monasticism without slow monasticism's vow of stability become more like monasticism-lite or fast. When some give more attention to trendy slow food (itself a helpful movement) than traditional slow sex you wonder how long such movements will last or merely replicate their parents' most divorced generation ever.

At the end of his seminal *After Virtue*, philosopher Alasdair MacIntyre predicted a new Dark Ages needing "another — doubtless very different — St. Benedict" to appear. For MacIntyre, "the barbarians are not waiting beyond the frontiers, they have already been governing us for quite some time".[39] He hopes for new, local forms of community, treasuring traditions for the stable formation of virtuous character against the atomising acids of modernity.

Anabaptist Gerald Schlabach took a vow of stability as a lay Benedictine oblate, following a modern monastic rule of life, influenced by MacIntyre, the early married Anabaptists, and Benedictine and Franciscan tertiaries.[40] Schlabach notes, following Hauerwas, that "the 'voluntary community' for which Anabaptists once died has degenerated — in this liberal society where most organizations are voluntary — into the marketing of churches and 'church shopping' among all sectors within all traditions".[41]

Schlabach, like Pentecostal Calvinist James K.A. Smith,[42] finds that a vow or rule of life involving daily worship is necessary because our bodily desires are constantly fuelled until completely captivated by a 24/7 conformist, consumerist culture, rather than continuously conformed to Christ. This operates, as Benedict and the later Finkelwalde monastic, Bonhoeffer, realised, even in our idealistic desire for community in our own image.[43]

I too have found this stability hard to live out in idealistic Christian communities. In 2008 I was in Melbourne Town Hall commending my friend and former student Sally Apokis and husband Con, for sticking it out for over a decade in a difficult ministry situation. She told me that my espousal of the Benedictine "vow of stability" had struck a chord. I was warmed by the comment but too heartbroken to say I was having to leave a place I loved after just 18 months, my shortest ministry spell ever.

Now, seven years later, I am experiencing the stability of leading St. Mark's Spotswood in Yarraville "Transition" Parish two days a week. Consequently, I'm able to share some of its story and struggle to stay put. Besides being committed to an Anglican parish that had a fraught history of conflict and clergy short stays, I'm also Anabaptist, with a commitment to non-violent reconciliation. Rather than commuting to a ministry location that panders to a customised church-style or lifestyle enclave, ministering to *everybody* within the parish boundaries helps Christians commit to deal with differences and conflicts (Matt 18:15–20). We should beware of the postmodern temptation to "move on" when our single-issue (ethical, doctrinal, or personal) or idolatrous identity marker clashes with another's. We're "in Christ", in the parish, let's persevere. I believe with Hauerwas that "The church does not have a social ethic; the church is a social ethic" by its very stickability, shape, and reconciliatory practices. To be prophetic is to persevere.[44]

Resisting postmodern "moving on" has physical and sacramental expressions too. When we determined to sell an expensive-to-maintain and poorly located branch church to an ethnic congregation with whom we'd built a good relationship, we put the money into a long-needed "makeover for mission" of our main church, hall, and tennis courts at St. Mark's Spotswood. My friend and former church chairman Peter Deutschmann exemplifies and cites Hauerwas' story in *After Christendom?*[45] Hauerwas describes his United Methodist church in a downtown area in Indiana putting on a new roof as a prophetic sign of their vow of stability, staying in the inner-city, and not joining the suburban flight of the church. We see our development that way.

In Melbourne's western suburbs, hard yakka for Anglican churches, we will have a 130-place child-care centre serving the community, enabling young families struggling to find good child care, to get a mortgage and put roots down in the area. We also have a church building big enough for hundreds of Burmese (Chin) Baptist refugees; a sign of ecumenical welcome, global hope, and a prompt to Australia to welcome more like them.

Building-wise, we're in transition, and also theologically transitioning towards being a Transition Parish. We're becoming economically sustainable — we would have been broke by now without the child-care centre — and have become a parish and regional centre for hospitality. We're shifting money and intellectual resources via *Ethos: EA Centre for Christianity & Society* from the eastern suburbs Bible belt to the west.[46] Almost annually we have an international speaker at St.

Mark's. At the gateway to the west our motto says: "Welcoming the West and the World". God willing we're here to stay, and in Jim Collins' terms, *Built to Last*.[47]

Our parish is also transitional through our intersection of the best global thinking and concern we can muster with local action, particularly around work/economics and ecological issues. Global thinking for the church, through time and space, means loyalty to the Creeds. Our trinitarian mission statement based on three credally connected commissions, or mandates, includes the creation commission of the Father in Gen 1:26–28 to rule or have dominion over the earth and guard the Garden (Gen 2:15) through service and stewardship; and the great missionary/discipling commission of the Son in Matt 28:18–20. Christ is the model God-man with all authority in heaven and earth. He fulfils the creation commission, through his life of service, nature miracles, sacrificial death, and resurrection, restoring creation. Making disciples involves all cultural spheres of creation as well as all peoples. The Great Commandment is written on our hearts by the Holy Spirit enabling us to love God (Rom 5:1–5) and neighbour (Matt 22) and accomplishing creation's renewal and completion (Rom 8). We are committed to supporting people in their work (paid or unpaid), ecological care, witness, and discipling, and their contribution to a reconciling Christian community that foreshadows the great multinational crowd gathered round the Lamb (Rev 5:9–14).

We have numerous ecologically informed and concerned people in the congregation. A number ride bikes to church. Some haven't found the greening (in a non-party-political sense) of the church easy. One stalwart member gave me an Andrew Bolt article against the idea of human caused climate change. That's fine, we're still friends. Our older ones are very gracious towards the younger activists. They know it was our advertised social issues series which started our growth spurt — social issues can be missional if the church *is* a social ethic! A creative kid's talk on water led to the building of a church community garden with water tanks, often a venue for Sunday club. The kids work side-by-side with adults learning about God's creation. We hope the appropriately named Bloom childcare will use the garden as a liminal, go-between space between the church and them, while we serve parents free coffee. Our Lautu Baptists also have a plot of Burmese spices. They use them for the magnificent spicy food they love to cook.

As a parish we seek to be a community for the community. We initiated the first Spotswood Festival in 2012, which celebrated the 20th anniversary of the movie *Spotswood* which we showed to a standing ovation. The movie, filmed on location, features Anthony Hopkins as an efficiency expert, coming from England to downsize a local moccasin factory, but being won over by the working-class community of the slot-car club at the factory. In a rapidly gentrifying area we wanted to celebrate and preserve where possible the parish's strongly communal working-class values. Spotswood Primary School, who hosted the festival, are now hosting us till the new church is built.

The transition parish concept also joins with the recent Ethos Oikos Project linking ecologists and economists. It uses the root term of both, *oikos* or house/home, to encourage ecologically sustainable communities. Jonathon Cornford's "The Shaking of the House" explains the household concept well. It is a more biblical, cosmic, communal, economic notion than privatised families and churches today.

Cornford argues that the biblical "household" fits well with a transitional, transparent parish model. Cornford explains our transitional eschatological position well as:

> ... fundamental to the vocation of God's people to embody and proclaim the reconciling of economics and ecology which is at the heart of God's great work of restoring all things, and at its heart is the intimate and practical reconciling of economics and ecology within our own homes... The Christian community should... speak with wisdom and insight into the challenges now posed by climate change — it has always been [our] core business to bring the future into the present... to instruct... how we ought to live now. We should be, but we are not. Before the Church can begin to more fully reclaim its vocation, it must go through a profound shaking of its own, "For the time has come for judgement to begin with the household of God" (1 Peter 4:17).[48]

The UK-based *Churches in Transition* (CiT) network conceived of the basic transition ecclesiology idea, initially using the more widely used but often misunderstood term "church" rather than parish. CiT represents many Christians and churches involved in Transition Towns projects transitioning to a low carbon economy. Their theological rationale explains how Christian communities live "in transition", in the now and the "not yet" of God's kingdom.

> The better future that God offers, and that we work towards, is a future of restored relationships and repaired connections.

Our present day relations with one another and with the Earth community as a whole anticipates that better future. We exist in two dimensions simultaneously — the present reality of brokenness, and the future reality of a redeemed Earth. We live "in between", in transition. And in that place, when we are truly thankful of God's blessings, we cannot help but share them.[49]

Conclusion

Whether in transition ecologically or economically, involving being in or out of paid work, the eschatologically oriented transition parish concept helps keep us earthed and connected with God's creative, redemptive, and restorative work. This occurs in the painful and potentially positive places of transition, as creation groans through the toughest transition of all, cosmic new birth (Rom. 8:18–30). Transition parishes refuse to allow us to move on, lift anchor, and be tossed like flotsam and jetsam on the turbulent seas of liquid modernity.[50] Parishes provide us with roots which can withstand the toughest storms. I hope I've provided sufficient stories of steadfastness and stability as parish parables of hope in the tumultuous transitions our world and parishes face. My prayer is that others, over time, develop their own experiences and stories, drawing on both old and new parish models.

Gordon Preece is Director of Ethos: EA Centre for Christianity and Society and leads an Anglican Transition Parish in Yarraville, Victoria, worshipping at St. Mark's Spotswood in Melbourne's industrial, now gentrifying, western suburbs.

Contemporary Spirituality and Mission

Philip Hughes

In a survey in 2009, more adult Australians identified themselves as "spiritual" than as "religious". The movement away from religion and towards spirituality is occurring in a variety of countries around the world. At heart, it reflects a major change in the ways people are thinking about the meaning and fulfilment of life: in the "subjectivity" of the individual rather than through fulfilling particular duties and responsibilities associated with gender, social status, and one's religion.

While the roots of this trend include a protest against religious institutionalism and dogma, there are many dimensions of contemporary spirituality that Christians can affirm. Mission and church life need to focus on helping people find fulfilment in their subjective life through Christian faith. The trend towards spirituality encourages Christians to recognise the sense of mystery in human life, the natural world, and the universe. Nevertheless, the fundamental message of the Christian faith is that people find fulfilment not in a focus on themselves but rather as they contribute to the lives of others and to the wider society.

The changing context of mission

One of the great challenges for mission in contemporary Australian society is the movement from religion to spirituality. This chapter is about exploring this trend and the challenge for mission. It will explore what it means for the population and how churches might respond to this change, taking up "spirituality" as a new wineskin in which mission might be developed.

The year 2009 marks a particular turning point in the way that meaning is being made in Australia. For the first time, a national survey of adults showed that more Australians identified themselves as "spiritual" than as "religious". The survey was conducted by the Australian National University among a random sample of 1712 adult Australians and included questions on religion designed as part of the surveys which are conducted in many countries around the world within the

International Social Survey Program.

The same question was asked in 44 countries around the world in 2008 and 2009: whether people saw themselves as spiritual, religious, both or neither. In Australia:

- 17.7% said they were both religious and spiritual;
- 15.4% were religious but not spiritual;
- 22.6% were spiritual but not religious;
- 29.8% were neither spiritual nor religious; and
- 14.5% said they could not choose or did not answer the question.[1]

If one adds together the "religious and spiritual" and the "spiritual not religious", one has just over 40 percent of Australians describing themselves as spiritual, compared with 33 percent describing themselves as religious. For some years, people such as David Tacey[2] have been talking about a "spiritual" revolution in Australia. This hardly amounts to a revolution. Close to half (44%) of Australian adults see themselves as neither religious nor spiritual, or can't choose. Certainly, for many Australians, neither religion nor spirituality receives much attention. Nevertheless, the growing proportion of people who see themselves as "spiritual", and particularly that group which sees themselves as "spiritual but not religious", demand close attention as part of the context of mission.

Australia shared in having more people identify themselves as spiritual rather than as religious with just four other countries of the 44 which participated in the International Social Survey Program. The other countries were New Zealand, Japan, United States, and Uruguay. In the United States, the proportion seeing themselves as religious and as spiritual was almost identical with large numbers of people seeing themselves as both.

A survey at one particular time does not make it easy to identify trends that are occurring over time. However, one indication of trends can be to compare younger and older people. The orientation of younger people is often suggestive of what may be predominant in the future. The proportion of younger Australians (under 60 years of age) who identified themselves as "religious" was 12 percent less than among older Australians (60 years of age or older). That pattern was repeated in every country which ran the survey with the exception of Israel, suggesting that religion may be in decline in many parts of the globe. It should be noted, however, that few countries in the Middle East and Africa ran the International Social Survey and some of these may show quite different trends.

In contrast, when compared with older Australians, younger Australians were 8 percent more likely to describe themselves as "spiritual". This trend was repeated in 19 countries out of the 44. These countries included quite a diverse range and included Taiwan, Israel, Sweden, Japan, the Netherlands, Great Britain, and Switzerland. In Australia, as in many parts of the world, it would appear that younger people are increasingly describing themselves as "spiritual" and less as "religious".

However, it should be noted that "spirituality" can mean different things in different places. Spirituality is not growing in a number of the Catholic countries such as Portugal, Ireland, Chile, Mexico, and Spain, because it has to do with the personal intensity of religious faith and with belief in the supernatural, rather than with the individualised notion of spirituality independent of religious institutions that is growing in English-speaking and northern European countries. In most of those countries where spirituality is not growing, the majority of those who say they are spiritual believe in God. In most countries where spirituality is growing, the majority of those who are spiritual say they believe in some sort of spirit or life-force rather than in a personal God.

It is important that Australian churches note these differences, for they are found among many migrants who come to Australia. Migrants from Asia, Africa, South America, and Southern Europe do not share the northern European sense of individualised spirituality. Indeed, there are some countries which have no parallel language for "spirituality" at all. This is true of Thailand and Burma. Religion is both personal and communal for these migrants. The idea of something that the individual owns and constructs personally is not meaningful.

The nature and origins of spirituality in English-speaking and Northern European countries

There have been a number of theoretical attempts to explain the growth of spirituality in English-speaking and Northern European countries. The sociologists of religion, David Voas and Steve Bruce,[3] for example, argue that there is little in the so-called spiritual activities, such as yoga, homeopathy, reiki, and other spiritual alternative activities which is spiritual in the sense that there is any reference to that which is sacred. They see these activities as by-products of the counter-culture movement of the 1960s, with roots in a long tradition of alternative spiritualities, but essentially being part of the process of secularisation. They hypothesise:

> The continuing unpopularity of institutional religion will lead more people to describe themselves as spiritual but not religious, at least for a time. Creators, importers and promoters of services for the mind, body and spirit will be able to sustain and possibly increase participation in the holistic milieu. Nothing in these developments, though, implies that social or even personal life is being sacralised. On the contrary, they are part and parcel of the process of secularisation.[4]

Two other British sociologists, Jeremy Carrette and Robert King, have argued that there has been a two-stage development of spirituality in northern Europe. The first they describe as emphasising "the association of 'spirituality' with the interior life of the individual", which, they argued, occurred in conjunction with development of the concept of the individual as "an independent, autonomous and largely self-contained entity within society".[5] The second stage occurred in the late 1980s and 1990s as "spirituality" was co-opted by corporate enterprise to meet its own demands for a flexible and compliant workforce and to replace religion with something more malleable and marketable that would not be critical of corporate capitalist culture.[6]

There is good evidence in most northern European, Australian, and American shopping centres of the capitalist adoption of the language of spirituality to sell its products. The language of holistic wellbeing has arisen from the spiritual milieu and is used to sell everything from cosmetics to holidays. It is also true, as Voas and Bruce argue, that many people are involved in the so-called alternative spiritual activities or the "holistic milieu" without much sense of the spiritual. Nevertheless, in the widespread adoption of the language of spirituality there appears to be something more going on in the ways people are seeking a sense of meaning in life.

The sociologists, Paul Heelas and Linda Woodhead,[7] undertook a major intensive empirical study of spirituality and religion in a town in northern England. They argue that the fundamental change in culture which occurred in the 1960s and 1970s had to do with a movement from life being seen primarily in terms of one's duty to fulfil roles that were given to one by one's gender, age, ethnicity, marital status, and social status and by one's religious heritage, to life being seen in terms of fulfilment of one's "subjective life". A clear example is the change in relation to the perception of gender roles. Prior to the 1960s, being a married woman meant that one had the duty to look after the home. With the rise of feminism came an awareness that married women could find fulfilment in life in many ways apart from looking after a home, and where they found fulfilment should be up to the individual to determine. The movement from religion to spirituality was part of a more widespread development of more individualistic ways of putting life together, less determined by social expectations and the sense of duty associated with gender, social class, and whether one was married or not.

The social theorist, Anthony Giddens,[8] has made a similar point using different terminology. He has described people in Britain as moving into a post-traditional age. It was an age when traditions were no longer seen as immutable and unchallengeable. Rather, individuals could determine what traditions were useful to them and what they wanted to make of life for themselves. Life came to be lived reflexively, as a developing biography, rather than as a fulfilment of a range of traditional duties and responsibilities.

Following the thinking of the sociologist, Peter Berger[9] and his colleagues, it seems very likely that one of the factors in the new way of looking at the world which emerged in the 1960s and 1970s had to do with changes in child-rearing practices primarily within the context of having smaller families. In the 1960s and 1970s, parents began to raise their children more as individuals, seeking to meet the needs of each individual child, rather than as members of a household. Family size shrank as infant mortality declined, as contraception improved, and as it became more expensive to rear children, with increasing expectation that families would support children not only to the end of secondary schooling but also through tertiary education. Thus, from a young age, parents began to ask children what they would like to play, to eat, and to watch on television, rather than telling them what they should do next. From early childhood, children grew up with the assumption that they could make of life what they wanted to make of it. They could choose not only their food and occupation, but also their political and religious preferences.

From this time, many young people began to drop their religious identity. Indeed, it was often more than that. In the counter-cultural revolution of the 1960s, they rebelled against religion. There were three major movements in that rebellion:

Rejection of religious beliefs. Many people felt that in an age of science, religious beliefs no longer made sense and were no longer necessary to explain what happened in the world.

Rejection of religious values. In particular, many people rejected the religious morality which held that sexuality was for procreation and could only occur within marriage. With the pill, it had become possible to distinguish sex for pleasure and sex for procreation, and sex for pleasure was fun! In more general terms, many people could not see the point of the asceticism inherent in religious morality. Why not enjoy life as much as one was able?

Rejection of religious institutions. Many people saw the religious institutions as authoritative, out-of-date, and as interested primarily in maintaining themselves. They disliked the fact that women and men were treated unequally by many religious institutions. Religious authority, like all other authority, had to be earned, rather than given by position, and religious authorities were not generally earning it.

Yet, within this world of the rejection of religious beliefs, values, and institutions, many people felt there remained something more to life than the material. There was more to life than simply having experiences of fun.

A few people found the institutionalised spiritual alternative organisations attractive. These provided a more systematic way of rejecting Christianity, but also of finding one's identity in relation to nature. Paganism, Wicca, and Druidism still have a following, but have generally remained very small. In the 2011 Census, a total of 32,000 people identified with what are generally referred to as nature religions. This includes 16,851 people who called themselves Pagans, 8,414 who used the term "Wicca", and 1,048 Druids, along with a number of others including Animists, many of whom were migrants from south-east Asia.[10]

Other people have looked to the religions of the East for their inspiration: to the Hare Krishna movement of Hinduism, or to Buddhism, for example. Small numbers of people have converted. However, many others have taken an interest in these religions without fully converting or identifying with them to the exclusion of other religious groups.

Many of the influences from these counter-cultural experiments of the 1960s and 1970s have dissipated into the wider society. Few people who today call themselves spiritual are involved in a spiritual group or participate frequently in alternative spiritual activities such as yoga or Eastern meditation.

At the heart of "spirituality" as distinct from "religion" is the sense that life is more than the material. Today, most people raised in an Anglo heritage assume that they can and should make their own choices about what they believe about life and whether they engage in any religious or spiritual practices. To that extent "spirituality" is seen as being an individual enterprise which may or may not include involvement in a community (as a matter of individual choice), although this does not imply that spirituality is individualistic in its ethic. Indeed, spirituality is often identified in the care people have for others. The fact that people look for that which will lead to personal fulfilment reflects consumeristic types of attitudes, but does not imply, of itself, consumerism.

Spirituality takes a variety of forms, to some extent, dependent on context. In Britain, there is an anti-religious strain in many forms of spirituality, as noted by Heelas and Woodhead. This is less the case in Australia. While some people have developed an identification with spirituality as part of their reaction against religion, others have used the language to stress the personal importance of religious faith. For some, there is little sense of "otherness" or transcendence in their spirituality, while for others it is a major dimension. Spirituality may be a step towards secularisation, as Voas and Bruce suggest. Nevertheless, in as far as it is the language many people use to describe themselves, it must be taken seriously. It certainly cannot be reduced to the small range of "holistic milieu" activities that Heelas and Woodhead note in their study and which Voas and Bruce reject as having little sacred significance in their critique.

A useful list of characteristics of contemporary spirituality which distinguish it from some religious traditions was drawn up by the Swedish scholar, Liselotte Frisk, and is reproduced by Antoon Geels.[11] She suggests that contemporary spirituality:

- is eclectic rather than particular in its identification of sources;
- focuses on experience rather than dogma in its expression;
- focusses on this-worldliness rather than on life-after-death;
- is practised and is owned personally rather than collectively;
- is egalitarian in its approach rather than recognising hierarchies in institutions or expertise; and
- takes an anthropological approach rather than a theological approach.

Drawing on a survey of Australian adults conducted in 2002, Kaldor, Hughes, and Black[12] identified two major types of spirituality in Australia. The first was eclectic, in which people saw themselves as drawing on a wide range of religious and other spiritual resources to find what was personally meaningful. These included New Age and Buddhist resources, but for many people also included Christian resources. About 8 percent of Australian adults could be identified as having such an eclectic form of spirituality. The second type of spirituality was nature-based. These people found their sense of meaning and identity in relation to nature, in a connection with land, or with living things, or with the environment. About 9 percent of Australians were in this group.

While contemporary spirituality may be closer to secularity than is traditional religiosity, there are no signs of it disappearing. Certainly its lack of institutional forms and expressions means it is weak and amorphous. However, Voas and Bruce's argument that it is just a passing fad among middle-aged women who have roots in the counter-cultural revolution of the 1960s is not supported by the statistical data. It is neither an institutional movement nor a specific set of doctrines about life, which have to be passed on across the generations, as are the nature religions. Rather, it is a sense among many people that there is more to life than the material, that there is mystery in inner life, in the existence of life itself, and in the very existence and nature of the universe. This sense is not likely to simply disappear, even though there are few communities built around these ways of thinking. Many people feel that a material approach to life is inadequate for dealing with life. There is a mystery in the very being of the universe which must be acknowledged, and personal spirituality is important in one's relationships and one's inner wellbeing.

People look for activities and events that will nurture their spirituality and contribute to their inner wellbeing. Some find activities such as yoga and meditation helpful in that way. Others find that art, music, drama, and film nurture the spirit. For some, holidays are important, not just for relaxation, but for activities that inspire, stimulate, or nurture. When one asks people where they most often find a sense of peace and wellbeing, the most common response is in the family and secondly among friends. A third and important source of nurturing the spirit is being out in nature. Some find surfing a spiritual experience as is bushwalking for others.

Meaning for mission

Heelas and Woodhead argue that some Christian churches are relating to people better in an age in which life is seen as the fulfilment of the subjective self rather than the adoption of traditions and duties. They suggest that the Pentecostal and charismatic churches respond to the subjective self because they place more importance on the personal experience as the entry into the sacred.[13] At the other end of the spectrum, they suggest that churches which place greater importance on the "truth without" rather than the "truth within" ask people to conform to that external truth. To that extent, they often give little place for the subjective life. The mainstream churches, for example, tend to focus on duty and self-sacrifice, rather than on freedom and self-realisation. Heelas and Woodhead suggest that:

> This emphasis on 'life-as' duties is often reinforced by the survival of hierarchical, directive and dominating ecclesiastical and organisational structures, residual clericalism, and formalized liturgical worship.[14]

While there are some more subjectively oriented activities and interests such as mysticism, Celtic spirituality, and meditation and retreat centres to cater for spirituality, these are generally marginal to the official life of these churches.

In responding to personal spirituality, then, the implication of the observation of Heelas and Woodhead would be that churches need to develop activities which nurture the subjective self, rather than seeking to impose structures and duties on people. Heelas and Woodhead note that the megachurches have been particularly successful in this regard.

Heelas and Woodhead are approaching the issue from a sociological perspective rather than a theological perspective. From the perspective of the church's mission, what is attractive to people should not determine how mission is conducted. Nevertheless, mission needs to take into account how people think and what is meaningful to them in its engagement.

Some of the emphases of contemporary spirituality are very much in line with some dimensions of the Christian faith. Firstly, contemporary spirituality recognises that there is "something beyond" this material world. A number of commentators, such as Antoon Geels, have noted that many forms of contemporary spirituality recognise the mystery in human life and in the universe as a whole. It is, in part, a protest against reducing the world to that which is material and mundane. Geels argues that this sense of mystery is very much in line with that described by the mystics of many religions including those in the Christian tradition. The recognition of mystery in contemporary spirituality may be an important antidote to the Protestant tendency to anthropomorphise God, as Karen Armstrong[15] has argued.

A recognition of the mystery and awesomeness of the natural world is not, in itself, antithetical to the Christian faith. It is certainly a common theme in the Psalms and in some of the prophets. The problem arises for Christians when the mystery is seen as inherent in the natural world rather than the source of the mystery of life and the beauty of the world. The Judeo-Christian tradition was critical of those traditions around it which worshipped nature in itself, rather than seeing the natural world as signifying something beyond. In times when the fragility of the earth has become so apparent because of its exploitation by human beings, contemporary spirituality reminds Christians of the importance of recapturing a respect for creation and a dedication to its care.

In recognising the essential mysteriousness of God, it becomes necessary to place the emphasis more on the experience of God than on dogmatic and propositional beliefs. This is also not antithetical to many parts of the Christian tradition, including the Orthodox and some aspects of the Catholic tradition. It has been argued that one of the reasons why the Pentecostal and charismatic churches have connected better with many post-1960s people has been their emphasis on the experience of God rather than a focus on propositional belief.[16]

Part of the protest of contemporary spirituality has been about the institutionalisation of religion and the development of structures and hierarchies. Contemporary spirituality reminds Christians that much of their energy is actually focussed on maintaining these institutions and of preserving positions, rather than focussing on the experience of the mystery of God. There have been many protest movements against the institutionalisation of the Christian faith throughout history, including those of the Reformation and Restorationism. This latest protest needs to be heard and ways found to lighten the weight of Christian institutional baggage. At the same time, the radical individualism of some forms of spirituality seems to have gone too far. People need to live in community and it is in the health and vitality of community life that personal fulfilment is found.

Thus, there is much in contemporary spirituality which resonates with the Christian tradition and which reminds Christians of aspects of their faith they had forgotten, such as the mystery of life and the universe, and the ultimate mystery of the divine, of the importance of the care of the natural world and of human experience, and of the tendency to over-institutionalise faith.

There is much at the heart of the Christian faith about the fulfilment of life and living life to the full. The term "salvation" carries overtones of health and wholeness. The idea of God's justice or *shalom*, to use terms from the Hebrew testament, contains the sense of whole communities living in purposeful harmony.

Where Christians need to make a stand over against some contemporary forms of spirituality is to argue that such fulfilment in life is not found primarily by a focus on self-realisation by obeying one's inner impulses, as Heelas and Woodhead seem to suggest, but through one's contribution in relationship with others. In contemporary society, each individual can develop their own biographies. But they will not find those biographies meaningful until they make their own personal contributions to the life of others and to the wider society.

There are certainly times when we need to re-charge our own batteries and care for ourselves. Human beings need time for reflection, times to step aside from the business of life. Again, contemporary spirituality reminds us here of something that has been present within the Christian tradition. There are times when we need to express our feelings through music, art, and drama. In the functionality of Protestantism, we have sometimes lost sight of these forms of reflection on life, and celebration of life and its roots in the mysteriousness of God.

Yet, ultimately we find fulfilment in life when we focus on the wellbeing of others and not just ourselves. As previously noted, in surveys and interviews I have conducted, mainly of secondary school students and teachers, I have found strong recognition of this. Most people say they find a sense of peace and wellbeing, a sense of meaning and purpose, primarily in close personal relationships with friends and family.[17] It is in these close personal relationships that people focus most clearly on the wellbeing of others and in which they find their major sense of fulfilment.

However, most people also find a sense of fulfilment in contributing to the wider society. This most commonly occurs through their paid occupations. Those paid occupations are particularly meaningful when they are seen as making a contribution to the wellbeing of others.[18] It also occurs through voluntary activities either with friends and neighbours or with community organisations.

In a number of surveys and interviews, I have asked school teachers what they would most like to do to enhance their spirituality, if time and money were no object. The most common response is to be involved in an international or local aid project of some kind. Some would like the opportunity to go on a pilgrimage. A few would like to explore life through a course of study, and theological colleges seem to be increasingly important in providing such opportunities. Others would simply like to spend more time at home with family. Most, however, recognise that a major way of enhancing their own spirituality is through giving of themselves to others.

To put it in Jesus' terms: the purpose of Christian mission is to call people to love God and to love their neighbours as themselves. Love of self, one's neighbours — who are not only one's friends and relatives but also the members of the wider society — and love of God form the spirituality to which Jesus calls us.

There is no sense, either in the teaching of Jesus or in the teaching of the early church, that the primary means of fulfilment of this love for God or for others was attendance at worship services. There are numerous ways that churches engaging in mission can open up ways for people to develop their relationships with God and with others.

One of the things that churches need to do is to find ways of engaging people who do not attend, and may not be interested in attending, services of worship. A survey of young people in Catholic schools in 2011 found that more were involved in social welfare, social justice, music and drama activities, sporting activities, and youth groups than were involved in attendance at Mass.[19] Many people I have interviewed have said they would enjoy being part of a small discussion group or would like to participate in a social welfare program, but are not interested in attending worship. Churches need to open paths other than through congregational worship to the exploration of the love for God, their neighbours, and themselves.

One form of ministry that relates well to contemporary spirituality is chaplaincy. Chaplaincy is usually non-denominational, places value on personal relationships, and treats people holistically. It does not focus on having the right belief, but takes seriously the personal experiences of people. It meets them incarnationally rather than expecting people to first become members of institutions.

The individualistic approach to spirituality probably means that, increasingly, people will connect with Christian churches and other organisations through short-term involvements in specific groups or activities, rather than through long-term involvement in congregations. There are many ways in which Christian churches can adjust for this. They need to train people to offer the variety of facilities and options. And they need to develop different financial systems so that "users pay" rather than these "additional" activities being developed on the back of the voluntary giving of small numbers of loyal congregational members.

Through the development of contemporary spirituality, God appears to be calling the church to renewal. We must put the holistic wellbeing of people first rather than our institutional structures. We do that as we develop a wide range of activities through which people can find spiritual nurture. The congregations which currently dominate our mission are likely to decline. I imagine them becoming trunks of great trees, with many branches, and many leaves, absorbing the light of the sun and turning it into energy with birds hopping among the leaves. Congregations will be the organising bodies, the structures which root the variety of activities into basic principles of God's kingdom. But beyond the congregations will be a great variety of activities through which people find that spiritual nurture for which they search as individuals.

One of the passages which sums up a vision of mission which may connect with the contemporary spirituality is Isaiah 42:1–4. It talks about the aim of "establishing justice". Justice should be read in its broadest sense of the ways which are right and fulfilling: the aim of peaceful and purposeful harmony, of *shalom*. The servants of God are filled with God's Spirit in order to participate in establishing God's *shalom*. How will they do it? They will not shout or make loud speeches in the streets. In other words, they will not do it through making laws or assigning duties. They will not break off a bent reed, or put out a flickering lamp, and thus they will not do it by pushing aside those who are wavering or who are weak. They will do it by persistence. They will not lose hope or courage, because God's *shalom* will prevail.

Rev. Dr Philip Hughes was ordained in the Baptist Church and served as a minister with the Uniting Church until 2016. From 1985 until 2016 he also served as the Director of the Christian Research Association. A prolific author and researcher, a major focus has been seeking to understand how schools, churches, and families can contribute to growing the spiritual faith of young people. A second focus has been the movement from religion to spirituality and what that means for the churches' mission.

Two Streams Converging "Families", "Households", and Their Critique of Individualism in the Missional Conversation

Beth Barnett

This paper seeks a convergence of two streams of thinking about family and mission: the relatively new voice of family talk, missional community, church planting, Fresh Expressions, and a historical case study of family mission in Scripture Union, Victoria.

A keen follower of the missional community and church planting conversation in any of the transatlantic hubs over the past couple of years will have noticed a new word entering the vocabulary, "family".

The level of thinking that is being given to understanding the domestic unit as an instrument in mission strategy is growing fast. Leaders and innovators of a new generation in missional movements are themselves more likely to have shared in the care of, and had more domestic engagement with, their children and their children's social environment than did a previous generation of task-focused leaders. The exposure of this generation of missional leaders to the community that their child inhabits has provoked the observation that children connect with more people each day than most adults. Moreover (and this is yet to be rigorously explored) children occupy a world in which ethics, values, and the wonder of life are the common grammar of conversation and interaction.

A quick review of recent developments in the missional conversation tends to underscore this point.

First, Mike Breen of *3DM* and other contributors to the *Verge Network* have been contributing to the "missional family" blog series over the course of the last year. Secondly, the Rethink group working out of North Point Community Church, Georgia, launched the *Think Orange* resource for church and family partnerships in 2009. Somewhat similarly, the Fuller Youth Institute's longitudinal research around the transition of young people to college and the impact of this upon their faith, led to the development in 2007 of the "Sticky Faith" cohorts and resources. These address parents and leaders with regard to the family role in faith formation. "Sticky Faith" is unashamedly grounded in the agenda of stopping the haemorrhage of youth from churched backgrounds, and almost exclusively assumes Christendom culture within the family of origin. Finally, *Fresh Expressions* in the UK recently reported that the popular intergenerational *Messy Church* model was the most successful model for engaging and holding non-church families.

To sum up, it would seem that "family" and "missional" are suddenly in vogue. Ten years ago it was rare to hear them mentioned together. During the first two decades of the emerging church movement, the young adult demographic was distinctly a-familial, unattached, and highly individual.

The last ten years have witnessed the dissembling of many of those emerging communities. As young adults have become parents, they have returned to mainstream churches in order for their children to attend Sunday school. While much was made of the "inadequacy" of Sunday school faith and the need to move past it in missional communities, parents and leaders in many cases were unable or unwilling to do the theological re-imagining required to create a missional community which would nurture faith across all ages. There are exceptions, but to date, the data, research, and reporting on differentiation of outcomes are extremely thin.

In mainstream denominational church plants, children and families have been an assumed foundation of new communities. I don't know of a single church planter willing to say they don't want any families in their new congregation or community. While many church planters have developed thoughtful, creative, and adept missiologies for their adult planting teams, the standard "Raikes" legacy Sunday school remains the default position for children.[1] This tends to establish a familiar pattern, which has often not kept pace with the theological framework of evangelism employed with adults. This is an important area for further research and reflection. We lack the space to detail this here, but it will be helpful to provide the briefest of overviews.

Christian communities tend to have pathways and conventions for belonging, believing, and behaving. They have their own cultures of spiritual maturity which align with certain kinds of responsibilities. Many church leaders assume that "faith stage theory" is relevant to adults who grew up in church and that it is normative for children of all backgrounds, including those with no church background. However, it is problematic if applied to an adult coming to faith. The theological dimensions of this conflict of models are largely neglected, and remain an important task for missioners who aspire to engage whole families with the good news.

There are also several sociological factors that must be mentioned briefly here, as they contribute to the shift in family profile. Generally, at least among evangelical church planters and missioners, the resurgence of more conservative family values has increased the focus on "right parenting" and resulted in the spiritualisation of the domestic space. The neo-conservative complementarian agenda has much more to say about relationships within the home, and this has led to leaders and writers addressing the family more often and more explicitly.

Secondly, "family" is increasingly important within the general community as a marker of social good and affluence. "Family time" is increasingly under threat and becomes an idealised goal in the face of its scarcity. While the narrative of "getting rid of the kids for a bit of relaxation" might hold appeal among parents, the complementary narrative of "something for the whole family" or "bringing the family together" (see the 2010 IKEA campaign) now has obvious direct dollar value. Missioners are beginning to recognise that they can leverage an appeal to "family time" as a connecting strategy to the non-church-going.

There are indications that multi-generational households are on the rise. Housing affordability, an aging population, and double-income families requiring flexible, reliable, and affordable child care support have created the necessity of three generations living together under one roof as a practical solution to a range of pressures. Missioners have noted the close proximity of some older church members to their grandchildren and some models of missional church (*Messy Church* and *Toddler* churches in particular) are experiencing the growing phenomenon of children attending church programs with their grandparents, without their (no-longer believing) parents.

Despite the persistence of one-dimensional images of the Australian family which involve a backyard BBQ on a quarter acre block, kids being licked by the dog, mum in the kitchen, dad with "tinnie" in hand swatting flies with the hamburger flip, and white skin showing sunburn red, Australia is now comprised of many different forms of family. These draw upon traditional, contemporary, hybrid, and emergent or contingent models from many cultures. To engage in mission with Australian families is no longer — if ever it was — to assume two married, or at least permanently partnered heterosexual adults, with two or more biological offspring, born within a decade of each other, and born in the parents' late twenties or early thirties. Absent parents, blended origin siblings, non-parental adult relatives, large age-gap siblings, same-sex parenting, single parenting, multi-household residency, and trans-city residency now make up a broader spectrum of family life. Contemporary missiological reflection must consider this more seriously.

Having briefly outlined the growing stream of family mission conversation within church planting and missional community movements, I turn now to the second stream, a case study of transformation of Scripture Union beach missions under the rubric of "family mission".

1987 was a watershed year for mission in the state of Victoria. This was the year that Scripture Union Victoria made the courageous move of renaming its beach mission programs. They were, in fact, the last state in Australia to replace "Children's Special Service Missions" (CSSM) with a "family-oriented" name — an indication of the theological and missiological deliberations that accompanied the decision.

Victoria had been a very early adopter of the Beach Mission initiative pioneered in Wales by Josiah Spiers in 1867. CSSM came to Victoria as early as 1880. More than one hundred years of history, public confidence, and affection for the Red Banners of CSSM were put at risk with Scripture Union's decision to rename CSSM as "Scripture Union Family Missions" or SUFM.

The move to the language of "family mission" was preceded by reflection upon the gradual shift of approaching children as a mission group, whom a team could "target", to a consideration of the developmentally grounded assumptions of contemporary childhood studies. These took a more adequate view of the cognitive, emotional, social, physical, and spiritual development of children. They also had due regard for the limitations and predilections of children. Best practice within Scripture Union mission came to be seen as a holistic endeavour in which the child, as a primarily relational being, was understood in the wider family context. To address the child without regard for the family became seen as ethically irresponsible and anthropologically naïve.

Further to this fundamental shift in the view of the child was the deepening influence of a set of theological and missiological imperatives. Affirmation of the relational structure of the gospel required a rethinking of the isolated, individualist application that had become prevalent in the "one soul at a time" style evangelisms of modernity. While most evangelicals would have agreed that a response to the gospel should intrinsically and empirically result in social transformation, in practice the social and communal elements of the evangelism process had been neglected. In fact, with some forms of conservative missiological discourse, including social components in a gospel response had become considered as a compromise of an authentic gospel decision.

In the face of this more conservative tendency, the reshaping of missional practice has been undertaken around the biblical narratives of family, household, siblings, and community. This has resulted in the recovery of proper attention to the ethical, spiritual, and practical aspects of sharing good news with children in the context of their families. It has also had the effect of resulting in evangelistic engagement with families in a more holistic fashion.

A commitment to family thinking and theology, at least in terms of those to whom we are being sent, has led to a re-evaluation of the quality of our family thinking and theology in terms of who we are as an apostolic community. The integrity and incarnational character of the gospel requires that we engage not as hearsay storytellers of a form of godly gossip, but that our missional discourse is shaped in terms of the credible witness of those with first-hand experience. A call to be apostolic is simultaneously a call to be a missional community, for it is the community which invites each one of us to be a part of it. Our witness is demonstrated relationally rather than individually. Moreover, the essential diversity of participants in the missional community corresponds to deeper biblical affirmations. The inclusion of children as participants and active agents finds its missional expression within God's covenant community.

Children in the biblical narratives are not souls divorced from God's grace, waiting out their time to attain sufficient strength of will enabling them to choose a personal saving faith in Christ. This particular theological evaluation of children within the Christian household follows the misappropriation of a narrow hyper-rationalist and individualist strain of Enlightenment philosophy soaked in post-Reformation, Christendom culture, and has little to offer a holistic, faith-formed missiology.

Even a cursory overview, drawing on over 1,500 biblical texts directly mentioning children, demonstrates that:

- Children are placed by Jesus among the disciples and elevated by him as a model of the kingdom of God (Matthew 18).

- Children are inspired by God to speak prophetically at a point in time when adults have grown calloused, defeatist, and negligent (1Samuel 3).

- Children are integral to the communal practice of the wholehearted love of God in the midst of everyday life (Deuteronomy 6).

- Children occupy the centre of our vulnerability and call us to acts of faith and dependence on God. (Luke 8)

In re-directing its focus, the Scripture Union movement in Victoria has embraced the theological reality of such biblical insights for its mission with, to, and among children. As a consequence, the concrete dimensions of its mission, teams, programs, activities, and its resources have undergone a profound transformation. Over the past two decades, Scripture Union's mission has undergone at least four major shifts that have emerged in response to exploring the theological implications of a family-shaped missional community. I will attempt to summarise these briefly in what follows.

a. Programs run for primary-aged children and teenagers

Some Scripture Union locations had encouraged parent discussion groups to engage with their mission. These were often patronised exclusively by Christian parents who saw themselves attending to "support" the mission. In practice, this frequently had the effect of orienting the culture of the parental group towards a form of "in-group Christendom norms" which tended to scuttle the missional potential of the group. In contrast, events now engage not only children and young people, but also seek to welcome the whole of the community — parents, grandparents, and passers-by, as well as preschool children who were previously too young to be involved in the structured program. Teams shifted their missional imagination away from "running a program for primary-aged children" towards becoming a whole community with "gospeling" presence in a particular location.

b. The role and contribution of the family

Teams had traditionally been comprised of young adults with an older couple, perhaps with their own children attending "on the side", as "team parents" fulfilling a pastoral care role for the team. A carefully managed daily timetable was geared towards ensuring effective teamwork between the able-bodied, independent adult members of each team, with families often reporting a sense of being isolated by the teamwork practices of the team. Teams are now more likely to have several families as team members and are more likely, for example, to have flexible options for accommodation. The presence of whole families with the teams has become integral to the formation of each team. This has come to underline the theological authenticity of community and provides plenty of experience for reciprocity of ministry between adults and children on the team. In this way the teams have moved away from a culture of viewing children as "targets" for the gospel, and towards them being valued as mutual participants in open and genuine relationships through which faith is shared. In turn, this has encouraged a culture in which the boundaries are less sharply drawn between families serving on the team (camping with the team and following fully the daily timetable) and other families participating in the program and present on the camping ground or in the local community where the program is being delivered.

These families, who are not camping with the team, have grown in numbers, diversity, and significance. They align themselves with the goals of the team and consider themselves to be contributors to and supporters of the mission. They might offer help with practical tasks, broaden the pastoral care of the team, or might exercise a significant evangelistic role in initiating contact with "fringe" adults or engaging in conversation with other parents present. A further benefit for these families is the experience of integrating mission with their experience of holiday, which one anticipates will encourage such routine mission within the family throughout the remainder of the year. These families, perhaps even more than those who are "on team", experience the reality that mission is not limited by role, program, or intention, but can be wonderfully interwoven into even the family's leisure time.

c. Opening families to the Bible

Scripture Union Victoria has moved beyond consideration of the needs of a particular target demographic in isolation from the family. It has come to recognise the need to resource teams with Bible engagement material that is shaped to all ages, flexible, integrative, but which retains particularised components. The series of resources published under the direction of Mavis Payne between 2008 and 2013 articulated a theology and associated methodology which equipped the whole mission community, including its constituent families, and re-oriented programming away from "thematic", didactic, and a simplistic "principles" approach, to programming that provided deep immersion in biblical texts, in connection with concrete contexts, as the central structure of missional engagement. The priority of mission was not to gain the mental assent of individuals to particular doctrines, but to authentically open the Bible in community and encourage listening and response to the biblical narrative.

d. Invitations to faith: increasing frequency and diversity

Ron Buckland's work in "Children and God" and "Children and the Gospel" provided strong theological material around faith and the child, particularly in non-church-culture families. With a post-Augustinian critique of "bounded set" conversion, and offering a flexible but biblical model of turning towards and away from God, Buckland's groundbreaking contribution required a reappraisal of the manner in which "response" was invited and narrated in mission team. The result, now reflected in Scripture Union resources, is that an invitation to respond to the gospel is given more frequently, but in a greater of variety of forms. Whereas "responding to the gospel" might historically have meant praying a formulaic prayer of repentance and commitment, a more appropriate response is now considered to be a commitment to an ongoing process, a practice that is appropriate every time the Bible is opened. Missiologically the goal is no longer to make mere converts (such as with a one-time decision) but to help families develop practices of discipleship which engage with and respond to the Bible in an ongoing missional relationship with the narrative, through which they can become followers of Jesus.

Conclusion

In conclusion, this is where two streams converge. Scripture Union Family Missions has taken a lead in initiating the task of families discipling other families towards and within faith. However, the mandate of Scripture Union has always been to work with churches. Where families are responding in faith, Scripture Union seeks to connect them with churches — hopefully missional communities. This has not always been an easy cultural transition for families to make, many of whom find themselves in conventional churches that approach families in a more atomised manner.

As the vocabulary of family develops and grows within the missional community and church planting movements, I am hopeful that some of Scripture Union's journey will find its counterpart within these movements, including:

- A deeper reflection on a theology of children — especially those theologies that do not move far beyond the "faith-stages" psychology of churched children;
- A stronger understanding of the various cultures of the family in society and of the healing and nurturing potential of the whole community;
- The development of a more nuanced and faithful evangelistic practice that encourages ongoing responses to the gospel by both long-term followers of Jesus and recent seekers. It should anticipate the need for continual responses to the gospel in ways not packaged by evangelists, but in ways suggested by the narrative of biblical texts and the call of the Spirit.

Beth Barnett is a PhD candidate at the University of Divinity, Melbourne.

Transforming Expectations

Frank D. Rees

How an expanded understanding of the priesthood of all believers can enrich people's experience of God's presence in the world around us and in turn give renewed substance to our gathered worship.

The defining challenge addressed in this chapter is the question whether people expect God to do anything or make any difference in the world today. What do we expect? There are indications that many Christians do not expect anything from God beyond their personal lives and local church. These trends reflect the preoccupation of contemporary ecclesiology and some missiology with the gathered church only, as if this defines the entire being and mission of the church. This chapter explores the potential of the classic doctrine of "the priesthood of all believers" to shift the focus towards the whole life of all the people. All God's people are the church and all of our lives are the "priesthood" we offer. A critical question is, then, where the priesthood of all believers is to be exercised and how we may discern that. To explore this question requires a reconsideration of the presence and activity of the Spirit in the world. What do we see God doing in the world and how does this activity help to define the priestly life of the church? The chapter begins with accounts of specific situations where some of these dynamics have been explored and the expectations of local Christians transformed by a greater vision of the presence and purposes of God.

Graham Hill is surely right. Despite the many books being published about the life and mission of the church in the postmodern era, there has been very little examination of the christological and eschatological basis of that mission. "The church is faithful to the messianic mission of Christ and to its missional nature when it is about the establishment of the kingdom of God on this earth." This means that the life of the church must be understood through "the theological grids of *the kingdom of God* and *eschatology*". In this light, Hill writes approvingly of Hans Kung's description of the church as *the eschatological community of salvation*.[1]

What this means is that the life and mission of the church must be defined theologically in terms of what we can and may expect from God and how we live into that expectation. The basis of these expectations is the life, death, and resurrection of Jesus and the mission of the Holy Spirit. It is in light of the Trinitarian mission of God, then, that the church may find and reach out for its own life.

In this chapter, we will explore the question of expectations, in the lives of Christians and local faith communities. The basic contention will be that transforming local churches into effective missional communities itself requires the transformation of expectations. In short, it is a question of what we expect: not just what we expect the church to be doing, but what we expect from God and what we may do and become in the light of those expectations.

One very clear indication of what we expect of and from God can be seen in our prayers of intercession — whether in fact we pray in this way and if so what we pray. Though it is a broad generalisation, it is, I think, a simple fact that with the shift from pastors leading services to others fulfilling this role, and the accompanying disappearance of "the pastoral prayer" in many church services, congregations have largely abandoned prayers of intercession. Where they do happen, we pray for our own, the members of our church who may be ill, dying, or in some other situation of need. We do not routinely pray for the world as such, the nations, the needy, and our governments, and this I suggest is because we do not expect God to do anything much in the world, or if we do we have no imagination of what that might be or how it might involve us.

What do we expect from God, in the world here and now? This question I suggest is a vital challenge to all that we call "church" and can in fact invite a transformation of local church life — a transformation of expectations. At the heart of this argument is a conviction that fundamentally the church is not about the church: it is called to be a community of faith, reaching out for God's presence and promised reign, transforming this world into God's commonwealth of justice, peace, healing, and joy. Jesus proclaimed this way of God and demonstrated it, through his healings and provision, his welcome to sinners and his inclusive gatherings, especially in meals of celebration. The church is a community of people who have received this message, the gospel of transformed expectations.

We begin our exploration of this theme with a series of anecdotes, describing how some people found an entirely different perspective on their own faith and the mission of the church, through such a shift in focus and expectations.

A shift in focus

It was about five years into my leadership in a local church ministry when one of the deacons came to warn me about a problem he could see developing. He was a very supportive leader, but he suggested to me that I was in danger of creating unfulfilled expectations amongst the congregation. The gospel message of the coming of God's kingdom, with its new age of grace and healing, was being received well — except that our local church was really not very different at all. The same old issues and struggles persisted. The new age was not dawning. This leader could see a danger of frustrated expectations, perhaps reflecting badly on my ministry.

I thought long and hard about this conversation and came to the conclusion that the problem was one of focus: it was a question of where people were looking. I had no doubt that God was actively transforming lives and situations, with or without our church. The challenge was to see this.

So for the next two years or so, we integrated into every weekly service a segment I called "Insights". Here one person from the congregation was asked to speak for three minutes about some situation or aspect of their life, often their work, in which they saw God at work. That short segment led into our prayers as well, for that person and the situation they mentioned. The very first such contribution was from a clinical psychologist who spoke of the challenges she faced in sitting on the Films Classification Board. This woman was obliged to view all the horrific films which were judged inappropriate for public viewing. That gave us a dramatically changed view of her life and work, and helped us to support her in different ways. Other people spoke about their work, family, neighbourhood, and so on. Very quickly, these segments led to people discovering so much more about each other and about the presence of God in an amazing range of situations around the city and indeed around the world. People began to see God at work beyond "our church". They also began to think about their own lives in this way, in anticipation of what they might say when I asked them to contribute one day!

A young man who is a social worker in an exceptionally demanding residential care situation, spoke with me this year about how he had come to see his work as the primary form of his Christian mission. In his earlier life within another denomination, he imagined that the primary focus of God's work in the world was the local church and its Sunday meetings. His role was to be part of that meeting and if possible to encourage other people to come along. Recently he has come to see that God is active in the world and it is the role of Christians to see that and to join with what God is doing, to participate in God's mission in society. I asked him how this change of perspective had come about for him. He identified two things. In the past, he said, the people gathered and prayed about people and situations far away, people they did not know and with whom they had no relationship. Now, his church prays about what is going on in the local community and "in the worlds of the gathered community", including his own work and his life. But this change was accompanied by the reading of the Gospels and by sermons which actually made these connections. The preaching and the prayers allowed him to imagine and then come to see God at work in his life, his work, and the world around him.

A third story derives from something I read many years ago, the source of which is now lost to me. At that time, there was a lot of emphasis in Evangelical churches upon the idea that everyone has a spiritual gift and we all should find that gift and use it in the ministry of the church.

In one church, the pastor was teaching these things, but one day a member of the church said to him that she just couldn't see it. She could see the gifts in others, but not for herself. Maybe she just didn't have a spiritual gift. The pastor encouraged her to keep praying about it and maybe she would find her spiritual gift. Then one day she came to see him again, with a very unusual request. She asked him did he have any ideas where she could get hold of a pile of children's story books, puzzle books, and that kind of thing. He was a bit surprised, as he knew she was an older person, with none of her own family living near her at all. Then she told him that the last couple of weeks she had realised that in her street all the families were households where all the parents went out to work, and so many of the kids came home from school to an empty house and often nothing much to do. So she had actually taken to inviting them into her house, giving them cordial and a cup cake or something, and she wondered if she could find some books and so on for them to read. This lady had started her own local after-school care program, in her own home. The pastor was prompted to consider what had led this lady to think that she did not have a spiritual gift!

What is common to all these situations is *a shift in focus* or perspective. In each instance, people were coming to see and expect that God is present in their everyday lives, whether at work or at home, in the world around them. They were all discovering God at work and their own lives were changed by coming to see that they did not have to create "mission", rather they were invited to join with what God was doing, or making possible, in that situation. This change in focus, in what people could see and become part of, is the basis of what I am calling transformed expectations.

It is worth noting here a number of the ingredients in this shift in focus, which can help us then to see how other groups and individuals might also experience a change in expectations. The first element to note is a change in the understanding of faith. All too commonly, we think of our faith in terms of believing things we cannot see and perhaps cannot even imagine. Often this faith has a focus upon another time: it's either about what Jesus did "back then", or what we trust God will do for us in the future, in the life beyond. So in this world and in this time, faith is about holding on to these beliefs, more or less in the face of how things are now. But in these stories, faith is about seeing and engaging with the present: with God who is present. Faith is about seeing what God is doing *now*.

In his classic study of the Holy Spirit and mission, *The Go-Between God*, John Taylor speaks of "bi-sociation" as a distinctive kind of seeing. It means being able to see things as they are, realistically and honestly, but also to see things as if "through God's eyes", to see the possibilities and potential of that situation, in God's creative and redemptive purposes.[2] Taylor says that the biblical prophets were given such vision, but Jesus exercised this insight to a unique degree. Jesus was at all times seeking God's presence and perspective on every person and situation of his daily life. He was asking: So in this dispute between brothers, or this anguished family with their epileptic son, or this crowd of confused and dispirited people, what is God wanting to do, to bring peace, healing, and hope — and how shall I engage with God in bringing this to reality?

Taylor suggests that enabling us to see God's presence in this way is the activity of the Holy Spirit. This transformation of our faith to a new focus, then, is the work of God making our faith more real and, in a sense, more immediately demanding. There are things to be done, situations calling for our engagement.

In all of the stories above, there is also the factor of the local church's teaching and preaching. This of course follows the pattern of Jesus' own ministry, raising expectations and inviting people to see that the kingdom of God was indeed among them (Luke 17:21). The social worker was encouraged and challenged by the worship and teaching of his new church to look in a different direction, to see God's presence and activity not simply in the meeting of Christians on Sundays but in the local community, in the world more generally, and very specifically in his work. His faith and his expectations of God's presence were changed through learning to see in a different way.

Luke's theology strongly encourages this kind of seeing. When Jesus sends 70 new disciples — raw in experience and told to travel light — they are not told to bring God's presence into the places they go to. Rather, they are to live with the people, eat and drink with them, heal the sick, and tell them that the kingdom of God has come near, or is among them (Luke 10:3–12). When they return to Jesus, their stories bring him great joy. They too have seen what he sees, the joyous presence of God already at work in the world. This way of seeing, with faith-filled eyes, is not only a source of joy. It provides the energy for mission. It transforms expectations.

It is also significant in this gospel story that the reports from the disciples' excursion into mission leads to praise of God. Jesus is ecstatic. There is a dynamic here that can also be played out in local church life. Our corporate worship is inherently the gathering together of our experience of God. We bring that experience into the gathered life and, when the process of the service allows it and works well, this experience is given voice. It may be thanksgiving, or regret, or hoping — and usually a mixture of all these. Similarly, when we go from the worship event into our daily lives, it is there too that we offer our worship. Mission is the outworking of what we said and sang about God and God's purposes back there in the worship space. It is the expansion of that worship into practical, living expression of what we think about God and what we expect from God, and it is our engagement with what we see God doing in the world around us.

Theological implications: the who and where of missional engagement

Findley Edge was a great leader of the Southern Baptist Convention's Christian Education ministry, who dedicated his ministry to the education of local congregations. At the heart of his outstanding book, *The Greening of the Church*, Edge writes: "It is imperative that we become a people who understand who we are, who God is, what God is about in the world and what God is calling us to be about in the world".[3] Edge goes on to suggest that the critical focus must shift towards a reclaiming of the doctrine of the priesthood of all believers. All these years later, his call is still needed.

The most important implication of Edge's call, at least for this discussion, is that "church" is not primarily about getting people "to" church, in the sense of the gathered community. That is indeed important, but the prior consideration is to change the idea of "church" from that focus to the people, wherever they are. The church is the people who know who they are, who God is, what God is doing in the world, and what they should be doing in the world.

We need to shift the use of the word "church" from a noun, especially from a noun referring to the activities of the gathered people, to a verb. Church-ing refers to all the activities of the community of faith, whether gathered or dispersed. Thus it refers to the activities and life of people at prayer and worship, but also at home, at work, at the gym, or at school. Together and apart, we are the church. "Going to church" may then refer to what we do when we leave a church building as much as what we do when we enter it. We go from the church service, to church — to be and do "church" wherever we are.

In the theological traditions of Protestantism there is a very helpful idea that expresses these insights. It is the idea of the priesthood of all believers. It is helpful to explore some of the history and applications of this idea, before we consider its application today. My contention is that this concept has immense potential, when properly understood, to transform local church life and the expectations people have. It is this idea which invites people both to see and to become part of what God is doing in the world today and thus to offer our lives, collectively and individually, as a priestly service of praise and commitment to God.

The idea of the universal priesthood of all believers arose in the Protestant Reformation of the sixteenth century. Indeed Timothy George asserts that this idea was Luther's greatest contribution to Protestant ecclesiology.[4] It is also an idea greatly misunderstood. It had a number of aspects worth noting. To begin, it is important that we do not read this concept through the highly individualist and "soul competency" emphases of later centuries. At the time of the Reformation there were other concerns. The doctrine of the priesthood of all believers arose from the fundamental emphasis of Luther and all who followed him upon the doctrine of justification by grace through faith alone. The important contrast here was with any implication that it was through the offering of sacrifices by the priests of the church that we come to salvation. Rather, Christ himself has offered a once-and-for-all, all-sufficient sacrifice, in his life and his death upon the cross. It is through faith in Christ that we are saved. As a consequence, the Reformers stressed that all Christians are called into an equal standing before God, which is both a privilege and a responsibility.

The use of the word "calling" is crucial here. Very commonly we still use the word "vocation" as if only some people have a calling. Many churches reserve this word for those who are called "into the church", to be pastors or priests or into some other "religious" office. But this is exactly the opposite of the Protestant emphasis. There, every Christian has a calling, namely to be a Christian, and there is no higher calling. As Jürgen Moltmann has put it, for the Reformers "Everyone who believes and hopes is *vocatus* and has to offer his [sic] life in the service of God, in the service of his kingdom and the freedom of faith". It is noteworthy here that our "callings" relate to service of God's kingdom (not immediately the church) and the *freedom* of faith.[5] The priesthood of all believers, then, was and is fundamentally about living a life that is a direct outworking of our faith in Christ and our trust in his gospel, the message of God's reign in this world — for which, in the words of Paul, we have been set free. For the Reformers, this meant a life of holy service and praise, in the practical realities of everyday life.

Thus the priesthood of all believers had a number of clear implications, both negative and positive. First, it meant that "the priest" or "minister", if there is such a person in the life of a local community of faith, is not a special person possessing a calling higher than other Christians.

Positively, the priesthood of all believers meant that all have equal access to God. All are called to know God and to exercise the priestly ministries of prayer, intercession for one another, and service to those in need. Luther identified seven responsibilities of priests which he now applied to all Christians.[6] This was not to say that there is no "office" in the church, for a pastor or "preaching elder" or "minister", as various communities named such callings. This, however, was but one of the callings amongst the universal calling of all Christians. All Christians have a calling, not only to the service of God through prayer but also to offer their lives as a living sacrifice, holy and acceptable to God (Romans 12:1) and this calling and service were taken to include people's whole lives. Today we might distinguish and separate work life, home life, and life in the community, but those separations were not the way people lived in earlier centuries. This is evident in the way "church discipline" was practised by early Baptists, for example. A disciple was expected to live a life "worthy" in every aspect, in the home, in commerce and industry (which was local), and in social relations. All of this was part of one's calling, the calling to the priesthood of all believers.

In later centuries, however, this doctrine became subject to what Timothy George calls a number of "perversions". These he identifies as the idea that no leadership structure or positions are necessary at all in the Christian community and the claim that every Christian has the right to their own individual interpretation of Scripture and matters of doctrine.[7]

A contemporary appropriation of the priesthood of all believers, however, requires a shift in focus from the gathered life of the church to what I have termed the church dispersed.[8] It is in the lives of Christians throughout the week, at home, at work, in the neighbourhood, leisure activities, and social engagements that this priesthood must find its primary significance. In other words, the transformation of expectations into mission requires re-thinking of the *where* as well as the *who* of mission. The priesthood of all believers means that every Christian is a minister, a person called into some service of God and the coming of God's reign. But this does not, primarily, mean activities in the worship services or other groups "at church". Rather, it is in the offering of our living bodies in reasonable service, as our worship, as Paul puts it in Romans 12:1. This is a priestly offering and therefore a form of worship. It is both individual and collective. Altogether it is the priestly service of the whole church. Thus, we follow Jesus who left the temple, not to abandon it but to develop a new body, a temple in which the Spirit offers this missional service.

The "who" and the "where" of this ministry or priesthood thus defines the mission of the church. It is the life of the church dispersed, engaged with what God is doing in the world. On the basis of the argument thus far, then, we must now ask what precisely this might mean. What are some of the things that might invite our participation, as the church dispersed, the priestly community on mission? The answer to this question takes us again to the question of expectations and, theologically, to the eschatological tendencies of the Spirit.

The mission of the church within the mission of the Spirit

Transforming expectations arise from seeing what God is doing. To describe something of what this means we turn to a brief description of the mission of the Holy Spirit in the world today. A number of theologians have written of the mission of the Spirit "within and beyond the church".[9] There is an important insight here, as well as a particular limitation. The insight is to recognise that the Spirit is not only at work in the church, but also may be seen in all creation and at work in specific events and opportunities all around us. The limitation of the expression "beyond the church", however, is that it implies that the church is only the institutional form or gathering, so that the presence of the Spirit in (say) educational settings is "beyond" the church. Our argument suggests that in at least some ways the church is present there, too, insofar as Christians are actively engaging with whatever the Spirit is doing or invoking.

Philip Rosato has described the activities of the Spirit both within and beyond the church, suggesting that the church can learn from the Spirit's activities "beyond" the church as well as contribute to those movements. Rosato describes the mission of the Spirit as life-giver, liberator, teacher, and unifier.[10] My own response to this piece added the idea of the Spirit as artist.[11] More recently, however, I have developed this argument further, adding the idea of the Spirit as healer. One of the things the Spirit heals is our vision, giving us the ability to see with the eyes of faith what God is doing around us. The mission of the Spirit includes the work of healing in all its forms and throughout the entire society, not only the activities of Christians.[12] The point is that we engage with what God is doing in the world and contribute our gifts to it. This is a vital part of the priesthood of all believers and therefore our worship.

Furthermore, I have argued that we need to see much of what we call "ordinary" life and work, such as our making of things, from the lunches our children take to school to the work of manufacturing, in factory or home shed, as part of the creative and life-affirming offering of all things to God, the giver and sustainer of all life. We participate in this positive living, which is God's will and purpose for us all. This too is part of the priestly life in which we may engage.

To see our thoroughly "ordinary" lives in this way is to lift up the vision of life as meaningful, wholesome, and worthwhile. It is to affirm these things as just as "spiritual" as when someone leads prayers or singing in the worship service. If we can affirm all of life in this way, as the priesthood of all believers, the collective offering of life with and to our God, this would be an immense transformation of expectations. Many people would find their lives valued and affirmed — and they would also find so much more to pray for and about.

It is a matter of where we are looking and whether we can see ourselves, all of us, as "ministers" or "priests", participating in what God is doing in the world here and now. To invite and encourage individuals and groups in this way is to evoke a veritable transformation of expectations. My conviction is that it is this transformation that will truly give rise to a missional church.

At another church where I was serving as pastor, a woman named Joy rang me one day to make a quite remarkable statement. She said that she had finally worked out what I was doing: I had not come there, she said, to persuade the church to adopt my particular strategy or set of programs. Rather, she said, now she could see that I was inviting the church to look for what the Holy Spirit was doing, all around us, and encouraging people to engage with that. I was overjoyed.

Frank D. Rees is Principal of Whitley College, University of Divinity and has served Baptist Churches in Melbourne and Hobart.

Re: Baptism
A Case for Removing the Requirements of Rebaptism for Membership in Baptist Churches in NSW and ACT

Ben Rodgers

For many years, baptism by total immersion of a believing adult has been a requirement for church membership in Baptist churches. With a growing number of people coming to Baptist churches from other traditions, this requirement has necessitated that believers baptised by the modes of other Christian denominations be rebaptised in order to gain membership. For many, this leaves them in the uncomfortable position of acknowledging that their prior experience of faith was insufficient or invalid because it has to be redone. On the other hand, by choosing not to be rebaptised, they are choosing not to participate fully in the life of the church as a member. In this work, Ben Rodgers presents the case for a new perspective in Baptist churches by removing the requirement of rebaptism on pastoral, theological, and hermeneutical grounds.

There has been growing discussion in Australian Baptist churches, particularly the Baptist Union of NSW & ACT (BUNSW), in regards to "open membership". This debate raises questions about the nature and role of baptism and the relationship between baptism and membership in the Baptist tradition. BUNSW has released a paper which identifies the problem at hand:

> While for many years Baptist Churches in NSW & ACT have had people actively involved who have come from other church traditions, in recent decades more people have joined our churches

from other denominations and have struggled with the idea of having to be baptised in order to become a Church Member.[1]

Baptist ecclesiology is structured around a regenerate church by a strong association between believer's baptism and church membership. In many cases, this has led to what is often called a "closed membership", where baptism as a believer by total immersion is required to gain church membership.[2] This is in contrast to a church membership that is "open" or "partially open" to those who have not been baptised, or who have not been baptised according to the Baptist tradition.[3]

When believers come to a Baptist church from a Christian denomination that does not practise total immersion of adult believers as its normative practice, some challenges arise in regard to the theology of baptism and church. Consideration must be made in regard to the way different groups understand baptism theologically, and more significantly, pastoral concerns associated with the idea of rebaptism.

Baptism and membership in Baptist churches

Many Baptist churches require attendees to be baptised by full immersion as an adult believer in order to be eligible for church membership. For example, the BUNSW has provided a sample church constitution stating, "Members shall be persons who give evidence of a sincere profession of faith in the Lord Jesus Christ who have been baptised as believers by immersion".[4] In addition to the requirement of baptism for membership, the BUNSW makes clear the denominational understanding of baptism in the BUNSW's statement of beliefs:

> Baptism is an ordinance of the Lord Jesus Christ. It is a public declaration of a person's faith in Jesus Christ as Lord and Saviour. In accordance with New Testament Scripture it should be administered only by total immersion which symbolises the believer's identification with Christ in death, burial, and resurrection, the remission of sins and the believer's dedication of himself [*sic*] to God to live and walk in newness of life.[5]

This statement indicates that the general Baptist view of baptism is exclusively practised by full immersion of believers upon declaration of faith. In the case of churches with a closed membership, this understanding is required not only for the practice of baptism, but also as an understanding of the validity of baptism administered in other congregations and traditions of the Christian faith. The historical roots of the Baptist movement expose the need, within a culture of religious practice dictated by the state, for a sign to identify the regenerated church membership and the desire to seek a biblical foundation for church theology and church practice over tradition. Hence the early Baptists "advocated a believer's church", as opposed to a state church.[6]

Historical context of the Baptist movement

The Baptist church and "faith emerged gradually in seventeenth-century England", and have developed into a diverse denomination.[7] The identity of this expression of the Christian faith can be characterised by certain distinguishing markers, including the authority of Scripture, the priesthood of all believers, religious freedom (liberty of conscience), autonomy of the local church, and, in particular for this discussion, the practice of believer's baptism.[8] Although these characteristics may not be exclusive to Baptist churches, and their role and significance may vary in different congregations, they provide a broad understanding of what it is to be Baptist. The Baptist distinctives discussed are interrelated and to some degree arise from a polemic against the state church, in the form of Catholicism or the Church of England. The title page of the *Orthodox Confession* of the General Baptists of 1679 clearly declares its intent "against the errors and heresies of Rome".[9] The first recognisable Baptist church began in the early seventeenth century under the leadership of John Smyth (1570–1612) and Thomas Helwys (1575–1616). Smyth, a former priest in the Church of England, "held that none of the former church's members had true baptism, for they had received it as infants before belief and faith, and they had received it from a false church (the Church of England)".[10] The full immersion of adult believers in baptism became, arguably, the clearest marker to distinguish this group of dissenters from other denominations, particularly those who practised paedo-baptism by sprinkling.[11]

The problem at hand

Though the Baptist church originates from a discontent with the practices and theology of institutional religion in seventeenth-century Europe, the theological and practical differences between such denominations are diminishing, with many Protestants agreeing on primary issues of theology and Christian faith. From the beginning of the Baptist church in Australia, what to do with believers who have been baptised in other traditions has been a contentious issue. When Australia was colonised, churches of an evangelical persuasion had become more aligned in theology and ecclesiology than their predecessors had been at the time of the historical context from which the Baptist movement had emerged.[12] John Saunders, one of the first Baptist ministers in Australia, duly acknowledged this and the denominational lines are even less clear today.[13]

In addition to the fading denominational boundaries, younger generations are becoming less concerned with denominational loyalty. The National Church Life Survey (NCLS) indicated that between 1991 and 2001 the growth in Baptist churches in Australia from denominational switchers was three times that of growth by conversion and of growth by young adult retention.[14] In further research "conducted among Australians by Edith Cowan University and NCLS Research, only 15% of Australians felt that loyalty to one's denomination was important".[15] The NCLS report concludes that the survey "provides solid evidence that denominational switching is a major source of growth in many denominations… it is also clear that there is not a culture of denominational loyalty among many attenders [sic]".[16] There are an increasing number of people coming to Baptist churches from traditions that have different requirements for membership and practices of baptism. "We live in a post-denominational age" and this raises problems pastorally, theologically, and hermeneutically.[17]

Pastoral concerns

Pastoral concerns arise when a person who has been baptised by a different mode to total immersion becomes involved with a church that holds to a closed membership. Until such a person is rebaptised they cannot fully participate in the church community to the same extent as those who have been baptised by immersion. This is not an issue if the person does not consider their original baptism, for example an infant baptism, to be a full expression of baptism. This person would not see immersion as a rebaptism.[18] However, if the person holds to a covenantal view of baptism and believes that their original baptism (and confirmation) is a valid expression of the rite, or if they have been baptised as a believing adult by sprinkling, then the requirement that they be rebaptised diminishes both their prior experience and expression of faith. It also constitutes an act that does not fulfil the intention of baptism, but merely becomes a hoop to jump through. If this requirement is not fulfilled, the person's ability to participate in congregational life is limited. One of the founders of the Baptist movement,

Smyth himself, would not fulfil the current requirements of many Baptist churches as it is likely that his baptism was not by immersion.[19]

When the requirements for membership are limited by the mode of baptism, one can ask what benefit the second baptism brings. Does the rite of baptism become a mere rite of passage to church membership, rather than the symbol of new life and regeneration following conversion that Baptists seek? Furthermore, how does one deal with this situation pastorally, if a church constitution implicitly invalidates, by omission, modes of baptism other than immersion, and then supports that invalidation by denying membership? If baptism is understood to represent identification with a new life in Christ and an initiation into the body of Christ, then the act of rebaptism suggests that "only at this point is the person really identifying with Christ and his church".[20] This diminishes or negates previous religious experiences, including baptism. Briggs rightly observes that "experiencing the life of the Spirit in company with other Christians has always challenged our theologies of exclusion".[21]

The pastoral concerns extend beyond the individual to ecumenical relations. Wright states that "it is a solemn matter for one church or body of Christians to decide that it will not recognise another's baptism, for this is tantamount to questioning the very character as 'church' of that other body".[22] In regarding a form of baptism as invalid, there must be a consideration of the consequences of that position in terms of individuals seeking membership and ecumenical relations.

Theological concerns

Theologically more questions arise. What are Baptists standing for in requiring full immersion baptism for membership? The theological agenda involves an endeavour to be true to the Scriptures, to allow for a liberty of conscience (the individual's choice to their religion), and probably most importantly to identify and protect a "regenerate church membership".[23] The Baptist movement "advocated a believer's church" as opposed to a state church,[24] and the act of believer's baptism provides the opportunity for a believer, post-conversion, to show that they have made a decision in their own right to follow Christ and are now prepared to live accordingly. Therefore, the issues regarding rebaptism arise not primarily from a Baptist theology of baptism, but from a Baptist ecclesiology.

Much discussion around the theology of baptism is related to the question of whether baptism is a sign or a sacrament.[25] Baptists generally take a Zwinglian position and regard the sacraments or ordinances as symbolic rather than a means of grace or salvation.[26] The act of baptism is an outward expression of the work of God in the heart of the believer, and therefore is a sign to both the believer and the community of what God has done in their life. In the Baptist understanding, baptism is a "symbol (rather than a sacrament) of grace".[27] Though symbolic, that symbol is important to the Baptist understanding of church membership, as only those who have received the grace, symbolised by their act of baptism, are truly members of Christ's body and thus the visible church. But what of people who have been baptised in a manner other than full immersion (whether as infants or adults), who show evidence of regeneration, and do not want to diminish the meaning of their original baptism by repeating the act? Stacey points out this inconsistency of the symbolic meaning of baptism and the requirement of full immersion believer's baptism (or rebaptism) for membership:

> Theologically, we seem oblivious to the logical inconsistency of claiming, as Baptists often do, that baptism is a "mere symbol," and then at the same time arguing that it doesn't 'take' if enough water isn't used.[28]

The limitation of membership to regenerate believers is essential to the Baptist church governance system in which decisions are made through a vote by church members. Thus, the position that a Baptist church takes in regard to baptism is inherently affected by the ecclesiology, which shapes the Baptist understanding of baptism and membership.[29]

Lorenzen identifies further theological problems faced in regards to a person being baptised for a second time. Most Baptist churches would affirm that baptism is a once off event, as the Apostle Paul declared, "There is one body and one Spirit — just as you were called to one hope when you were called — one Lord, one faith, one baptism" (Ephesians 4:4–5).[30] Why then should a Baptist church require a person to be baptised for a second (or third) time to become eligible for church membership? Beasley-Murray states that "Infant baptism is not the baptism of which the New Testament documents speak", and thus "The Baptist considers the Paedo-Baptist unbaptised".[31] This view may not be pastorally sensitive, but has a theological grounding in the Baptist understanding of baptism as requiring the individual's choice. However, the effectiveness of this argument diminishes when a person who has been baptised as a believer by a method other than immersion seeks membership. This person's baptism would fit within a Baptist theology of baptism in regard to the meaning of the baptism, but not the amount of water, which leads us to hermeneutical considerations.

Hermeneutical concerns

Hermeneutically, one's interpretations of Scripture are influenced by cultural and historical factors, and when it comes to the issue of baptism by immersion there are biases on both sides in regard to approaching the Scriptures. The BUNSW statement of belief presents baptism exclusively by full immersion in "accordance with New Testament Scripture".[32] Without an explicit mention of full immersion baptism in the New Testament (beyond debate), let alone an imperative declaring it as the exclusive mode, such a statement raises questions of hermeneutical approach.

Furthermore, there are issues of hermeneutical consistency when the Lord's Supper, the other ordinance recognised by the Baptist church, is taken into consideration. If we, as Baptists, are so committed to imitating the symbolism of Scripture, why do we drink juice when we celebrate the Lord's Supper? The Scripture clearly says wine. Why drink from separate glasses when Paul speaks of "one bread", "the cup", and "this cup" (1 Corinthians 10 and 11)? Is not wine from a communal cup a fuller representation of the symbolism of this ordinance than apple and blackcurrant juice, just as immersion is a fuller representation of the symbolism of baptism than sprinkling or confirmation? Is not the prescriptive teaching of the New Testament that we share bread and wine as a meal in remembrance? There seems to be an inconsistency between the commitment to the New Testament mode of the ordinance of baptism and the mode of the ordinance of communion. If we are going to hold to immersion as the only mode of baptism prescribed by the New Testament and the only one qualifying us for church membership, shouldn't we, a least for the purpose of consistency, require the Lord's Supper to be a regular remembrance meal incorporating bread and wine? Considering these hermeneutical, theological, and pastoral concerns it will be helpful to further investigate the meaning and modes of baptism.

The meaning and timing of baptism

There are two points in Scripture which are explicit in regards to baptism, and immersion is not one of these. The first is the *meaning of baptism*: baptism reflects the death and resurrection of our Lord Jesus Christ. For "all of us who were baptised into Christ Jesus were baptised into his death… we were therefore buried with him through baptism into death in order that, just as Christ was raised from the dead through the glory of the Father, we too may live a new life" (Romans 6:3–4). Our baptism is into Christ Jesus rather than into water. Baptism is symbolic of our knowledge that "our old self was crucified with him" (Romans 6:6), and that "if we died with Christ, we believe that we will also live with him" (Romans 6:8; cf. Colossians 2:12). From a New Testament perspective, we are baptised into Christ and into his church, "For we were all baptised by one spirit into one body" (1 Corinthians 12:13).[33] Baptism is an initiation into new life in Christ and into the community of believers at conversion. As the inward change occurs at conversion, it is only fitting that the outward reflection be associated, in time, with the inward work of God, which it symbolises.

The other observation of baptism in the New Testament is in regard to the *timing of baptism*. "New Testament baptism always marked the beginning of the new Christian life and entry into the Christian community. It was at conversion."[34] Examples of baptism upon conversion can be found in Acts 2:41; 9:8, 16:15f. 18:8; and 22:16.

The modes of baptism

It is difficult to find in the Scriptures a prescriptive formula for the method of baptism. Wright speaks of baptism in the New Testament as "involving at the very least a baptiser, one or more persons being baptised and water".[35] Though even in this statement, one can question whether water is necessary, or if baptism in the Spirit without water is sufficient. Witherington correctly observes that since the "New Testament does not tell us explicitly when the children of believing parents should be baptised, both Baptists and Paedo-Baptist are arguing from inference, not evidence".[36] It appears that most arguments for both believer's baptism and paedo-baptism have been made on historical grounds,[37] or by discussions of what was meant by the term "*baptizo*", where both Paedo-Baptists and Baptists cannot gain enough evidence to conclusively support their positions.

This being said, there are theological grounds for different modes of baptism. Douglas Wilson, for example, presents sound arguments for a number of different modes of baptism that he believes to be present in Scripture, including baptism by immersion, pouring, dipping (or partial immersion), sprinkling or affusion, and identification (in which one could include confirmation).[38]

Baptism by total immersion presents the fullest symbolic expression of identifying with the washing of the individual's soul, and of identification with the death, burial, and resurrection of Christ. The First London Confession (1644) affirms that for Baptists, "The way and manner of the dispensing of this ordinance the Scripture holds out to be dipping or plunging the whole body underwater: it being a signe [sic], must answer the thing signified".[39] As Ellis argues, no other method of baptism represents the picture of baptism painted by Paul in Romans 6:3–9 as well as immersion.[40] Again, immersion is likely in the case of Jesus' baptism as the imagery of immersion fits with the description in Matthew's Gospel that Jesus "went up out of the water" (Matthew 3:16).[41] But, in his commentary on Matthew, Morris states that, "Matthew does not describe the baptism" and nor do any of the other gospels, and a partial immersion, pouring, or even affusion could have occurred with Jesus physically in the river.[42]

Douglas Wilson[43] points out that even if there is a strong case for immersion baptism, whether theologically or scripturally, a case must still be made for the inappropriateness of other forms of baptism if one is to limit church membership to those baptised exclusively by full immersion. This is a difficult case to make. Wright argues that infants being baptised in the New Testament church "cannot... be ruled out", though he acknowledges that in arguments for certain paedo-baptisms in Scripture "the case falls short of proof".[44] Douglas Wilson affirms this lack of conclusive evidence to support an exclusive mode of baptism in Scripture: "there is no dispute whatever about the propriety of immersion as a true form of Christian baptism. But as Scripture makes equally clear, we cannot limit ourselves to immersion only".[45] Not only is it hard to argue for an exclusive mode from Scripture, it could be argued against. Paul declares to the Galatians, "Neither circumcision nor uncircumcision means anything; what counts is a new creation" (Galatians 6:15). It would be fair to contextualise this passage to the current Baptist setting and say, "Neither immersion nor sprinkling means anything; what counts is a new creation in Christ". There are passages that are clear about growing in the unity of the body, loving one another, serving God and others, preaching the gospel, bringing justice to the oppressed, and freedom to the captives that require action without letting an unclear, peripheral issue such as the mode of baptism hinder the aforementioned explicit directives of Scripture. If one holds firmly to the mode of baptism, they are at risk of erring in a similar manner to the Pharisees who are condemned by Jesus in Matthew 15:3: "Why do you break the command of God for the sake of your tradition?"

These pastoral, theological, and hermeneutical issues leave closed membership Baptist churches with a dilemma when a person actively attending or even participating in leadership is not a member of the church because they have been baptised according to a different tradition which they believe to be valid and significant in their personal journey of faith. So where do we go from here?

The way forward

The real issue: membership

In discussing a way forward it is important to note that the central issue at hand is not the theology or practice of baptism, but rather the restrictions placed on church membership. With the Baptist model of congregational governance, there must be some way of defining who is in and who is out in regards to the membership roll. Baptism has been that measure, or at least part of it, in Baptist churches with closed membership. In the current setting, we need to ask a number of questions: Why is baptism so heavily linked to membership? Does it really provide the best criteria for eligibility for membership? Is a different expression of the rite of baptism a valid reason to exclude people who would otherwise be considered for church membership? These are questions that need to be answered in the context of each congregation.

Open or partially open membership

To avoid the uncomfortable position of insisting that, while baptism is not essential for salvation, it is essential for membership, a trend in Baptist churches in NSW over recent years has been to shift to an open or partially open membership.[46] Where open membership would allow people who have not been baptised, yet show evidence of regenerate life, to become members of the church, partially open membership can place a number of restrictions on membership.[47] This may include membership being extended to those who are baptised (or maybe even confirmed) in other denominations as believing adults, but not as infants, or require some sort of initiation rite with the person publicly declaring their faith and affirming the commitment that they made at their previous baptism. Another form of partially open membership involves a tiered membership where those who have not been baptised are granted an "associate membership" and are allowed to vote on certain issues but not others. However, there are problems with all three of these options.

The tiered structure of membership separates the responsibility and privileges of the church membership according to the amount of water by which they were baptised. This implies a sort of second-class citizenship in the church. It is difficult, if not impossible, to work out where to draw the line between full membership and associate membership, and the amount of water seems to bear little relationship to the spiritual maturity of the member and even more importantly to their spiritual standing as children of God. Either one is part of the body of Christ or one is not. There are no partial or associate members of the church universal or of the invisible church. Why, then, should there be such designations and division in the visible church membership? This is clearly contrary to Paul's argument in 1 Corinthians 1:13, "Is Christ divided? Was Paul crucified for you? Were you baptised into the name of Paul?"

When it comes to a partially open membership, the question of where to draw the line for membership is also difficult to answer. If it is a separate initiation rite affirming the previous baptism, then the member attests to faith in Christ and regenerate life, but the Baptist understanding of baptism as "an act of obedience" to Scripture[48] is not fulfilled. If the line is drawn at the inclusion of believer's baptism, but not accepting infant baptism as fulfilling the membership requirement, the pastoral problems still exist for those who believe their baptism as infants to be valid and significant. To still seek rebaptism for such people is to degrade the rite of baptism, making it merely a legal hoop to jump through in order to gain membership.

The concept of open membership is not new. It has existed in Baptist churches since John Bunyan in 1673,[49] and it is likely that it was practised by early Australian Baptist churches. However, this is not even an option for many Baptists as "believer's baptism is God's appointed way of entrance into church membership". Hulse continues, "Believer's baptism safeguards that nature of the church and preserves her from being nominal in character."[50] A fear of many Baptist churches is that if membership becomes open, then the church will be open to the nominal religion of the state churches out of which the Baptist moment rose on polemic grounds. Limiting membership to those baptised by immersion is a way for Baptists to protect the regenerate membership for which they fought so hard. There are two flaws with this argument. Firstly, infant baptism does not inevitably result in a nominal Christian. Since the religious freedom and liberty of individual conscience that the early Baptists strongly pursued have become a reality, an individual has the ability to choose their denomination and congregation. There is no longer a requirement to distinguish between believers baptised by immersion and those who were compelled to be baptised as infants by the state. In our post-Christendom age, there is no longer the expectation that all people are baptised into a state religion. And, in fact, closed membership impinges on the liberty of conscience, which should be granted, especially in regard to an issue with so much debate over what the Bible teaches. BUNSW declares that, "The church does not try to tell anybody exactly what they should believe, but each individual seeks the truth of God personally".[51] Hence liberty of conscience, which once led to a closed membership, can now be used to support an open form of membership.

Secondly, baptism by immersion does not inevitably result in a regenerate church member. Neither does it prevent nominal members, it merely requires that members who are nominal be baptised. As Wilson[52] contends, "putting a person under water is not necessarily believer's baptism". A person may have been baptised by immersion, then lost interest in the faith, but now seeks church membership with an alternate agenda. This idea of protecting a regenerate membership may hold more weight in a sacramental theology of baptism, where baptism is a means of grace which has a spiritual effect, but with the Baptists generally perceiving baptism to be a sign of what God has already done in a believer there is a lot less at stake in removing the requirement for membership.[53] Closed membership does not protect a regenerate membership as we have no means or rite by which one can judge the human heart. Only God can know, beyond doubt, who belongs in the true church. It is from this position of humility that the constitution for the Downs Chapel, Clapton (London Baptist Association) of 1869 was written expressing the grace and invitational nature of God, as cited by Payne:[54]

> Membership of the church is open to all who confess faith in Christ. We desire to have the church as open as the Kingdom of God, and its gate neither broader nor narrower than that by which men enter into life… The question of baptism is left entirely to individual judgement and conscience. The immersion of believers is the only ordinance taught or practised as baptism, but we make no difference in the manner of cordiality of our reception of Christ's disciples.

As observed in this constitution, a more open criterion does not and should not diminish the commitment to teaching and practice of full immersion baptism in Baptist churches. Accepting into membership those baptised in other denominations does not change the practice of baptism within Baptist churches. Baptist churches in Australia must reassess their position on baptism and affirm the rich biblical and spiritual significance of believer's baptism by immersion, but also seek a position of acceptance of divergent views taught and practised by other evangelical denominations. In doing so, the Baptist church can embrace a valuable distinctive, validate differing Christian religious experience, and look towards an era where church growth is not limited to those who hold to a single mode of baptism, especially when the Scriptures are not clear in terms of a mode, particularly an exclusive mode, of baptism. These steps will avoid "the position of saying that a person can be acceptable to Christ, but not to our Baptist churches"[55] in a time of growing fluidity in denominational allegiance.

Appendix: The author's experience of baptism and membership

From my personal experience of salvation I decided, at the age of 15, to be baptised in the local community of believers with whom I was in fellowship. This happened to be an Anglican church. I expressed a preference to be baptised by full immersion in living water, as in the *Didache*,[56] as I saw a fuller representation of the symbolism of baptism (though I was more concerned with the presence of the Holy Spirit than the amount of water). This was not an option for the date I had requested due to practicality, so I was baptised by having water sprinkled on my forehead after publicly confessing my faith, and was then welcomed into the community of faith. Following this I was confirmed, again making the public declaration of my faith.

I have since been baptised by full immersion, thus fulfilling the requirements of membership at a Baptist church in which I was in leadership and on staff. The requirement to be baptised again led me to feel that some others within this community perceived my previous experience of baptism as "invalid" or "illegitimate". Such an experience could cause hurt and diminish the significance of genuine steps of faith that active participants in our congregation have made in other traditions who administer the same ordinance, with the same purpose, by different means.

Since 2004 Ben Rodgers has been serving at Ryde Baptist Church, where he is currently acting Senior Pastor, and has previously ministered at St Peter's Anglican Church Weston (ACT). He completed a Bachelor of Ministry with an Honours project in pastoral theology at Morling College and a Master of Theology at Charles Sturt University. He is married to Kim and has two children Micah and Luciella.

The Lord's Supper as Meaning-Full Sacrament

Anne Klose

Current beliefs and practices concerning the Lord's Supper in the Australian Baptist context suggest that its significance has been largely pared back to a particular form of individual piety. This emphasis on memorialism does not, however, fully represent the rich range of meanings associated with the Lord's Supper among early Baptists. Awareness of this facet of our Baptist heritage challenges our tendency to disregard our "tradition" which, in this case, provides a basis to explore the many possible meanings of the Lord's Supper as it takes its vital place in the life of the local church: in its worship, the ethical demands of its life lived in Christian community, and its mission. In each of these areas, reclamation of the meaningfulness of the Lord's Supper may provide a locus for transformation in Australian Baptist church life.

Many of us who attend Baptist churches in Australia seem to have a somewhat ambivalent relationship to the event we designate "communion" or "the Lord's Supper". On the one hand, we invest it with great solemnity and significance, but on the other, its meaning seems to rest largely on the adequacy of our own individual acts of remembrance. This ambivalence, I would suggest, stems from a paring down of our understanding of this ritual to a form of personal piety in which the roles of God and the local church are diminished. Whilst this memorialist view may be credited as "traditional" Baptist thought concerning the Lord's Supper, it does not reflect the rich range of understandings which were held among early Baptists, and which may yet form the basis for a broader sense of the many ways in which this church event may make a significant contribution to Baptist congregational transformation.

This chapter will briefly outline contemporary Australian Baptist practices and beliefs concerning the Lord's Supper, and then contrast these with the range of understandings which were held by early English Baptists. This contrast will then be used to form the basis of an exploration of the Lord's Supper as an event which, whilst involving personal acts of remembrance, is also profoundly theo- and ecclesio-centric, forming and transforming the church community in its worship, its ethical life together, and its work of mission.

Contemporary practices and beliefs

In practical terms, Australian Baptist church communities tend to celebrate the Lord's Supper or Holy Communion twice monthly, once in a morning service and once in an evening service, so that most attendees will have access to it once per month. At most such times, "everyone who loves and wants to serve the Lord" will be invited to share in this "symbolic meal", so that church members, regular attendees, visitors, and children may all be seen to partake in the elements.[1] These are offered in the form of small pieces of bread and, out of deference to those who prefer to abstain from alcohol, very small individual glasses of red grape juice or cordial.[2] There may or may not be any indication that the bread is from "the one bread" (1 Cor 10:17). The celebration is often presided over by a pastor, though this responsibility and privilege may also be delegated to other persons, and is likely to include a Bible reading (usually from the Gospels or Pauline accounts of the institution), a short homily, and a quiet time for self-examination and grateful remembrance.[3]

The documents of the various Baptist state associations provide a consistent sense of the beliefs which are entailed in these practical arrangements. In summary, the Lord's Supper is an "ordinance": that is, it is recorded in Scripture as ordained or commanded by Christ during his earthly ministry and carried out as a memorial to his sacrificial death.[4] It is not a "sacrament" in the sense that it conveys salvation or grace.[5] It is individual believers who are the main actors in this ordinance as they celebrate, remember, and declare their thanks for Christ's substitutionary death which is portrayed in its elements and actions.[6] There is some sense in which, in doing so, believers "share in", or are reminded of, their fellowship with Christ and one another, and anticipate an eschatological fulfilment, but the emphasis is, for the most part, on individual believers who, here and now, obey and remember.[7] In all this, the significance and meaning of the Lord's Supper in the contemporary Australian Baptist context is, to a significant degree, pared back to a particular form of individual piety.

The Lord's Supper in early Baptist thought

This was not, however, always the case. The Baptists emerged in England in two strands, just a few years apart in the early seventeenth century. The General Baptists, who were influenced by an Arminian or "general" form of atonement theology, tended to follow a Zwinglian or memorialist approach to the Lord's Supper using the language of "ordinance", whilst the Particular Baptists followed Calvin in both their Reformed or "particular" atonement theology and their more "sacramental" approach to the Lord's Supper. The point of difference between General and Particular Baptists on the Lord's Supper was, unsurprisingly, the same as that which stood between Zwingli and Calvin.

The Calvinist position was one which more closely followed the broad Christian heritage which affirmed that it was God who was the "principal agent" in the sacraments: it was God who undertook the oath or "sacramentum", pledging Godself to God's people, and thereby consecrating those means by which God conveys the promises which are made to God's people.[8] This view was initially affirmed by Zwingli, but in seeking to strengthen the sense in which baptism and the Lord's Supper demonstrated human loyalty to the established church (and, in Zwingli's particular context, the state of the Swiss Confederacy), he later placed the emphasis in such covenantal oath-taking on the activity of the human rather than the divine participant.[9]

To state the difference this starkly, however, is to fail to recognise that there was still much common ground between the beliefs of the two strands of the early Baptists, and this was reflected in their confessions. Both General and Particular Baptists affirmed the necessity of personal faith on the part of the communicant in receiving the Lord's Supper, and both used the terminology of sacrament and ordinance, not in a contradictory sense but rather as "broader ("ordinance", which included at least the word and prayer in addition to baptism and the Lord's Supper) and narrower ("sacrament", which described only baptism and Lord's Supper)" terms.[10] Hence, despite the shift to the language of ordinance, the Particular *Second London Confession* affirmed a Reformed position, declaring that "Worthy receivers, outwardly partaking of the visible Elements in this Ordinance, do then also inwardly by faith, really and indeed, yet not carnally, and corporally, but spiritually receive, and feed upon Christ crucified & all the benefits of his death".[11] On the other hand, *The Orthodox Creed*, whilst employing the term "sacrament", was more circumspect.[12] It used the Reformed language of "seal" and yet equivocated on a Calvinist doctrine of the Supper, neither committing to nor excluding it.[13]

According to David Bebbington, despite these differences, for both General and Particular Baptists, "the belief that Christ is present at the communion service, spiritually rather than physically but in a way that he is not elsewhere, remained a part of the inheritance down into the nineteenth century".[14] For both General and Particular Baptists, the Lord's Supper was a sacred meeting place with God and with one another; a unifying act shared by the church community.

How then did we arrive at the contemporary Australian Baptist position? I would suggest that from the eighteenth century on a process of a post-Enlightenment Baptist forgetfulness was underway which impacted Australian Baptists as it did others around the world. Bebbington argues that a range of factors were at work in this:

- the ecumenism which followed in the wake of the Evangelical Awakening resulted in Baptists being willing to agree with the statements of their fellow Independents on a range of issues rather than maintaining their own grasp on "first principles"[15]
- a pragmatism and rationalism which undercut any sense of mystery in the sacraments[16]
- the growing influence of Romanticism within the Evangelical movement which placed an emphasis on personal experience and "a heightened supernaturalism" which looked within rather than beyond the self to such physical elements as the bread and wine[17]
- a profound suspicion of everything associated with Roman Catholicism.[18]

I would add to these points the coalescence of the British General and Particular Baptists which occurred at the end of the nineteenth century, and marked a further diminution in awareness of historical diversity amongst Baptists and an even greater unwillingness to engage in what might be perceived as inter-Nicene theological debate.[19]

In the midst of these processes there were isolated Australian voices which continued to raise the possibility that God was at work in the sacraments, but, for the most part, Australian Baptists followed British trends of the period in conceiving them as "an 'ordinance' *as opposed to* a 'sacrament', an act of human obedience *as opposed to* a means of grace".[20]

The role of Baptist tradition

It is perhaps debatable whether this diversion into Baptist church history is of any relevance to our current circumstances. Paradoxically, it is a well-recognised aspect of the Baptist *tradition* that *tradition* has very little role to play as each new generation of Baptists attempts to find its own form of congruence with the church of the New Testament and, though this generally receives less attention, of the eschaton. James McClendon has argued that this is in fact the main distinctive of Baptist theology which has as its *"necessary and sufficient organizing principle"* the *"shared awareness of the present Christian community as the primitive community and the eschatological community"*.[21] Martin Sutherland has envisaged this in terms of a lengthy train moving along a curved track which provides each generation's carriage with a view of the engine and other carriages. In Baptist theological method, he suggests, time is similarly curved, so that Baptists in any age may look directly to the engine of "the Christ story" and acknowledge that the carriages of previous generations are thus seen "as what they truly are — fellow travellers, fixed to the same engine but not of themselves giving us either motion or direction".[22] On the other hand such generational carriages *do* supply a necessary link to the scriptural "engine", the story of Christ, providing "continuity and a profundity of experience and discovery from which any contemporary theology constantly draws".[23]

In this Sutherland is perhaps more willing to acknowledge the "traces" than the "tracks" to which Paul Fiddes points in his *Tracks and Traces: Baptist Identity in Church and Theology*.[24] According to Fiddes, whilst "traces" are only "shadowy after images", "tracks" are the "pathways trodden in the past which still have definite meaning and relevance for the present": they do indeed represent a tradition.[25] These have, he acknowledges, been dealt with "characteristic impatience" by Baptists across all generations, yet, and here I would argue that Fiddes certainly points beyond Sutherland's conclusion, they still possess the potential to "offer guidance for the present day".[26] Whilst then we may laud, with Sutherland, the fleetness of foot which our predilection for discounting our church history lends us as we "morph and shape the emphasis of our witness",[27] we need to beware that, at its worst, this may also represent "a neglect of the lessons which the Spirit has wanted to teach the church during its history".[28]

Perhaps our reluctance to engage at this level, however, is not just a matter of degree, but also an issue of tone. So often it appears that our Baptist heritage speaks with a unanimously negative voice; we do not drink alcohol, we do not fellowship with Roman Catholics, we do not recognise sacraments. And it is these negative assertions to which some Baptists have become most vehemently attached and against which others have reacted. In either case this negativity has tended to obscure the richly diverse and affirmative nature of much of our heritage and its potential to provide both tracks and traces for our belief and practice. These are the features to which and beyond which the remainder of this chapter will point in proposing a reclamation of the Lord's Supper as a meaning-full sacrament for Australian Baptist churches in relation to their worship, their ethical life together, and their participation in God's mission to God's world.

Reclaiming the Lord's Supper as a meaning-full sacrament

The Lord's Supper as worship

There is a sense in which our whole concept of worship is thrown into question by an examination of the Lord's Supper. Much of what Australian Baptist churches practise would appear to indicate that it is believers who are the primary and active agents in worship; in the case of the Lord's Supper, as *they* obey and remember. God, having acted in history and quintessentially at the cross, is the passive recipient of this worship, and the church as God's gathered people is simply the incidental context in which believers make their individual acts of worshipful remembrance. Such a pattern, I would argue goes against the grain of McClendon's and Sutherland's formulation of Baptist theology: that is, that it is God who *continues*, in an immediate sense, to be graciously present and to act by the Holy Spirit in and through those who gather in Christ's name. It is with this in mind that this section is structured around the nature of the participation of each of the possible acting agents in relation to the Lord's Supper: God, church, and communicants.

a) The Triune God as primary sacramental participant

As was noted above, one of the key issues which is raised in claiming that "Baptist sacramentalism" is not an oxymoron is whether God might indeed be an active participant in the event of the Lord's Supper.[29] The underlying objections which were raised historically against such a possibility have largely passed from awareness, and yet the shadows they cast still need to be addressed.

Firstly, it would seem that to expect God to be at work in a sacramental sense is to limit God's freedom: it is to demand that God be present and at work at particular times and in particular ways. But, according to John Colwell, God is far more dynamically at work as the "one who loves in freedom" and who chooses, to be "freely and graciously here".[30] God's presence and work in the sacraments may therefore be received as God's faithful, gracious, and ongoing gifting of Godself to God's people. Secondly, the mystery and physicality of the Lord's Supper might be weighed against the rationality of listening and responding to Scripture, and found wanting. Calvin himself faced such criticism, and responded to it in terms of the sacraments acting as "seals" for the written testament of God: they are another dimension of God's commitment to us, and not to be disdained on the basis of their materiality. This last objection to sacramental theology is, thirdly, based on what is perceived to be a fundamental dualism between the material and spiritual, and a preference for the spiritual in unmediated, experiential terms: the Spirit's presence and work may be sought, but manifestations of these are generally expected to occur on an individual, internal, and experiential basis.[31] Yet this, as Colwell argues at length, is to deny the persistent pattern of "God's apparent predilection... for physical, material means of mediating his presence and action".[32]

b) The church as sacramental participant

Most essentially, as Sutherland points out, however, Colwell's Trinitarian model is most helpful in that "it establishes mediation through *persons*, rather than objects", and it is this form of mediation in particular which is consonant with the early Baptist conception of the church community.[33] On the basis of Matthew 18:15–20, Christ is understood to be present with the local church in their gathering together in his name, and it is in the context of this central Baptist form of sacramentalism that the sacramentality of baptism and the Lord's Supper is grounded.[34]

The (one) bread and wine/juice are offered (both in the practical provision of them beforehand, and in the physical act of offering them at the time of communion) by representatives of the church community for God's use amongst God's people. Together, the church community confesses its sins and shares the resulting reconciliation and peace, and in doing so enacts "appropriate forms of the supper [which] provide appropriate acts of renewal of the covenant ties that bind us not only to the Lord but to our covenanting sisters and brothers".[35] For McClendon, Christ's presence not only ensures our union with God, but also the reality of believers' union with one another: "Such union with Jesus is re-membering, it is reconstitution, being made part of the whole".[36] It is then in this recognition and acknowledgement of its role in administering the sacraments that the local church community is thus re-dignified, according to its responsibilities and authority before God.

c) Community members as sacramental participants

If these are the roles accorded to God and God's gathered people, it becomes apparent that the role of communicants is to personally receive God's gracious presence and work in the sacraments through faith, as they are administered by the church community. Such receptivity is not passive in the terms critiqued by Nigel Wright as part of the maintenance and enforcing of the Constantinian "sacral order".[37] Rather, it is an active exercise of obedient trust that God is uniting each believer with Godself in Christ, and with Christ's body, the church, by the Holy Spirit. Firstly, communicants actively participate with the community in their confession and in sharing the peace.[38] Then, as with baptism, they undertake the Lord's Supper, not as a "self-service" event but, rather, by faith they receive the spiritual nourishment of Christ's body and blood from the human hands of the church. There is, indeed, remembering to do which has a profoundly personal element, but it does not primarily have an inward focus which must rely on an individual summoning up of thoughts and feelings, but is rather an outwardly focused hearing and seeing which results in participation in a sense of remembrance and thankfulness in the midst of God's people. As such, the sacraments act as "triply enacted" signs, in which God, the church, and each personal participant, all have a vital role to play.[39]

The Lord's Supper as ethical life together

Evidently then, the purpose of the sacraments is not to remove participants from the realm of the church community into their own private world with God, but to reaffirm their place amongst God's people. It is therefore unsurprising that the Lord's Supper is laden with ethical implications: the life of the church community is empowered through the sacraments by the Holy Spirit, and God's way of being is reflected, taught, and formed into the lives of that community in its worship. On this basis, the ritual of the Lord's Supper embodies the proclamation of those things which are already true for participants (indicatives), and the exhortation for them to live according to those truths (imperatives).

Such indicatives of the Christian faith which come to expression in the Lord's Supper include union with Christ in his suffering servanthood and death and, thereby, union with Christ's body, the church (1 Cor 10:16, 17); participation in the eternal life of the kingdom, both now and, in anticipation, at the eschaton (John 6:53–57; Matt 26:29); and membership of the new covenant and its community (Luke 22:20). The event of the Lord's Supper rehearses each of these indicatives in the power of the Holy Spirit, so that they are never just a remembering, but a participation in what is represented.[40]

The imperatives which accompany these indicatives come in two forms. Firstly, they reflect, not specific ethical exhortations, but a sense that the whole foundation and nature of the believing community has been/is being transformed. Being "in Christ" through the sacraments, entails a "moral miracle of faith… which finds expression in a new way of life in Christ by the power of the Spirit".[41] This not only applies at an individual level, but calls the church "to be a different kind of community".[42]

Secondly, specific examples of how this character-forming participation in God's life is worked out within the church community *are* also provided in Scripture; in relation to the Lord's Supper as the equitable sharing of resources, firstly within, and then as we will see below, beyond the church community. Most evidently, in 1 Corinthians 10, the meal which the community shares must be shared appropriately in order to bring its unity to "visible expression".[43] Paul's writing suggests that he is outraged that, in the very setting where God's people were to gather together "as one body" in expression of what Christ had done amongst them at enormous cost, they were continuing to express their factionalism and dishonouring the poor (1 Cor 10:16–17).[44] In all this, they were in danger of acting "without discerning the (Lord's) body" (1 Cor 11:29).[45]

More recent work has also sought to take the principles which are bodily enacted in the Lord's Supper and apply them in contemporary ways. Carole Stoneking, for example, seeks to develop sacramental forms of ethical reasoning around euthanasia, suicide, and dying in relation to the Lord's Supper.[46] She begins by describing the very apotheosis of such reasoning as it appears in the guise of rational individualism which is unable to "tolerate moral ambivalence or recognize meaning in suffering".[47] Fundamentally, such individualistic ideology results in the belief that "we are the determiners and possessors of our own life".[48] For the church community, on the contrary, as they *receive* the bread and wine they learn that they are not "the determiners" of their own lives but God is, and in this light, receiving the cup of Christ at the Lord's Supper is "deadly work".[49] In the context of this ethic, the church community patiently bears (with) its sick and dying, and makes the hopeful proclamation that its existence will culminate in the resurrection and an end to suffering of every kind.[50]

It cannot be assumed by Australian Baptist church communities that their members have somehow absorbed Christian forms of reasoning around such issues as suicide and euthanasia. The prevailing cultural milieu is pervasive even within such church communities and promotes the individualistic language of rights and self-determination which, as this example has demonstrated, are at odds with Christian ethical reasoning formed by sacramental practices. It is the very nature of these participative practices as repeated events which, when appropriately narrated, slowly and steadily form God's people into "a community of character".[51]

The Lord's Supper as sharing God's blessing in mission

It may well be perceived that the Lord's Supper, as an event which in one sense reinforces the membership boundaries of the church community, is quintessentially a place at which the community closes itself against the world and the possibility of sharing God's blessings with it. This, however, is to fundamentally misunderstand the nature of the church community which, knowing itself to be called by God to live in community with God and with one another, is also responsible to remain open and ready to share God's blessing with God's world. This determination to share God's blessing is expressed in a number of ways through the Lord's Supper: as an expression of solidarity with and openness to the world; as preparation and nourishment for the community in its role of service to the world; and in witnessing to the world concerning the quality of life in community which God gives.

Firstly, both baptism and the Lord's Supper are events in which the baptismal candidates and communicants representatively bear the world before God. This sense is particularly captured by Brian Haymes for whom baptism, far from being a sectarian act of exclusivity, proclaims that the baptised are, and continue to be, in solidarity with the world: "'To be baptized into Christ is to be baptized into one who, at the Jordan and the cross, totally immersed himself in human life".[52] In the same fashion, as communicants make their confession of sin, receive the bread and wine, and are re-membered in Christ, they bear God's world before God and hold it provisionally in God's blessing,[53] even being willing to renew their "sacrificial commitment to make up what is left over of Christ's sufferings (cf. Col 1:24) — to be part of God's own costly mission to humanity".[54] This they do with the great hope that many "outcasts" will be present at the great eschatological feast (Luke 14:15–24).

As the church community stands together in such an event, they also affirm their openness to God's world. Whist baptism is the "evangelical sacrament" which affirms that any and all who come to faith are welcome to join the community,[55] Anthony Clark proposes that, under a "mission imperative which is eager not to exclude", the Lord's Supper may be a place at which even those who are just beginning to explore the possibility of faith are welcome.[56] If the emphasis on what is occurring in the Lord's Supper lies on God's gracious presence and work, this makes good sense: even in the presence of very little faith, God is, according to Christ, able to do great things (Matt 17:20).

Secondly, the sacrament of the Lord's Supper prepares and nourishes the community for its role of service to the world in sharing God's blessing. As the bread and wine are served to the church community by its deacons, such commissioning and sending are portrayed and modelled in this diaconal movement and service.[57] In the Lord's Supper, God's people are nourished by the Holy Spirit as they feed on Christ, and so are strengthened "in the spirit of suffering service to bear the word of life, to continue Christ's own work of reconciliation" (John 20:21).[58]

Thirdly, as the church community participates in the Lord's Supper, it acts as witness to the world of the quality of the life in community which God gives, and to that which enables human flourishing whether within *or* beyond the church community, because "the people of God is called to be today what the world is called to be ultimately".[59] Particularly as the actions of the Lord's Supper are narrated by the church community, it becomes apparent that such practices are undergirded by an alternative form of ethical reasoning to that which operates in the wider culture. Such witness must not then be confused with the imposition of outcomes which make no sense in the wider cultural context, but must rather demonstrate alternative possibilities of what can be seen and heard to make a life-affirming difference in the lives of both individuals and their communities.

Conclusion

To memorialise Christ's death on an individual basis is indeed a significant aspect of our response to the Lord's Supper, but this most adequately finds its context in the range of other meanings which come to light as we explore our heritage. In terms of participation in the Lord's Supper as an act of worship, the promise that God in Christ by the Spirit is present recalls the church to faith that God is still at work in their midst as they worship; the church itself, as an ecclesial reality, has a significant role to play as it gathers and as it distributes the elements, and is thereby re-membered by Christ; and it is those who in the presence of both Christ and his people remember his saving death and resurrection.

Such a sacramental understanding of the Lord's Supper, rather than rejecting the physical and social milieu of participants, provides an alternative set of practices and forms of ethical reasoning which enable and shape the discipleship of the community. And this ethical life, together with God's other blessings, rather than being bound up within the church community, are made available to God's world as the Lord's Supper is celebrated; as the community and its members remember their solidarity with and their openness to that world, as they are prepared for their work in and for that world, and as they act as God's witness to that world.

These meanings, rooted in Scripture and following the tracks and traces of our heritage, are manifold, and thereby have the capacity to hold together the tensions which come to light as the community celebrates the Lord's Supper. Sometimes and in some contexts, the focus may fall heavily on God's gracious action in the Lord's Supper. At other times and in other contexts, the emphasis may be almost entirely on the ethical implications and responsibilities of human participation. Or again, the emphasis may rest on openness and welcome. But, over time and with careful attention, the rich meaningfulness of the Lord's Supper will play its vital role in the transformation of our church communities.

Anne completed a PhD in Baptist ecclesiology at the University of Queensland in 2013 and is a member of faculty at Malyon College, Brisbane.

The Liturgical Participation of Children in Small Churches

Alison Sampson and Nathan Nettleton

The concept of the priesthood of all believers underpins the participation of children in worship. Children who are part of the life of the church are regarded as members of the priesthood; as such they have pastoral and ministerial gifts to share. Like adults, they need to worship God; and as catechumens, they need to learn about faith. By being enabled to participate fully in the worship service, children have an opportunity to share some of their gifts; they are encouraged to engage in worship; and they learn the patterns of the faithful. This paper explores these convictions, partly in theory but primarily in the practice of one small congregation, the South Yarra Community Baptist Church. This church has developed ways of more fully involving the children in the liturgy. Most of our small group of children are now regularly present and participating in most or all of the service.

Once upon a time there was a little girl who was sick. She spent the week drifting around the house and dozing in sunspots. Hot with fever, she slept the afternoons away. Her throat was sore; her head ached; she was quiet as a mouse. But on Sunday, at church time, she got up, got dressed, and got ready to go out.

"But you're sick," said her parents. "We're staying home."

"What?!" she wailed, "I want to go to church!" She threw herself down at the front door, and hollered and yelled.

"Darling," said her parents, "Dear heart, sweetie pie, no…" but their pleas and entreaties fell on deaf ears. There she sat, their cross little girl, weeping and wailing and begging to go to church. Her parents didn't like to see her cry. "Whatever shall we do?" they asked.

"Church!!!" she yelled.

Her parents looked at each other, and sighed; then one fetched the car keys while the other packed a bag. Seeing this, their daughter calmed down. Her parents popped her in the car and off they went; and they were only a little bit late.

This is a true story, and has been told by more than one parent at our church. Such a story should be heard in every church, but it's not. Too many children hate going to church, or at least are indifferent to it. Rather than racing out the door, they are dragged along by stressed parents — when their families bother to come at all. But things don't have to be this way. What follows is the story of a little church that decided to incorporate even very young children into the worship service. As a result, and to everyone's surprise, most of the time most of the children now love to come to church.

Background

It's no great secret that churches across the board have found it difficult to involve children. In small and under-resourced churches, the challenge is obvious. Most large churches can pay to make the problem go away: people are employed to educate and entertain the children while the adults get on with the worship service. These children grow up, most of them leave the church, and we wonder why. But, of course, they didn't grow up in the church. They grew up in the Sunday school program while the adults did their thing.

However, alternatives aren't easy to find, and so wealthy churches often continue to pay for big programs. But what of small and under-resourced churches? Most small churches try to copy the patterns of big churches, perhaps hoping that that way they'll become big, too. In many areas this doesn't work too well, and this is especially obvious when it comes to children.

When you have only a few children, it's hard or impossible to create age-appropriate programs and activities, and it's hard or impossible to find people to run them. In a small church, you may have no adults in the congregation with the gifts or interest in running the children's program. Even if you do have people, when there are so few of you in the first place, taking them out of the service to look after children feels like a high price to pay.

At our small church, even the idea of running a Sunday school was creating tension. For many years our average Sunday attendance has fluctuated between 20 and 35 people; of them, between half a dozen and a dozen are children. If we had run a Sunday school program, at least a third of the congregation would have left halfway through the service each week to attend or run it, which would have had a devastating effect on the worship service.

We tried various options. We hired babysitters, parents took the children out, and so on, but nothing worked well or felt right. And so, after much thought and conversation, we decided to have the children stay with us during what is admittedly a long and wordy service. And most of the time, most of us are glad that they do!

Why include children?

There is no question that we want our children to have faith, which is why we examined traditional models of Sunday school.[1] However, we concluded that these models imply that the elements of faith can be taught and that children can be educated in these elements.[2] Yet faith is not something we earn when we have learned enough doctrine,[3] and so, like others, we came to the conclusion that trying to convey faith through teaching was useless.[4]

Instead, faith is a gift from God, encouraged and nurtured by exposure to the patterns of the faithful. Moving away from dogma, then, we began to think about how our children could learn the culture of faith as expressed through ritual and worship, loving across boundaries, and acts of hospitality and service. Sociologists, anthropologists, and child psychologists have long argued that children learn culture by mimicking the adults around them, in an approach which resembles apprenticeship.[5] Therefore, we realised that children and other catechumens will learn the culture of faith when they stand alongside those who are engaging in the cultural practices of faith: ritual, relationships, and loving service.[6]

In other words, our children needed to be exposed to the culture of faith as practised by the adults in our context. Forming a Sunday school which set up teacher-student or entertainer-audience relationships, such as one often observes in the programs of larger churches, would not achieve this. It would remove children from the primary place we gather as a congregation, the worship service, and it would risk obstructing the formation of genuine two-way relationships between adults and children across the whole faith community in the ways children need to have their faith ignited.[7]

Furthermore, as noted above, the very idea of Sunday school created tension in our church. Nobody felt called to go out with the children. Nobody wanted to be a Sunday school teacher. However, when we began to approach faith development as a process of enculturation, no one person was required to step up. Instead, all adults in the congregation became responsible to varying degrees for the faith development of the children.[8] Individually and together, everyone could act as facilitators who provide the environment and space needed for children to enter into the story of faith, and for the Holy Spirit to do the Holy Spirit's work.[9]

The central gathering point, most significant cultural activity, and most formative experience of our church community is worship, and so we began to realise just how important it was for the children be present with us during the service. There they could watch and copy the adults[10] and gradually absorb the habits and culture of faith.

Of course, we are not suggesting that a child's faith will be ignited solely by mimicking the adults during the worship service. The formation of Christian identity involves much more than mastering the mechanics of worship, particularly if the worship service is not well thought out. It also involves immersion in the stories of faith, learning why we do what we do, offering hospitality and service, and having opportunities for critical reflection and dialogue.[11]

However, participation in the worship service is a good starting place, as it can address many of these needs. For example, the weekly Scripture readings tell the stories of faith. The sermon might explain one of those stories or an element of church practice; provide an example of critical reflection; or, through narrative means, write the congregation into God's story.[12] The Eucharistic feast is an opportunity to participate in the church's central act of hospitality. When it is constituted as a range of people from different ages and social backgrounds, the congregation itself embodies God's radical loving across boundaries.[13] Conversations after the service, when members of the congregation raise questions, seek clarification, or grapple with the stories or the sermon, are also important. Therefore, a child who participates in a thoughtful service and the conversations afterwards has many opportunities for faith development. Moreover, the stories, patterns, and relationships experienced during the service carry into other aspects of church life.

The idea of welcoming children into the worship service coalesced with our congregation's existing ecclesiology. We have long proclaimed the priesthood of all believers, affirming that every participant in the life of the church has gifts to offer and gifts to share, and we don't just pay it lip service. Instead, we seek to express it in practical and symbolic ways. For example, every regular attender has a job or two. It may be as simple as folding the notice sheet or as complex as keeping the accounts; whatever their level of ability, every member has a practical role. In addition, as described in more detail below, every regular attender contributes to the weekly conduct and performance of the service so that the priesthood of all is made manifest.

Reflecting on our children, we began to realise that, like many churches, we had unconsciously and inadvertently excluded them from this priesthood. Yet whether or not they are baptised (and in most Baptist churches they are not), children, too, are members of the body of Christ. As such, like adults they have gifts to share as well as a need to worship God.[14] When they are taken out of the service to go to a children's program, no matter how excellent the program, their gifts are withheld from the full worshipping community and they are no longer worshipping God. Nor is the remaining congregation forming the complete body of Christ. Therefore, we concluded that proclaiming the priesthood of all believers meant welcoming our children into the worship service.

In summary, then, having considered and rejected traditional forms of Sunday school, having come to understand children's faith development as a process of apprenticeship and enculturation, having identified the worship service as the most significant opportunity for this to happen, and having admitted that we had not recognised the priesthood of children in our own worship service, the conclusion was clear: our children had to be present during the whole of the worship service each week. The next step was to find ways to put this into practice.

Putting it into practice

To enable the full participation of children in the worship service, we had to interrogate our worship practice. Our service style is very formal, and we weren't sure how accessible it would be to children. Yet we were clear that we didn't want to turn our service into one of those "family friendly" affairs. There was little point welcoming children if it meant infantilising the rest of the congregation or giving up the liturgical structure which so many of us had found so enriching.

Instead, we sought to shape the service so that it could be accessed on different levels simultaneously and thereby meet the needs of both children and adults. We found that we could achieve this by offering children roles in the service and by adding more music and movement; by providing activities for the children to do during the silence and sermon; and by changing some of our adult views on what constitutes a worshipful stance.

Roles, music, and movement

We already used a formal style of liturgy, and we began to realise that it is particularly suited to children. There are several reasons for this. For one, we use the same liturgy for a church season: Advent, Lent, Pentecost, or common time. The only things which change within a season are the lectionary readings, a few prayers, the sermon, and the hymns. The rest of the service repeats each week. Moreover, many of our prayers are sung, whether they are short refrains or the more complex creeds and Lord's Prayer. This use of repetition and song makes the service easy to learn over time, even for those who cannot read. In our church, many children join in the congregational responses from the age of two or three.

The text of the liturgy is spoken, paragraph by paragraph, by different voices from the congregation. Every regular attender has several parts during the service, which they speak each week. Therefore it was easy to assign spoken parts not only to adults, but also to children. Currently, the youngest child to have a regular spoken part is five years old. Each week her high voice pipes up, "Blessed are you, Lord God of all creation, and blessed is the communion into which you gather us" — hardly a dumbed-down part!

Of course, these responses and spoken parts are all very verbal. Given that most children like and need to move about, we also sought to develop more physical actions that were relevant, important, and valued by the rest of the congregation.

Therefore Nathan sat down with the service booklet, which includes the text of our liturgy, and went through it page by page. He tried to imagine what could be happening in movement and action on each page, and came up with a series of actions which enhance the service. So, for example, early in our liturgy we have a prayer invoking the presence of the Spirit which is spoken with a sung refrain. Now, as that prayer is spoken and sung, we have added a dancing procession around our central altar. We have a processional cross, a processional kookaburra (the kookaburra being Australia's avian symbol of the Holy Spirit), and dancers waving symbolic flames made of sparkly fabric. Our youngest child recently started joining in the dance, often going around in the opposite direction to the rest and at twice the speed, but that's all good. The Spirit blows where the Spirit wills and you cannot know where that will be. The flame dancers appear twice more, as the Bible is processed for the readings, and during the preparation for communion.

When the gospel is read from the centre of the room, it is now surrounded by children holding icons of the four evangelists. As well as giving them an important symbolic action, it also compels them to listen to the story. When it's time to set the communion table, the children line up at the side table, bow before the bread and wine, and then carry them to the central table and set it out.

We also changed the way we do the prayers of the faithful. We had been praying aloud from our seats, but we moved to using prayer stations. Now, after an introductory exhortation to pray, we allow about five minutes for people to move between the various stations to offer prayers for different needs. These stations invite both a prayerful symbolic action and some words. For example, there is a symbolic brick wall, and people are invited to pray by pulling a brick from the "wall of oppression" and writing a note or drawing a picture-prayer about a situation of conflict, injustice, or oppression. One young child prayed for "LA" every week for about a year. She had been there and observed the poverty — and it was a city she could spell. We have small cloth prayer flags fluttering on a line, and both children and adults write prayers for particular people on labels and stick them to the flags; and there are other stations. It is not all private devotion, because the words and pictures at the stations prompt other people's prayers.

As well as during this five minute period, it is not uncommon to see a child, or an adult, go to one of the stations and offer a prayer at some other point during the liturgy. The station of a garden and small animals, where we pray for the earth, is especially popular with the little ones.

So in these congregational responses and individual parts, symbolic actions and joyful dancing, and in other ways, we invited children to participate in and contribute to the performance of the worship service. Young children have small parts, while older children have increasingly important roles, reflecting what Mercer describes as the movement from "peripheral positions of participation to increasingly full levels of participation in community practices".[15] And at our church, the most significant community practice is the worship service.

Activities for the silence and sermon

Our service includes ten minutes of silence for contemplation and reflection, which is followed by the sermon. We provide an activity sheet for the children to use during this time. It presents a paraphrase of one of the lectionary readings and suggests some possible responses. The children can choose to do one of the suggestions, or they can develop an activity of their own. Inspired by some of the thinking behind Godly Play, we explicitly name the open option to allow for children's authentic responses to the story.[16] For this, they have access to art and other materials. They can draw, mould plasticine, make paper craft, act out the story using Biblical figurines, look at picture books, or solve jigsaws. The books and jigsaws pick up themes from the week's lectionary readings. The activities are self-directed by the children, and occur in the same room and at the same time as the rest of the worship service.

We did wonder whether the activities might distract the children from the service. However, since introducing them we have observed two things. First, the children often choose not to use them. Instead, they stand with adults — rarely their parents — and participate in the liturgy, thus demonstrating their ability to apprentice themselves to adult experts in the culture of faith.[17] It also demonstrates their increasing levels of participation, which suggest their growth in faith.

The activity trolley might be thought of as an example of scaffolding. Scaffolding usually refers to the mentoring activities of adults or expert peers as they help children build up from what they already know and do to more complex insights and abilities, gradually moving from assistance to independence.[18] However, we wonder whether the activity trolley provides the "in" that young novices need when first confronted by a long church service. It provides them with comfortable ways to engage with the service which can be shed as they become more familiar and engaged with the practices going on around them.

Second, we have noticed that even when the children do use the activities provided, they often use them to help tune in. It is not unusual for a child to come to the preacher after the service and ask questions or make comments about the sermon, or share a relevant story. It seems that, even while they are moulding plasticine or zooming plastic camels through the air, many of them are paying attention.[19] Moreover, their questions and comments can be very challenging! These conversations provide an opportunity to engage in the reflective practice and dialogue Mercer sees as crucial to a child's faith development[20] — although there are times when it is the adult's faith and theology which are being stretched by the questions and insights of a child, and not the other way around.

Let's take a quick step back. Knowing that the children might listen challenges our preachers to prepare sermons which are accessible, at least in part, to children, while also being sufficiently stimulating and theologically rigorous to engage the adults, many of whom have studied theology at a tertiary level. We have found that pastoral and narrative preaching styles are especially effective at communicating across the generations.

In summary, then, we provide quiet unstructured activities for children to engage with during the service. Even so, we have observed that, as children become accustomed to the service, they tend to make less use of the activity trolley. Further, some children seem to use the activities to help them focus on what else is happening, leading to some astute questions and comments afterwards. Conversing with these young theologians has been an opportunity to engage in reflective practice, and has challenged our preachers to think about how to communicate on multiple levels while preaching.

Changing our views

Including the children hasn't been completely straightforward, of course. Our children have surprised us with their ability to respect the event, but their presence has raised the level of background noise and sudden unpredictable movement, and this has bothered some people.

Over and over, though, the adults' concerns are driven by a misunderstanding of what public liturgy is. Most of us have grown up assuming that the liturgy should be performed as well as possible so that nothing draws our attention away from God. We also often assume that it is purely an aid to private devotion. However, although public liturgy and private devotion inform one another, they are different activities and should occupy different time-slots.

The public liturgy is about offering the communal gift of the entire congregation to God. It is not about what pleases us, but about "what pleases God"; and what pleases God is to receive the worship of the full community.[21] Everyone has to be part of it, or it will not be the offering of us all. If in our pursuit of perfection we exclude the contributions of those who are messy or chaotic or only semi-articulate then we are offering something which may be beautiful to adult human eyes. However, it is beauty achieved at the expense of God's little ones, and that is a sacrifice we are no longer willing to make.

Therefore, as part of the process of welcoming children, we not only sought ways to physically include them, but also sought to educate the congregation. Alison distributed copies of her essay on the agency of children in the church.[22] This essay was used as a catalyst for conversations about our theology of children and how this might be expressed in our community. Nathan used the preaching slot to clarify the distinctions between public and private devotion, to remind us what constitutes the body of Christ, and to talk about the place of children in our corporate life. In time, the congregation came round to the idea of welcoming the children; or, at least, they were willing to give it a go.

Once the adults were ready, we prepared the children. We helped those who wanted to dance make sparkly Holy Spirit flames, and we obtained and set up the activity trolley. We asked the children what things they thought would be useful, and included them on the trolley.

We also talked with the children, explaining their new roles and our expectations. For example, we explained that when they weren't doing their bits they were free to move about quietly and light candles, hang up prayer flags, play in the sand tray, or sit under the communion table. They did not need to sit still or maintain absolute silence. However, they were not to run around, become too noisy, or try to be the focus of attention during the service. Instead, they were to help focus attention on God.

Finally, one Sunday, we were ready. The adults and children were prepared, and so the children stayed in. In surprisingly little time the children settled into their new roles and the adults adjusted to the slightly higher levels of noise and movement, and the children have remained in with us ever since.

Assessing the approach

The fact that we continue to worship with our children present shows that we have found the approach fruitful. When we began, many adult members of the congregation were sceptical. "It will never work," they said. However, after discussion, and to their credit, they were willing to give it a try; and they were quickly converted. Some of the staunchest opponents are now the loudest advocates for having children present in the worship service.

Several years after we first welcomed them in, adults still regularly attest to being moved by something one child or another has done during the service. It is often simple: hearing an eight-year-old's voice raised in song; reading a child's prayer on the prayer wall; or being warmly welcomed on arrival by someone small. Visitors, too, remark on their surprise, even shock, when one of the first voices of the service is that of a child. Their reactions remind us just how rarely children's voices are heard during worship and other public events; they are a largely marginalised and silenced sector of our population.[23]

Worshipping together appears to have deepened relationships between children and adults. It is very common for a child to worship with an adult who is not their parent, even standing on a chair to place themselves at adult height during times when the congregation stands. We have not collected data on this, but the sharing of songs, prayers, and communion bread seems to have led to increased forms of sharing outside the service: adults and children working in the kitchen together to prepare supper; nutting out a hymn together on the piano; knitting blanket squares together for a mission project; or planning the church camp or an annual boat trip together. Seeing adults and children worshipping, working, and playing together suggests that they are forming the genuine intergenerational relationships which are the seedbed of children's faith.[24]

Another healthy sign has been the enculturation of new children. We had been concerned that, while our own children would learn how to "do" church, the approach might not work with newcomers. We wondered how we could educate visiting children in the few minutes between their arrival and the start of the service, but we discovered that we needn't have worried: our own children take care of things.

In her study of the passing on of cultural expertise, Rogoff found that peers and older children have a significant role to play in the enculturation of other children.[25] We see this played out in the way our children welcome visitors. When new children arrive, the regular children spontaneously welcome them in. They explain what is happening, they show them the activity trolley, and they invite them to dance with the flames of the Holy Spirit. Our children demonstrate how to follow the service booklets, how to light a prayer taper, how to use the prayer stations, and how to pass the communion bread. When new children or young children become raucous, it is not always adults but older children who hush them and explain that they need to be quieter just now. Such actions suggest that our children are mastering the culture of faith as it is expressed in our context, and are confidently passing on their expertise. We see this as significant. It shows that our children do not regard themselves as passive recipients or consumers of worship. Instead, they consider themselves cultural experts who are willing and able to pass on their cultural knowledge to others.

At the outset, welcoming children into the worship service felt risky but also intellectually necessary. However, they settled in quickly and have greatly enriched the performance and experience of the liturgy. Furthermore, worshipping together appears to have multiplied the ways adults and children work and play together in other aspects of church life; and our children's approach to visitors suggests that they are becoming cultural experts in the ways of faith. Thus bringing children into the service has been more than worth the effort, for their presence has deepened the faith of us all, individually and communally, adult and child.

Final observations

Our liturgy style is very formal, which many of us once thought of as "adult". However, our children have surprised us with what they are capable of. For example, as mentioned above we have a ten-minute period of silence every week. We were not sure the children could manage this, but as we talked about expectations and provided quiet activities for them to do, the children showed us they can keep silence too. We adults have also learned that sitting in silence means learning to embrace noises in the background as signs of creativity and life.

For the most part, having the children in the service has been a great gift. We included them primarily for their sake, but the rewards have been abundant. In their freedom of movement, the children have given us permission to move around the service more freely ourselves. In their curiosity and absorption, we have been challenged out of our distraction and encouraged to pay attention. In their hugs and in the way they welcome people in each week, they have modelled loving hospitality and care. In their absolute trust, they demonstrate very real faith.

At times, the actions of one child or another has shocked and challenged us, even brought us to tears. One memorable Good Friday, a four-year-old threw herself at the foot of the cross and sobbed, a poignant reminder of the women who stood watch while Jesus died. We name these actions as gifts, even when they feel like interruptions and challenge our preference for quiet participation.

In this society of ours, which is largely segregated by age, it is easy to gloss over the physicality of the incarnation and the characteristics of real children.[26] But Jesus came to us as a little baby who cried and wore nappies and kept his parents up nights; and as a grown man, Jesus welcomed little children, encouraged them to draw near, and instructed his disciples to become like them. When we include children in the worship service, we are reminded what it is to be childlike and, whatever our age, we are challenged to explore what it means to be a child of God.

Alison Sampson and Nathan Nettleton are the pastors of the South Yarra Community Baptist Church. Alison also researches child–adult friendship through the School of Public Health, La Trobe University. Nathan also teaches liturgical studies at Whitley College in the University of Divinity.

Growing the Seeds of Emergence
Congregational Leadership Development in the Baptist Union of Victoria[1]

Darren Cronshaw and Stacey Wilson

The Baptist Union of Victoria (BUV) is committed to developing an organisational culture that enables successive generations of leaders to emerge and be empowered to lead. This project interviewed a group of emerging/emerged leaders and leadership development experts. It identified seven important factors for the emergence and practice of mainly Generation Y emerging leadership. To grow the seeds of emergence requires a culture of leadership development focused on mission; giving leaders opportunities with an apprenticeship of learning by doing; intentional mentoring; an empowering and collaborative leadership model; inclusion of gender, age, and cultural diversity; financially sustainable training and ministry; and a reframed definition of leadership.

Introduction

Developing the next generation of leaders is a challenge for all local churches and denominations. This chapter explores the critical contextual issues which affect emerging leadership in Baptist churches. We interviewed some Victorian Baptist emerging (or emerged) leaders and members of the leadership development community associated with BUV churches. This is an action-research project, investigating how younger generation leaders emerge and proposing principles and strategies for fostering leadership development.

To examine emerging leadership development, it is appropriate to consider what supports or inhibits the connection of young people with church. The church is aging and generally has a greater proportion of older people than the general population, and a lesser proportion of younger people. Baptists in Australia have a younger profile than the church overall, but still older than the general population.[2] This underlines the urgent need to connect with younger emerging generations.

The church needs younger leaders to guide us in how to connect better with younger generations. BUV recognises the critical need to engage younger leaders. For one level of leadership — pastoral ministry — many of our current serving pastors are approaching retirement: 58 percent are aged over 50; 33 percent are between 49 and 36; and only 9 percent are under 35 years old.[3] Within 15 years more than half of the current, serving pastors will retire. BUV currently has less than 10 percent of pastors under 35 (Generation Y are currently aged 21–35, born between 1980 and 1994). To reach younger generations we need a greater proportion of Gen-Y pastors and youth workers, and an emerging group from Gen-Z (those currently aged 6–20, born between 1995 and 2009).[4]

Generations Y and Z are increasingly mobile, but National Church Life Survey (NCLS) results warn that people who have been in church for fewer than five years are less likely to have a ministry role or feel their gifts and skills are encouraged.[5] Moreover, Victorian Baptist churches are comparatively less likely to appoint younger people and newcomers to ministry roles or encourage them to use their gifts and skills. Only 23 percent of 15–29 year old Victorian Baptist attenders in 2011 felt "their gifts and skills are encouraged to a great extent", 9 percentage points below the 32 percent of all Australian attenders. Of people who switch or transfer from another church into Victorian Baptist churches, 16 percent feel greatly empowered, less than the 23 percent national average. The figure is worse for newcomers: 11 percent of Victorian Baptist newcomers feel greatly empowered, compared with 20 percent overall. For long-term attenders, the Baptist figure of 21 percent is identical to the national average. This raises the need for discerning what blockages we have against welcoming and integrating newcomers (and switchers and transferees) into leadership roles. It is unfortunate, especially for younger generations who want to be involved, that it is easier to sit and be preached at passively, than find a place to stand and contribute. Baptists say we believe in the ministry of all believers, but in Victoria we seem to adopt the ministry of mature believers.[6] What will it take to adopt a more proactive role in identifying and empowering leaders who are younger or newer to our churches?

Principles for emerging leadership

To gain a deeper understanding of the experiences and practice of leadership amongst the next generation, we interviewed fourteen leaders aged 18 to 39, and 11 people involved in developing leaders. We wanted to explore how they developed as and/or develop leaders, and seek their insights about what could better foster leadership development in Victorian Baptist churches.

From our interviews, seven themes emerged as significant factors for the development and practice of leadership. These are principles that emerging leaders value and that we suggest are essential components for a Next Generation emerging leaders' development program.

A culture of missional leadership development

Foundationally, churches and denominations need to prioritise cultivating a culture of leadership development that is focused on mission. One helpful model that some churches use is to imagine themselves as a "leadership farm", existing to nurture and grow leaders. This is not merely or even primarily about growing leaders for "full-time ministry", but helping the whole people of God to lead in their spheres of influence. We need mission-hearted leaders in the church, but also in government, business, and non-profit organisations.

A number of the leaders we spoke to are passionately eager to develop themselves and others for missional leadership. Some expressed frustration and disconnection from a leadership culture whose focus was to "shore up their own patch rather than putting the resources into pioneering expressions and innovations and doing things that are outward".[7] They have little patience for reluctance within the church to acknowledge and face society's changes. Urban Seed's Andreana Reale commented that churches often make little space for innovation and hold a traditional view of ministry with:

> the idea of the teacher/pastor/leader who kind of does everything and other people kind of fit around the edges but are relatively passive … even though we could have a theoretical conversation about "OK the world has moved on, the system is broken, we need to try some different things", it is actually really hard to have the space to try those different things.[8]

Beth Barnett appeals for leadership development to be reframed away from a preoccupation with professional (usually male) full-time ministry and instead focus on developing leaders for missional contexts — in the world. She suggests ministers, who themselves have been called into full-time ministry, look at younger people with leadership qualities, passion, and integrity and think, "what I should do is encourage that person to become a full-time professional minister. That will be encouraging." But in a post-Christendom context that is not the most empowering and usually not the most missional advice. Let's encourage emerging leaders to dream about how they can remake their world more in line with God's dream, from within work roles, and "connected to business and culture and the local tennis club ... rather than pulling all of our best articulators, evangelisers, and mobilisers into the Christian world vortex."[9]

Emerging generations become an asset and a gift to the church when they challenge the church to be true to its missional identity. We need an organisational culture in our churches that promotes leadership development that is focused on mission.

Apprenticeship of learning by doing

A second principle of leadership development is learning by doing. Gemma Bell said that being given the opportunity to try or "being thrown the keys" was crucial for leadership development.[10] Sam Hearn observed that he started developing as a leader as he was released into mission opportunities:

> Lots of other leaders I've talked to ... the moment in which we actually stepped into leadership was the moment we first engaged in mission or in joining in God's purpose ... Where we started our leadership journey ... was when we stopped just getting stuff from God and we started wanting to be a vessel for him to use.[11]

To develop leaders, churches need to create space for young people to learn while doing.

Interestingly while participants mentioned specific courses or training they had undertaken, few Anglo leaders identified these as key to their development as leaders. For example, Simon Burnett:

> Certainly my theological training helped with my formation, but I would say that helped my formation far more as a believer... but didn't really touch much on my formation as a leader.[12]

Arrow's Emerging Leaders Director Julian Dunham affirms that Bible College prepares people for understanding and teaching the Bible, thinking theologically about issues in the church and the world, and pastoral skills for a church of fewer than 150 people. But he suggests colleges do not usually prepare people to lead outside the box of a single staff church and broader leadership complexities.

Leadership formation is not primarily about teaching and acquiring more knowledge, but giving people experiences of service and ministry, and the opportunity to learn and grow through that. Benji Watson, in his leadership at Crossway, values this apprenticeship approach:

> It's very much bringing back that New Testament model of discipleship. It's done through relationship. It's not just visual teaching ... It's come alongside of me, I'll show you what it looks like and then you do it.[13]

Several leaders from non-Western backgrounds especially appreciated their theological education at Whitley College, but underlined that their formation was valuable because their studies were combined with ministry experience. They also seemed to appreciate theological studies because it helped enculturate them into a new Australian system for church. However, one of their challenges is when their culture expects emerging leaders to be older before being given leadership opportunities.

Robert Banks appeals for re-envisioning theological education along missional lines — by which he means more field-based, related to everyday life, and empowering the mission of the whole people of God.[14] He argues that the best formation stretches students to *do* what they are studying. Many colleges have developed Supervised Theological Field-Education (STFE) programs which facilitate this action-reflection cycle well, and structure units in ways which foster learning while doing ministry. Students of Whitley's STFE program, such as Chin pastor Mang Hre, appreciate the space to present cases of their ministry experience, whether difficult or risky, to a supervisor and peer group for encouragement and support.[15] Informal leadership development programs cannot do all that theological education providers do, but they can apprentice disciples as leaders and help them to learn while doing.

Mentoring to support learning

The results of a "learning by doing" approach are most successful when supported by mentors who offer resourcing, support, and evaluation.[16] In describing processes that were helpful in their leadership development, participants stated it was mentoring relationships which have been most formative. Andy Mitchell said he has not had formal leadership training but credits his opportunities for experience with the support of people alongside them: "the small handful of people who have come alongside me and seen some potential and decided to mentor me or disciple me".[17] Reale similarly states, "It's that balance of space and support. Give them space to try things but also give them the support to be able to reflect and refine".[18]

Mentoring is a qualitatively different approach to training — helping people to articulate their goals, develop strategies, and connect their experience with their own learning. It is not incompatible with tertiary education, but it does not depend on a classroom. It is more like an apprenticeship, where someone who is more experienced in the craft of leadership can guide emerging leaders in their development. Tim Devlin described his training happening more through learning with the help of mentors than through a classroom curriculum or textbook.[19]

Mentoring helps leaders develop character and spirituality as well as skills and strategies. Rowan Lewis explains:

> There are two parts to the leadership game, there is the external, extrinsic being a leader amongst people and the things that you do and the actions that you take. And then there is the inner life growth and the character which can support being in a role.[20]

Mentoring is usually one on one, but can also happen in a group. The Victorian Council of Christian Education is developing Communities of Practice as a model for developing children and families' ministry leaders. VCCE assumes most leaders do not need another expert course as much as a cohort of colleagues they can trust and learn with. Leaders need space to bring their own questions and issues, and the help of a facilitator to guide them to reflect theologically and develop ministry responses.[21]

Identifying and training mentors in an organisation is one direct way to help foster leadership development. Some interviewees identified the challenge of "finding people of character who want to invest in generations below them".[22] They suggested the Western church is lacking the art of intergenerational discipleship. Watson expressed this concern:

> There are certain instances and cases where God will call people to pioneer something that they can't model off someone else… when we have lost the discipleship process there is no one to imitate. So you have got these people bursting with potential and absolutely, clearly anointed by God but no one really knows how to lead them and empower them and help them develop.[23]

Assisting churches to develop networks of trained mentors who are committed to leadership development and linking them with emerging leaders facilitates opportunities to learn through doing while reducing the risks of going it alone.

An empowering and collaborative leadership model

Our interview sample reflected a preference of Generation Y and Z for empowering and collaborative leadership. When asked to define leadership the interviewees described an open, collaborative process whose focus was not to get things done but empowering people to act. They defined leadership as "helping others to take effective action",[24] "to steward surrendered trust",[25] and "responsibility for the wellbeing of a group of people".[26] Burnett emphasised the importance of empowering others rather than self-achievement: "For me I see leadership as something that empowers others to be leaders, and my role as a senior leader is to relinquish the desire to try and get it all done myself".[27] Watson stated, "Leadership is not about you, it's actually about serving other people. If it's about you then you are not a leader".[28] These leaders showed a strong sense of responsibility, caring for, and leading for the benefit of others.

Lewis suggests part of empowering leadership is being willing to let go of outdated approaches and re-contextualising leadership for new contexts. He urges being attentive to what God is doing and what leadership is popping up, and cooperating with that:

> Instead of saying we have God and we need to give it to others… God is bigger and larger and more mysterious and active all around us. Sometimes he might even redeem the church but he's definitely redeeming the world and so we can go on and try to participate with that.[29]

Thus ultimately our collaboration is with God and what God is doing.

Many of those interviewed expressed the frustration of working within a less collaborative system. They are looking for not just the rhetoric but the reality of empowerment, as Steve Echols warns:

> While the proponents of this great-man theory of leadership, chauvinistic even in its title, are virtually extinct as theorists, in practice elitism in leadership is still unfortunately more prevalent than we would care to admit.[30]

The inability to "fit" these often unspoken leadership criteria limits access to opportunities. It can also result in negative early experiences.

Generation Y are more comfortable expressing leadership in empowering ways, and expect to be led with an empowering posture. Australian schooling aims to help children become empowered learners, to acquire attitudes and skills for self-directed learning for their whole lives. The Australian government whitepaper "Bridging the Gap" examines workplace intergenerational interactions, and how to engage and retain Gen Y employees:

> (Generation Y) have been raised in an environment where they have been given leadership opportunities throughout their schooling and encouraged to challenge and independently evaluate other's decisions. As a result Gen Y has brought new values to the workplace. Gen Y's expect to be treated as equals, they expect to have choices and input into decision-making processes, and such expectations run counter to hierarchical systems of leadership. Indeed, 97% of Gen Y's surveyed valued a leadership style that involved empowerment, consultation and partnership, and would leave if they did not get it.31

Church attenders and leaders are not "subordinates". Their role is more often voluntary, and as such they even more expect consultation and empowerment.[32] Hierarchical leadership models no longer function adequately within groups whose members believe they can actively contribute.

Inclusion of gender, age, and cultural diversity

Steve Echols, Professor of Leadership at New Orleans Baptist Theological Seminary, proposes that inclusiveness is a key leadership quality for Christian leadership:

> The inclusive leader rejects the notion that certain groups have no place at the table in regard to decision making. Leaders who practice inclusion often believe it is not only morally wrong to marginalize certain groups within a constituency, but it is a grossly ineffective

means of leadership that will minimize or even destroy the potential energy and creativity of any organization.[33]

Without inclusion the interaction and interdependence required to foster emergence cannot exist.

The interviewees identified three areas where they feel the church struggles to demonstrate inclusion in leadership: gender, age, and cultural diversity.

There is a vast difference in the expectations of gender equality for Generations X, Y, and Z compared with some traditional church views.[34] Young tertiary educated women are often surprised if their local church debates their role in church. Gender-based limitations to leadership are still prevalent. For example, of the 503 current serving pastors on the BUV database, only 18 percent are women.[35] The societal context in which these generations have grown up is much more gender inclusive.

Women in church who experience restricted access to leadership roles also experience deep pain.[36] One young woman, outside of the interview process, described to us the profound hurt she feels knowing that there are people within the church who see her training and knowledge as not just wasted but dangerous, because she is a women.[37] Others, if they are leading, feel the pressure and expectation to lead in masculine ways. Kafieris commented:

> I just want to be myself as female… I feel like "You're asking me to be masculine here in order to be heard, you need to see me as a man in order to validate my opinion". I don't like the fact that I have … to make that shift in myself to be heard on behalf of others … I don't think we have a feminine style of leadership (in the church) yet. Not one that is healthy and works and is one that even I would like to try and emulate.[38]

Emerging generations also see the need for involving the contribution of children and all ages, and people of all cultural backgrounds. This is critical for a church on whom God pours out the Holy Spirit on and through all nations (Acts 2:5–11; Rev 7:9) and sends the Spirit so that "sons and daughters will prophesy [and] old people will dream dreams [and] young people will see special dreams" (Joel 2:28). The church, however, often segments ministries along age and ethnic lines; thus breaking God's kingdom into "bite-sized components"[39] but missing interdependence and mutual learning.

Barnett is an advocate for worship that incorporates all ages, cultures, and stages of faith. She invites different voices into the community to learn from one another. She affirms the voice of emerging generations who "bring a different kind of intelligence, I love the skills of critical thinking, the nuances of literature; they bring a hermeneutic of suspicion that's just natural to them. There's lot's we can learn from that."[40]

Hre and other culturally diverse leaders explain that Asian groups, as communal cultures, benefit from a group approach to leadership development, rather than extracting individuals from their context.[41] BUV Chin leadership development days have benefited from inviting pastors and existing congregational chairmen to attend together. A next step for BUV is for culturally diverse churches such as the Chin and Karen to send their young adults for training. BUV's Meewon Yang was serving in a Korean church but realised she needed to broaden her Australian experience in order to care for her Korean church in its new context. She urges churches to release their young adults to have the freedom to go out for broader experience: "Being a leader means you have to stretch. It's a vast land. We often pressure our kids … We need to give home more freedom to go out and come back."[42] Camps and retreats for churches or networks may work well across cultures. Mixing Chin with Anglo and other culture emerging leaders and exploring together how to relate gospel to culture offers the benefit of learning from one another.[43] It is important for culturally and linguistically diverse (CALD) leaders to engage in more conversation about how best to collaborate for leadership development.

The broader church will suffer from cultural captivity if we do not learn from non-Western sisters and brothers. This suggests the importance of linking mentors and emerging leaders from different cultural backgrounds, but also considering the cultural diversity of preaching, worship, and leadership teams. Local churches can tend to default to white male older leadership, and need intentionality in including the leadership contribution of others.[44]

Among the gifts younger generations bring to church is their commitment to inclusiveness — they expect it, will notice its absence, and can lead us in more inclusive directions.

Financially sustainable leadership development and ministry

Another element of leadership culture raised by a number of interviewees was the financial cost of ministry, training, and the expectation of voluntary work. Emerging leaders, particularly those not pursuing ordination, report working in insecure, short-term, partially funded positions. Many of our interviewees hold two or three part-time roles, including paid and unpaid positions. Bell commented that living costs are higher today than twenty or thirty years ago, and support for leadership development is usually minimal. Emerging leaders often get a start in their development through self-financed, volunteer, or part-time roles, which may be possible for young single people for some time, but once older or with families it becomes less sustainable.[45] Some ministry roles require raising financial support from churches, which develops partnerships but takes effort.

Beyond the pure budgetary concerns it is also a matter of value and recognition. The assumption that "young adults have all this free time … that if we need something doing we will get the young adults to do it because they don't do anything",[46] that young people can be expected to work long hours for little or no pay shows a disregard for the work, study, and family contexts, and the economic realities of ministry.

Internship programs which totally remove young adults from the workforce and give them few marketable skills can be irresponsible, taking advantage of the interns. We need alternative models for leadership development that leave space for young adults to stay connected to their work world — for financial and missional reasons. This is not to suggest the middle-class dream of a secure career and financial self-sufficiency is a gospel value. But it is better if churches can offer training and patterns which are sustainable in the longer term, and be transparent about the costs involved. Mitchell said that his colleagues are critical of internships that do not lead anywhere, or what he sceptically labels the "Cool, we will burn you out for a year then you're done, goodbye!" year-long internship process. If there are no ongoing support and training options then interns are sometimes left feeling used. The church needs to "give them something that they can take away that's more than just, 'oh yeah, I had this really awful year at church and now I don't go there'."[47] Internships can be valuable learning experiences for the interns and enhance fruitful ministry for a church, but they ought to primarily add value to the future work and ministry of the intern. Programs which function alongside part-time or full-time work are also needed. It may also be helpful for churches to explore alternate, entrepreneurial means of funding their ministries beyond Sunday morning offerings.

Reframing leadership

The church needs to develop leaders appropriate for our twenty-first-century cultural contexts. One of the characteristics of many in this group was a reluctance to think of themselves as leaders. For some the magnitude of the responsibility weighed heavily on them. They do not perceive themselves as an authority figure who has the right to lead others, particularly in ministry. They are aware of the damage which can be the result of poor leadership. Many have felt pushed into leadership positions without adequate support or clear expectations. Merryn James, Children and Families Pastor at Crossway, acknowledges the difficulty achieving a balanced approach to leadership development:

> For some young leaders they feel frustrated because they can't do what they are feeling God wants them to do, they don't have that opportunity because there is a lid on leadership. But for other young leaders it feels like they are given so much responsibility as a young adult that they burn out.[48]

Consequences of this include a reluctance to embrace the title of leader, distrust and rejection of leadership theory and training, and "profound scepticism about leadership material".[49] These leaders are seeking a deeper interpretation of leadership beyond merely "running programs and trying to build a mega church".[50] They want to address the misconceptions of leadership that are common amongst young people and the wider church. Mitchell commented:

> Coming into leadership now in the church, I see a lot of young people who think it's about having a platform and suddenly you have to be like Francis Chan and you need a YouTube channel and you need a book deal and these are all signs that you have made it in leadership. It's all very events-based and you have to be running the next biggest and best thing but people seem to neglect discipleship and meaningful forms of leadership.[51]

Unless somebody fits preconceived "successful" notions of leadership, misconceived as they often are, their leadership gifts may be overlooked. Bell observed:

> If the only foothold you have is within a church and if you're not a showy up-front-type person you get missed. I work with young adults who have been extremely discouraged by that type of approach.[52]

Dunham described how Arrow teaches that leadership is not just for A-type, loud, courageous leaders who fit the stereotype of conductors, persuaders, or promoters. Quality leaders can also be introverts, detail-oriented, supporters, and coordinators.[53] Leadership development needs to help develop strengths, rather than expect people to be shaped into pre-existing moulds. Reale suggests that BUV should subvert preferred types of leadership and challenge stereotypes:

> If a group of people can say "yeah we know what a Baptist pastor looks like they are … they wear … and their haircut is …". then people will self-select out and go "I don't fit that". So being able to subvert that and say leaders come in all sorts of shapes and forms is fabulous.[54]

Reale encourages others to affirm the potential for anybody to lead, even if they do not hold a position; and to discern options for leadership in all different spheres, not just ordained pastoral ministry.[55] There is an eager openness from younger leaders to be guided and coached, and not just for traditional church leadership but for leading the church, and leading in society, in fresh directions.

Leadership development, at its best, will guide leaders-in-training to reframe leadership in directions that cooperate with God's mission. Hearn describes leadership as helping people move in the directions God is calling them:

> I feel that being a leader is being in between where God is and where he's calling and leading, and where people are, who might not quite be as far along yet, who I can call to head in the same direction as I feel God is calling me.[56]

Leadership is not about dictating vision and direction, but needs reframing in our churches around an invitation to help people imagine and implement God's vision and mission for them.

NextGen emerging leadership mentoring

BUV is starting to plan and evaluate its emerging leadership development approaches with these principles that emerging/emerged leaders identified as important as a checklist. That is, we are asking to what extent the BUV, our programs, and our churches help foster:

a. A culture of missional leadership development

b. Apprenticeship of learning by doing

c. Mentoring to support learning

d. An empowering and collaborative leadership model

e. Inclusion of gender, age, and cultural diversity

f. Financially sustainable leadership development and ministry

g. Reframing leadership.

Moreover, in the context of these principles and other available programs, BUV is exploring a program of mentoring and "communities-of-practice" group coaching for Gen X, Y, and Z leaders. This recommendation reflects the importance of mentoring that all emerging/emerged leaders discussed. Moreover, it reflects the fact that this is one area not served by other organisations, and most local churches would benefit from a denominational network of mentoring.[57]

The BUV vision is "to advance the kingdom of God by empowering leaders for mission". Fostering a culture of missional leadership development is thus core business for BUV. The best way that BUV can add value to emerging leaders, and complement existing available programs, is to facilitating mentoring and the group coaching of "communities-of-practice" for Gen X, Y, and Z leaders.

Darren Cronshaw is Mission Catalyst-Researcher with Baptist Union of Victoria and pastor of AuburnLife. He teaches as Associate Professor in Missiology and Head of Research with Australian Colleges of Ministries (SCD) and adjunct faculty and Honorary Research Fellow with Whitley College (University of Divinity), and is an Adjunct Professor at Swinburne Leadership Institute. Email: darren.cronshaw@buv.com.au

Stacey Wilson is a Research Assistant with BUV, Special Projects resource worker with Victorian Council of Christian Education and Regional Coordinator for the CBM Australia Luke 14 program. An occupational therapist by training she is passionate about championing inclusion for people with disabilities in churches. Email: stacey.wilson@vcce.org.au

The Trinity and the Ontology of Worship
Re-sensing Sacredness

Jeff Pugh

This exercise is an attempt to reappraise theologically what some could perceive as an anthropocentric trend in contemporary evangelical worship particularly, through the dual lenses of Trinitarian and ontological categories. These lenses are entirely compatible and the Trinitarian in fact enriches the structures of a biblical ontology. The lack of these depth dimensions is attributed to the lacklustre mood and modest participation rate of many in so-called evangelical churches within the Baptist or other congregational traditions. This malaise curiously has deepened despite the intense move toward more technologically innovative and professionally savvy musicianship. The way back to sacredness is not more of the same but a theological re-imagination of the whole worship event, particular the place and meaning of preaching and the sacraments for Baptist people.

A recent recollection

A couple of years ago I was fortunate to sit in the audience of a well-patronised church leader's conference. At a midpoint in the conference, during a plenary session to do with trends in worship, a theme emerged in the dialogue among the experts on the panel. These experts shared the one characteristic, namely, that they were in charge of worship at some of the largest churches in the city. The surprising theme was that despite all the sophistication of musicianship at their disposal these days, there was still something missing. They all testified to a ubiquitous sense of passivity in their congregations who were not as ignited by the passions of these talents to be actively engaged in the worship. It would appear this malaise was city wide as the stylistic sameness of the majority culture in liturgical expression. Two assumptions stood out strikingly in the panel's explanations. The first being that worship is what happens as the music is playing;

a very recent deviation from historical liturgical thinking. Worship, or at least "praise and worship", is almost a perfect synonym for singing. Secondly, although one expert contributed a perceptive sociological analysis based on a keen sense of contemporary trends that affect expectations, the focus was conspicuously on the worshipper and their world. This was matched by a corresponding lack of mention of God or anything resembling a theological framework for addressing the issue. The assumption was that the issue was entirely pragmatic, understandable on the human plane alone and, therefore, would sometime soon be resolved through technological solutions.

This essay seeks to address this lack of mystique that typifies so much worship in so many typical contemporary Baptist churches Sunday by Sunday. I adopt a Trinitarian perspective whereby the ontological categories which frame this event are placed front and centre in the discourse. While these phenomena could be traced historically, culturally, or sociologically as many have already[1] it is the purpose of this article to argue that the critical factor in the rejuvenation of the worship of our churches is more adequate theological thinking.

The erosion of ontological categories in evangelical analysis

Some cultural comments are in order. As grandchildren of the Enlightenment, post Emmanuel Kant, a reductionism is bound to occur in our analysis of worship. The lenses of the surrounding culture become all important ways to understand what is happening and, when worship "works", contributing factors can be identified. Several limiting lenses conspire to divert attention from the crucial ontological awareness of the worship event.

The first value, "scientism" means that all that is not demonstrable empirically is unimportant or even nonsense. Only science can give information about the world and what happens in it. Only those things which have demonstrable causal linkages can be believed or trusted. This rules out any possible place for mystery in worship altogether. It means that solutions to the malaise will be better examination and know-how.

Another strand inherited from popular American culture, "romanticism", equates the most valued experience as the most evocative emotionally so that the sense of knowing another intimately is paramount. The spiritual evidence that the divine-human encounter has or is occurring is equated to whether the passions have been moved or feelings of intimacy stimulated. Recent apparitions in worship language include the fact that some today are encouraged in worship not only to love God with heart, mind, and soul but to "fall in love" with Jesus, a highly erotic demand indeed. What is important is not so much to trust in God's covenant love but to capture the feeling of being loved.

"Individualism" focuses obviously on the elevation of the inalienable rights of the individual to self-fulfilment and aspirational values consistent with a political economy of opportunity afforded in the West. Such aspirational values are ingrained in the mindset which is inherent in today's American Evangelicalism and imported smoothly as the Australian contemporary church, in typical cultural cringe, uncritically accommodates the moods and modes of that context as if they are universal, transcendent principles.[2]

"Consumerism" joins these grids together as the review of the components of worship as attempted in the plenary session above are brought to bear to induce the sort of emotional stimulants through the musically accompanied evocation of the moment. All this is with a view to appeasing the tastes and shifting whims of the religious customer. This is indeed a rationale to pursue if the goal is to build market share in the religious marketplace. The trouble is that even this market analysis is not producing an adequate explanation of the passivity and predictability of contemporary worship.

The upshot of this is an inevitable "reductionism" of Christian worship. These categories dominate interpretation of the gathering of the saints into a mundane affair that can be captured at the level of empirical analysis. But they are insufficient to begin to grasp the larger aspect of the event we call "corporate worship".

History drift

These approaches to worship in Western evangelicalism also represent a shift in perspective in the area of theological ontology. One cannot explain the shift from the sacramental view of the liturgical experience in the Reformation without the influence of American revivalism of the eighteenth century and beyond. This era links more closely with scientism than sacramental realism or the scripturally based reflection of the Reformers. Evangelicalism had already found the value of accommodating the emerging aspirational values of the New World. The nineteenth century played into the hands of late Enlightenment with "worship" being viewed as a prelude to the inspirational message followed by a call to respond. That which is most spiritual or real is the evocative climax of the message. The revivalist sacrament is the movement of emotions to extract a decision to move out of the seat of conviction to the front of a meeting house. It was no accident that the revivalist evangelistic heroes, despite being effective evangelistically, reduced their ministry to a published technology that could be employed to produce spiritual effects elsewhere.[3]

In this stream the priestesses and priests of the contemporary evangelical or charismatic worship service recapitulate this same tendency whenever the MC's commentary is added to the worship "vibe". This may be seen at those points when music leaders confidently announce at moments when the emotional contagions surface that "God is really in the house tonight" or similar affirmations of faith. It is no accident that the means of grace within today's worship service are no longer the preached gospel or the sacraments but the artistic skills of the musicians and the persona of the preacher or leader.

We maintain, however, that genuine Christian worship is, or should be, that unique social space where this suffocating domination of popular culture is not replicated but instead brought to heel. Worship is that space where these unexamined cultural constructions are brought into proper alignment with ultimate reality; the unknowable almighty God.

Ontologies of worship

All theologies of worship contain unspoken ontologies in the background. A fine connection here has been recently articulated by John Jefferson Davis.[4] He identifies the problem as a failure primarily in the area of theological ontology. Simply put, this would imply that there is a confusion of the ultimate with sub-ultimate reality. Those ontologies which are "thin" or from too low a horizon produce correspondingly inadequate theologies of worship. Adequate ontologies are "dense" or thick with significance. These theologies of worship may also represent inadequate eschatological, soteriological, or sacramental notions at the same time. This framework is useful for understanding the less than satisfying experiences and the passivity that bedevils contemporary worship in so many situations.

A biblical ontological perspective according to Davis involves discriminating between five levels of existence or domains from the most to the least real. Davis's ontological distinctions are as follows. These also need to be enriched by cross-referencing the implications of the triune nature of God as this affects the capacity to interpret God's personal presence within these categories. This interplay of theological lenses can serve the purposes of a theological analysis here.

Level 1 Reality

A theologically adequate ontology of worship must involve a view of reality that apportions the highest or most real to the interpersonal, eternal, perichoretically expressed, life of the triune Godhead. The unbegotteness of the Father and the uncreated persons of Son and Spirit are not reproducible in the lower orders of reality. This alone should sound a warning to those expositors of group worship experience who would too quickly identify group contagions with divine presences. Generation of the Son and spiration of the Spirit have no direct correlates beyond the Godhead.[5] An incalculable reduction in reality occurs as one moves from the eternal infinite realm to that of created contingent realities. We must not think of reality as a smooth continuum from most to least real but as a radical disjunction from the creator to the creature.[6]

Level 2 Reality

Davis argues that this level of reality includes those spirits, malevolent as well as obedient, along with the departed saints whose similarities are that they possess centres of consciousness, self-consciousness, wilfulness, and, I would add, a limited yet unambiguous vision of the level 1 reality. They walk by sight not faith and in this sense are living out a higher order reality than level 3.

One could also argue on the basis of the writer to the Hebrews that this level with these inhabitants was not initially God's ordering of existence. This level is meant to be the level of those humans made in his image (Psalm 8:5 MT cf. Gen 1:26) and who being *"a little lower than God"* exercise dominion over angels. In Adam this opportunity to exercise vice-regal subsisting has been squandered and this world was, according to Jewish tradition, parcelled out to angelic overlords (Dan 10:21). Not so for the world to come. Level 3 reality is only regained through Christ who *"became a little lower than the angels"* as a means of transcending these spirits in the age to come (Hebrews 2:8, 16). God's concern primarily is for those sons of Adam who become "the sons of Abraham". We should also add that the Scriptures are open to the possibility that the demonic is a willing substitute to a genuine divine orientation in worship. Such level 2 fiats have the capacity to give level 3 reality a sense of transcendence. Tangible "sight-based" encounter can be mistaken for the Creator's revelatory Word or personal presence.

Level 3 Reality

Humanity inhabits this set of beings as not only, constitutionally speaking, through being conscious centres of will and self-awareness, but also through divine appointment as bearers of God's image in a secondary and inferior sense to the imaging of the begotten in the unbegotten. Being image-bearers, humanity in this level of reality alone has the commission of reflecting, meditating upon, and exalting the qualities of level 1 reality.

Level 4 Reality

This level is a distinct drop again from the level of being in level 3. These are both the inanimate and animate creations of God granted to level 3 inhabitants for stewardship and enjoyment. Such inhabitants reflect the glory of the creator artlessly but unknowingly and have lives determined by their natures but not the capacity to self-reflect or worship.

Level 5 Reality

This is lower in the sense that it contains the constructs of the creature, the artefacts, institutions, cultural artefacts, career and work identity, and all those reifications that we as humans invest with meaning and treat as if real. In fact humanity never relates to the other levels except in a mediated way, through technologies, tools, language symbols, and various dominant logics. Ironically it is these constructs that we assert "give our lives meaning" when in fact we project meaning into them. What we mean ultimately can only be received from a level 1 perspective.

This taxonomy should serve as an immediate caution for those who would attempt to revive worship through a more adequate choreography or scientific analysis. This problem of a level 3 imagination cannot be resolved by analytical methods derived from the same level. In fact, our own secular society provides evidence of this. A real sense of transcendence occurs when level 3 reality is taken as the highest ontic level.

For instance in local sporting culture, which many have identified as our national religion, we frequently observe the phenomenon of a religious interpretation of transcendent experience of the events even though level 1 is rarely given a second thought. We note in particular those times when a sports star, coach, or their immediate relative dies, and they are accorded due honours even "bookending" the match-day event itself in liturgical acts of crowd and participant alike. The departed are depicted as able to access the present spectacle "from above" — while the living God is never given a second thought. Likewise level 3 ontology in those group events and moments which appear to be ultimately meaningful especially when winning is involved. In the sporting arena players and those in the crowd of the premier team suddenly feel they share the same psychological skin as the final siren sounds or the winning goal is scored, the long-shot wins the cup, or the budding talent progresses through the stages of the talent quest. The after-match elation of the typical champion when interviewed by the media is "It doesn't get better than this". Such is the indicator of the impact of a transitory but somehow super-real moment even though consisting entirely of a level 3 reality. It is just comparatively more real and personally affirming than life at the normal level of subsistence. But as worship this is a psycho-social fraud that does not engage the above or the beyond despite its mystical evocation. And despite (or because of) the attempts to refuel the moment with "sponsor's product" in the after-match partying, the moment is bound to fade into another season and simmers as a faint nostalgic glow in the memory of the devotees.

In summary, a biblical ontology implies that a focus upon any of the levels as if this is ultimate reality is symptomatic of our carnality, not just our creatureliness. If the problem of passivity or the meaningfulness of our worship is due to a lowering of our ontological horizons the solution cannot be found by a more rigorous fixation with level 3 technology that brought about the issue in the first place.

Pragmatic parallels to ecclesiology

Just as worship is liable to be misconstrued as a level 3 or 5 reality this only matches the notion of the church when it is construed in less than Trinitarian terms as a merely level 3 event. The "how to…" pragmatics of the Church Growth movement grew out of the same soil as revivalist evangelicalism and the proponents of both were largely overlapping sets.

If a level 3 ontology is applied to the growth of the church then its logistics can be discovered, mathematised, and manipulated. Lenses of management science and social psychology supplied the modernist hope that this would bring the culture of world and church together in a painless docking manoeuver. For three decades up to the early 2000s, Baptist churches and other non-liturgical "traditions" were hell bent on making the religious client feel at home at church. But this comes at the cost that the numinous presence is often a discomforting reality which may not feed the elevation of mood to which the religious customer subscribed.[7] This science of evangelism being locked into level 3 concerns eventually ensures that mystery will be insured against rather than encountered by faith.

The postmodern heirs in the emergence mode of church while *au fait* with postmodern discourse, are often bereft of an adequate theology of worship in this regard being more concerned with cultural resonance than fidelity to revelation. The critical element of worship is the transcendent encounter which is impossible to traverse unless level 1 condescends to intersect level 3. No amount of empathy for the present cultural mood can draw across the infinite gulf from level 3 to appreciate the level 1 reality. This is not to say contextualisation is pointless. But despite the antipathy between proponents of emergence and their modernist grandparents in the Church Growth movement the pressing issue for both these views is that worship ceases to be the "chief end of man" in itself, and cultural appeasement instead of spiritual confrontation is more the order of the day. Wherever worship is evaluated in utilitarian terms,[8] as a means to achieve something else, something higher, such as the painless attraction of persons into the church or coffee-serving non-church, ontological confusion has occurred and ecclesial irrelevance is assured.

But the New Testament Trinitarian metaphors remind us that the church is the bride, body, and building which Christ is constructing, the temple of the Holy Spirit, and the covenant family of God the Father known from eternity. These metaphors cannot be reduced to mere ideas or techniques, but are ontological statements of how level 1 reality intersects with the creaturely level 3 through our union with Christ. Worship is that time when one "discerns the body" properly (1 Cor 11:27–32) lest judgement is dispensed instead of grace. Eating rightly is preaching! It is the place where the Son adores the Father but now amidst the company of those whom Christ is *"not ashamed to call brethren"* (Hebrews 2:11,12 cf. Ps. 22:22) and in whose assemblies he delights to sing praise to God the Father! The Trinitarian contribution to worship is that the object of worship becomes subject in the worshipping community created by the Spirit. This is how the church assembling for worship is involved in sacramental action; acting by faith as it is itself being acted upon by grace. By its union in Christ through the person of the Spirit, the church, consciously or otherwise, is pneumatically constituted as an event of the eternal Spirit, incorporating the worshippers not just into each other, but into the eternal fellowship enjoyed by the triune God!

How pointless it is then to think we can orchestrate such a mystery with the level 5 constructs of our own level 3 minds. Congregational worship is a mystery, not in the sense that our feeble minds cannot put the pieces of the Scriptural witness together, but in the sense that it has to be grasped by the means supplied from level 1 reality, by faith alone; that is, with a posture of complete renunciation. Such things are completely antithetical to technological cleverness.

Worship time and modernist problems with sacramental discourse

It is here that one senses the deficiency of a Zwinglian/Baptist up-bringing regarding the ordinances, or what the mainline calls sacraments. This terminology reflects that our mindsets are influenced by secular post-enlightenment culture. This is not to thereby endorse substantialist views of grace or the sacerdotal ministry of the solitary priest. We worship at a table not an altar and the whole church is the priesthood (1 Peter 2:9,10). But scientism distrusts any level 1 discourse of sacred mystery and elevates the objectivity of one's level 3 senses. Ironically the metaphors which inform our analysis of the worship event are informed just as much by our socially constructed interpretive grids from level 5 as by "raw data".

A Trinitarian view of worship reminds us that if we encounter level 1 at all it is via the intersection of the incarnate Word with our creaturely context. Barth reminds us in his treatment of the three forms of the Word that the ongoing encounter with the eternal Word is via that word proclaimed into our midst and becomes the word of revelation at the sovereign intervention of God's Sprit.[9] An adequate ontology of worship affirms that the most real level has penetrated the depths of level 3 reality and redeemed this with his presence in history. What has happened definitively in the unique Christ event continues to recapitulate in the corresponding worship event. So, there is indeed "real presence" when we worship deliberately in Christ's name, but this has to do with who is at the table, not what is on it. And this presence is both three and one. It is because of the perichoretic interpenetration of the persons of the Godhead, the one God, that this very God is able to be accessed in worship. It is because of this triune nature of the one God that the thick ontological reality of level 1 can reinforce the thin ontology of level 3 without demolishing its integrity. The immutable being can interrupt the mutability of creaturely procession toward non-being. The critical issue then is where this intersection of levels is to be found in this aeon. Here is where we must address our theology of word and sacrament.

The popular Baptist view of the sacraments as aid memoirs or "ordinances" matches the view of the proclaimed word simply as a word of encouragement or anyone's cherished notions.[10] These things are true but not true enough. Such views will not sustain the presence of either expository preaching or sacraments on the worship running-sheet into future generations if these are viewed as options competing for the limited space that customer patience permits. Neither will the mystique of the worship event be sufficiently sustained by the communion meal or the baptism of the saint as a command of Christ and the apostles, though it is that. Nor again will the realisation that the practice can be traced historically in unbroken sequence back to the first hands who gave thanks for cup. As inspiring as these notions may be they provide insufficient insurance against cultural degradation of these practices in our current context. Too much is made in these rationales of our psychological processes and our memory, and not enough of ontological reality and Trinitarian nature.

Mundane regular worship looks to the uninitiated eye as if that is all it is. But our worship practices as we deliberately meet in Christ's name are actually ontologically transformed or better, transposed into an event within the experience of the triune fellowship in level 1. As regards the ongoing life of the infinite God, the important thing is that our moments in time are also where his cosmic eternity tracks with our time and space, so that every point and moment, regardless of our consciousness of the fact, is a point of immediate access to God's life and God's to ours. And likewise, as our orthodox brethren affirm, this is a glimpse also of our own future life. It is as Christ makes a body of us that we remember whose we are. The same Spirit who produces our saving union with Christ within our space-time experience of human history produces another level of fellowship through the most real presence, in the midst of our worship. This is the work of the God who is the Spirit of Christ.[11] The writer of Hebrews, no stranger to "realistic" categories, has the audacity to inform us that in our time and space

> You *have come* to Mount Zion and to the city of the living God, the heavenly Jerusalem, and to innumerable angels in festal gathering, and to the assembly of the firstborn who are enrolled in heaven, and to God, the judge of all and to the spirits of the righteous made perfect, and to Jesus the mediator of a new covenant, and to the

> sprinkled blood that speaks a better word than the blood of Abel.
> Hebrews 12:22–24

In a "real" sense, it is appropriate that we exist in a level 3, one-directional time frame. Whatever this level 5 construct "time" may be in a post-Einsteinian world, what is done in time cannot be undone later. We no longer look longingly forward to a new covenant to replace the conditional covenant of works, nor need to wonder if the declaration of our righteousness in the resurrection of Christ (Rom 4:25, 5:10) may be eventually worn away by the cosmic winds over time. Christ only can die a level 3 death *"once for all time"*. And this simultaneously registers at level 1, as Christ's self-offering was *"through the eternal Spirit"* (Heb 9:14). But this does not mean we cannot enjoy the fruits of the life of the future while we look forward to the future trans-historical life which is as far as our perspective now is concerned. What is future can be spoken of as *having come*. We as of this moment "shared *in the Holy Spirit and tasted the goodness of the word of God and the power of the age to come"* (Hebrews 6:4b, 5). Salvation grace is nothing other than the interplay of ontological levels *"via the eternal Spirit"* of the risen and ascended Christ who is equally "at home" in both levels and thus in both "times". Mundane worship is nothing less than the subordination of one level to the salvific potential of the other. The Spirit straddles history and both domains of reality and as the third person possesses all the warrants of the Father and victory spoils of the Son. Thereby our own worshipping selves become the acceptable offering to the one God as will be the case even with the Son at the ontological terminus (1Cor 15:23, 24) that "day" when the very notion of dominion will have become redundant. Christ promises his church, in its compliance with the command to enact the feast of remembrance, or to proclaim the word of the gospel, to gain access through the shared Spirit to the founder of the feast, the Word of God enfleshed. This is not through some level 2 transcendental time-travel but down to the condescension of the Lord of level 1, binding himself to the covenant he provides and signified personally through these promises: the sacraments of baptism, the feast, and Word present in preaching and the community itself. He himself is present, uttering these promises, the Word himself, afresh.

The critical point: what place then of level 5 creativity?

If level 1 is the "most-real-reality" then we can symbolise this reality as worship in the most-true sense. The interrelationships between the distinctive persons of the Trinity are likewise role- and person-specific as well as reciprocated. They are interpersonally from first to second to third persons described as

1. Father to Son who relate eternally via generation and reciprocal adoration
2. Procession or spiration of the Spirit from the Son and reciprocal glorification of the Son
3. The Spirit's procession from the Father and reciprocal revelation of the Father.

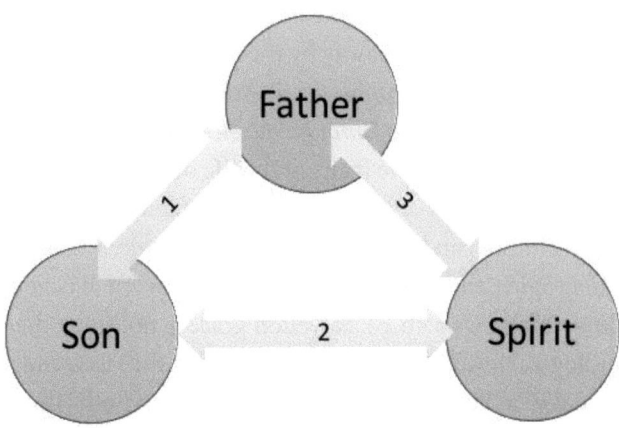

Diagram 1: Level 1 Reality

But at level 3 the experience of the worshiper by faith could be construed as

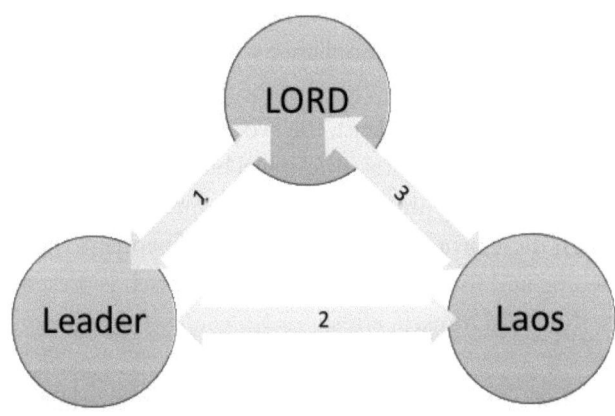

Diagram 2: Level 3 Reality

The intersection of level 1 with level 3 is through three dimensions again in an interplay of roles or dimensions of the encounter. The three dimensions are

- The charismatic dimension
- The catalytic dimension and
- The cataclysmic dimension.

This requires several radical movements to occur simultaneously through these dimensions.

The Charismatic dimension

This is to affirm that in the eternal decision of God, the uniqueness of some individuals are pressed into the service of gathering up the attention of the people of God, the *laos*, and turning these toward Christ as Lord, to induce prayerfulness. They are a unique workmanship created in Christ for this particular goodness (Eph 2:10). To the uninitiated this may be confused with an "X factor" personality or singing voice. More than mere talent, it consists of a theologically sensitivity.

The Catalytic dimension

This dimension allows for the interplay of sub-ultimate to ultimate realities to the extent that both leader and *laos* as gathered worshippers understand the leader role as merely instrumental or catalytic of a powerful reaction within a far more mystical communion. Those who, like the effective sporting umpire, while visible should "go unnoticed" as they are not the game but necessary for the game. In other words that this catalysing function occurs is not a scientific law or a foregone conclusion but still a decision of God. It is not a technology that can be measured, controlled, replicated, or demanded. But it can be discerned, petitioned, and received with thanks.

The Cataclysmic dimension

The goal of worship is that it breaks through rather than reinforces our enculturated views of reality. Participants cease to be consumers, becoming alert participants, brothers and sisters of the Christ present. When this happens they would not only be discerning the body of human community present, but the greater body, the focal object, and the always adoring subject. If we want to appraise any worship product, it is the transforming faith in the Christ encountered in this of domain transposition. Like the Samaritan at the well, once freed from her symbols of mundane living (John 4:26) and the constraints of her oppressive cultural place, she is renewed with a compulsion to bear witness to one she has just encountered. This interplay of domains may be expanded as an embedding of our thin worship space into the corresponding but thick interrelating within the triune society.

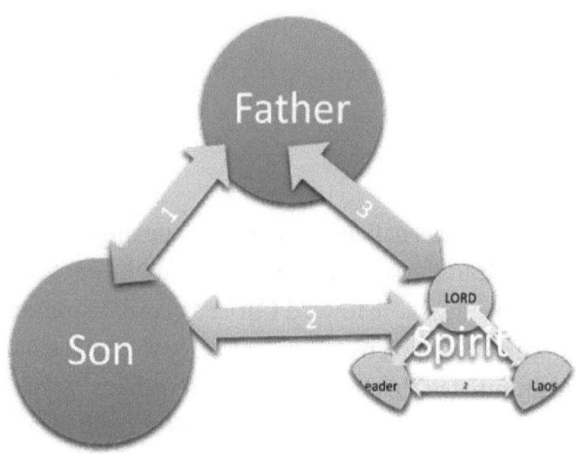

Diagram #3: The Ontological Moment Laid upon the Eternal Reality

If we are brought into this ultimate reality of spiritual union with the Lord, this humanly impossible dynamic, then it is mandatory that all media must match the mood of the miraculous moment. This catalytic leader is functionally "priestly" if not ontologically so. She needs to realise she is the servant of the Spirit of the triune Lord. This poor soul is the one who straddles awareness of both the consciousness of the human participants and the righteous yearnings of the divine worshipper par excellence. Instead of striving to fill the agenda with thoughtless words or getting through enough music to satisfy the expressive needs of the music team, the designer-leader should seek to focus deliberately upon the preparation of a people for the nature of the encounter with level 1 that is happening in this domain. Then, having been a fellow witness to the mediated revelation that does occur, move to the facilitation of response especially as the word calls for a specific obedience. And of course this involves a spiritual preparation and willing obedience of themselves.

Worship construction becomes more a diagnostic exercise than a directive exercise; a work of space-making than space-filling, as dreadful as it is privileged. As long as this is the case then "the world is our oyster" as level 4 artefacts and level 5 imaginations can gather inspiration from any of the levels from 3 or below in ways that exceed the monochrome reliance on praise music that is currently flattening our mystical horizons. Their profound role must be radically reformative if we are to interrupt the down-slope to non-being that is the current boredom with worship. This is a far more refined and rare skill set than being able to sing in key. When such a posture is imaginatively constructed out of a co-creative consciousness, the more likely we will begin to apprehend what we already are, the body of Christ, discern the Word being revealed beneath the mundane words and humble symbols. The triune voice would not then be impeded by our noise, and, I dare say, parched secular souls who would not otherwise believe may rejoice with us that *"God is indeed with you"* (Zech 8:23). Our own dark "thin" level 3 hearts may again perceive the light of level 1 dazzling in its density. One transformed poet has captured such a tension moment:[12]

Taking any route, starting from anywhere,

At any time or at any season,

It would always be the same: you would have to put off

Sense and notion.

You are not here to verify,

Instruct yourself, or inform curiosity

Or carry report.

You are here to kneel!

Where prayer has been valid,

And prayer is more than an order of words, the conscious occupation

Of the praying mind, or the sound of the voice praying.

And what the dead had no speech for, when living,

They can tell you, being dead: the communication

Of the dead is tongued with fire beyond the language of the living.

Here, the intersection of the timeless moments

England and nowhere.

Never and always.

Jeff Pugh is a practical theologian who has pastored several Baptist Churches in the 1980s and 1990s and since then has taught in Baptist seminaries in three states with roles as a denominational consultant in church development. In recent years his main role has been in developing the postgraduate research school with the Melbourne School of Theology. His research interests focus mainly upon organisational culture change and homiletics.

Improvising a Renewed Story at AuburnLife
Utilising Biblical Narrative for Congregational Transformation

Darren Cronshaw

The biblical narrative is a resource for congregational worship and transformation. N.T. Wright adopts a high view of Scripture as the narrative that the church finds itself in, and suggests the mission of the church is to "improvise" how to continue the storyline of the Bible in a new context. This chapter considers the case study of how AuburnLife Baptist Church has used this approach in Sunday worship to engage with the biblical story and how it engages with our story and mission. In a post-Christian society, it is important to explore a church's story within a foundational Christian metanarrative, and its relationship to other competing (counter-)narratives of late/post modernity. The aim of the exercise, ultimately, is to improvise a renewed story — to utilise the biblical narrative for congregational transformation. It aims to help a congregation get in touch with the biblical narrative (and how they can continue that, using the Acts 29+ metaphor of improvising the ongoing story of the mission of God), in order to enhance the formational quality of Sunday worship and help the church improvise new ways of doing church and mission.

Who's for a story?

Paying attention to the guiding narratives of a church can enhance worship and foster congregational transformation. Missional-culture architect J.R. Woodward teaches that a church can gain insights into where God is calling them by paying attention to their church's narrative. His challenge is to ask: "As you consider the congregation you serve, is the narrative of the community shaping people to love Christ more, be more like him and deeply engage the world in order to see God's kingdom become a greater reality?"[2] Woodward suggests there are three groups of stories which shape a church. A church is shaped firstly by the Bible stories it focuses on. It is worth asking how these stories help the church love God, love their neighbours, and love their enemies. A church is also shaped by the historical stories and memories of the church that are rehearsed, and thirdly by stories of mission from current experience that are retold. Analysis of these three sets of stories can help identify what a church sees as important, and where a church might best focus its vision and mission.[3]

In a previous chapter in the first *New Wineskins* volume, and inspired by Woodward's revitalisation frameworks, I explored the historical narrative of AuburnLife Baptist Church and some of our contemporary missional stories.[4] As a congregational worship exercise, we used "appreciative inquiry" and a historical storyline to map our local church history. This revealed distinctive features of our church's history which are also shared values that inform our current mission and vision. The aim of the exercise was to imagine a renewed story. The key features of our vision draw on key assets of our history — especially being a "leadership farm" that grows a new generation of leaders, offering multicultural hospitality space, and being generous with our buildings.

This chapter discusses our experience with the other framing narrative that shapes our congregational life — the narrative of Scripture. At Auburn we followed up the congregational timelines exercise with a teaching and learning series on "This is My/ Our Story". We wanted to start exploring how our church's historical narrative fits in the context of the biblical story.

What's your biblical narrative? (Act V/Acts 29+)

Any church story begins not with the plant or start of the local congregation, but with the story of the Bible. The church's story is God's story to begin with. The first part of a church's narrative is to reconnect with the biblical narrative. This is not just about reading Scripture to master it, but letting Scripture read and master us. A good teacher, Woodward argues, helps people understand that the Bible is a voice to hear, not merely a book to read.[5] Good teaching helps a church to be like a Berean. Luke reported that Bereans "were more open-minded than those in Thessalonica, and they listened eagerly to Paul's message. They searched the Scriptures day after day to see if Paul and Silas were teaching the truth" (Acts 17:11).[6] Part of not just engaging Scripture but dwelling faithfully in its story is about asking what the truth of Scripture is for a particular local congregation.

N.T. Wright urges Christians to adopt a high view of Scripture as authoritative, but he suggests a different and more dynamic way of viewing its authority. It is not so much full of rules to obey or creeds to believe, nor even timeless truths to instruct, devotional snippets to inspire, or evangelistic summaries to quote, but more of a narrative that we find ourselves in. Wright does not belittle laws and truth, devotion and evangelism, but argues we approach Scripture best by dwelling faithfully in its story. He suggests a model for reading and responding to Scripture as like a five-act play:

> Suppose there exists a Shakespeare play whose fifth act had been lost. The first four acts provide, let us suppose, such a wealth of characterization, such a crescendo of excitement within the plot, that it is generally agreed that the play ought to be staged. Nevertheless, it is felt inappropriate actually to write a fifth act once and for all: it would freeze the play into one form, and commit Shakespeare as it were to being prospectively responsible for work not in fact his own. Better, it might be felt, to give the key parts to highly trained, sensitive and experienced Shakespearian actors, who would immerse themselves in the first four acts, and in the language and culture of Shakespeare and his time, and who would then be told to work out a fifth act for themselves.[7]

The first four acts are authoritative. As we improvise the fifth act, we are guided by the plot and characterisation of the first four acts — Creation, Fall, Israel, and Jesus, and by understanding how the fifth act — the story of the church — will finish. The fifth act is begun in the New Testament as the first scene of the final act, but the church through history has been improvising and performing the following scenes. We do not make up the script entirely out of our own imaginations. Rather we let our imagination be formed by the story of what God has been doing in history, and of where Scripture tells us history is heading. The ways in which Jesus brought life and wholeness, and how Jesus sent the church to continue the story and mission of Jesus (John 20:21), are formative for how God invites us to continue the story.[8]

The Bible is the story of *missio Dei* or the mission of God, and as a story it has potential to capture people's imagination. N.T. Wright suggests this is why God used so much narrative in Scripture: "Throw a rule book at people's head, or offer them a list of doctrines, and they can duck or avoid it, or simply disagree and go away. Tell them a story, though, and you invite them to share a world-view or better still a 'God-view'".[9] Old Testament scholar Christopher Wright encourages us to see the purpose of our lives wrapped up with the mission of God:

> We want to be driven by a purpose that has been tailored just right for our own individual lives ... when we should be seeing the purpose of all life, including our own, wrapped up in the great mission of God for the whole of creation.[10]

Part of what really is good news about Christianity is that God has a purpose, a mission, and an ongoing story which God invites us to be part of and cooperate with. But it is an ongoing story that we co-create. God's will and purposes for us are not a set script, although the story of Scripture points us in helpful directions from which we improvise.

Biography as theology, and as narrative ethics, was pioneered by James McClendon.[11] John Millbank contends the task for Christians today is not to "out-reason" opponents, but to "out-narrate" them — to tell a better story that draws them into a compelling vision of human flourishing.[12] Or in the words of Paul Fiddes:

> The Christian strategy is not to imagine that we have a point of vantage above or beyond culture, from which to survey other stories. It is rather ... the persuasive power of our story that will judge other stories. And it is not just telling; we are to out-perform others by *living* by a better story.[13]

The story of Scripture is the clarion call for a local church to become all it can be as a partner with God in the *missio Dei*.

Missionary statesman Lesslie Newbigin urged leaders to let the tradition dwell in them, and dwell themselves fully in the tradition: "The Christian understanding of the world is not only a matter of 'dwelling in' a tradition of understanding; it is a matter of dwelling in a story of God's activity, activity which is still continuing".[14] Scripture helps us understand God's story. But congregational life also offers us clues about God's story, and our congregations are a vehicle for communicating the uniqueness of the biblical story. In answer to the question of how the biblical story can challenge competing worldviews, Newbigin comments: "it can do so through the witness of a community which, in unbroken continuity with the biblical actors and witnesses, indwells the story the Bible tells".[15] More famously, in answer to how the gospel can be communicated, Newbigin declares: "The only answer, the only hermeneutic of the gospel, is a congregation of men and women who believe it and live by it".[16]

Martin Sutherland argues that a distinctly Baptist way of doing theology focuses on church as gathering and becoming, more than merely developing philosophical ideas that are more highly regarded in the prevailing scholastic model of theologising. For Baptists, church manifests primarily in local visible form, where Christ is dynamically present in the community. This is the "beating heart" of Baptist theology.[17] Nevertheless, Sutherland asserts the importance of paying attention to the narratives of Scripture as well as the congregation:

> The church experience is never just local, never just one story. Rather it is the dynamic interplay of *two* stories — the contemporary, local, "gathered" one, and the Christ story as revealed in Scripture. These stories are not equal partners. As the church gathers "in his name", it is seeking to align its story with Christ's story in all its scandalous particularity. Thus, in this dialectic, the Christ story is primary and normative.[18]

Sutherland suggests the story of the church aligns with the story of Christ, not in direct correspondence or imitation, as if to answer "What would Jesus do?", but more like the musical concept of "coherence". Our theological task is to bring the story of the local church into harmony and consonance with Christ: "The story itself calls us forward and outwards rather than backwards or inwards".[19] But our beginning reference point is the storyline of Scripture.

The story of Scripture is something God invites us to continue to improvise. The early church's story is told in Acts but finishes at Acts 28. It is the calling of the church since to continue the narrative and live out Acts 29+.[20]

AuburnLife — putting ourselves in the story

AuburnLife has had a few worship experiments to help understand how the Bible fits together as a narrative, and where we fit in the story.

In 2012 we hosted a "Bible and art" series where different speakers shared a piece of art and talked about its significance. Each piece of art was then hung on the wall. The art was from different cultural backgrounds. The different pieces represented a different part of the biblical story — from creation through to Israel's exile, to Jesus, the last Supper, and the early church. For example, an indigenous speaker, Safina Fergie, introduced creation for us with her indigenous dot painting. Jenni Cronshaw invited us to engage with Jesus through his parable of the Sower, and invited us to reflect on what seeds God wanted to plant in each of us. Each Sunday offered a meaningful reflection on a different part of Scripture, but our Sunday Stuff co-coordinators that year, Julia Rhyder and Mark Payne, helped us also to see how the stories fitted together in the overall narrative of Scripture. Now each Sunday we are still surrounded by our biblical story, as a reminder of the story we inherit and of what we learned in that series.

When we came to 2014 we wanted to revisit our biblical story, in particular with reference to N.T. Wright's concept of reading and applying the Bible as improvisation. Here are some questions we used as a church to imagine a renewed story through biblical narrative:

a. To what extent is the Act V or Acts 29+ metaphor of improvising the ongoing story of the mission of God helpful for reading the Bible?

b. In what ways can we read the Bible in order to help us deeply understand our story and help us improvise Acts 29+ today?

c. What parts or passages of Scripture are especially helpful or formative for us in our story as a church? What is your church's biblical story that you are living, and why does it belong particularly to you as a group? (This question is a good "homework" or retreat exercise to invite people to consider and discern.[21])

Discussing these questions was prompted by sixteen-year-old Tim Barnett's comment on a sermon from a guest speaker one week:

> That guy was good — he told interesting stories, though he didn't mention the Bible at all, which was kind of weird. Still that's better than when they just say obvious stuff about the Bible that anyone who just reads it could see. That's so annoying when they just tell you what you already just read, as if you couldn't read it for yourself. What's the point of that?

This "fairly brutal honesty of youth" led Beth Barnett, one of our teachers and worship leaders, to ask on our church Facebook page: "how might this help us think through how we spend our time together in listening to stories (and whose stories) and how we help each other hear God's Story in opening the Bible?" I wanted to open up the conversation, beyond Facebook, about how we can deeply engage Scripture and relate it to what God is doing and inviting us towards.

My story/ our story

When we discussed these questions one Sunday, connected to our congregational timeline exercise (11 May 2014), participants said that seeing the Bible as a basis for our improvisation was a novel but helpful framework. It also helped members make sense of reading some parts of the Bible that seem less relevant today — such as Levitical codes, or even offensive parts, such as calls for genocide. These parts of our narrative from Act II are not things to repeat as part of our script, but they are part of our background story for how we express faith today. Finally, Beth Barnett commented that N.T. Wright's language of giving "the key parts to highly trained, sensitive and experienced Shakespearian actors" was daunting, but another writer reminded her that we have a helpful director and prompter in the Holy Spirit who guides our improvisation.[22]

An important footnote to this presentation was added by Alex Sangster who has a strong background in acting. Sangster shared the following "rules" for improvisation as an actor:

a. *Say "Yes"* (When someone suggests something begin with "Yes".)

b. *And say "Yes AND not Yes BUT.* (It is too easy to undermine a good idea with too many "buts" ... but who would come?")

c. *Stay in the moment.* (Don't get distracted by what went wrong last time or what is supposed to happen next week. For an actor this is critical; for the church it means being attentive to God's calling now.)

d. *Make your partner look good.* (We are a community and called to build each other up.)

These acting rules can quite easily be translated into a notion of "missional improvisation". We read Scripture and do church together, at our best, when we affirm and build up one another, help each other to thrive, and do not dwell on past mistakes or future fantasies. We are planning on discussing this further, at Auburn, as we journey through the gospel of John. We will be asking, "How can we best support and bounce off one another in improvising this life of Jesus we are learning about?"

Improvisation is a fresh invitation to really engage and indwell our biblical story. Dave Male, related to his work in Fresh Expressions of Church, explains that pioneering leadership is not just about looking for new and novel ways of doing church and leaving tradition behind, but getting to the heart of our tradition. Like those who can best improvise in music, sport, or art, we do well to understand first the foundations of musical forms (or movement or artistic expression), and then experiment in new and vivid directions. Male encourages us to rediscover the heart of our history, not to default to the status quo but on that foundation to imagine constructive change for a radical future. This is our hope for Auburn, as we reshape as a signpost of the kingdom for our context and times.[23]

We followed up our first exploration of the stories of the Bible and how they connect to our stories with Beth Barnett teaching on Genesis 1 and 2 (18 May 2014).[24] From the perspective of biblical studies, the Bible is not one consecutive narrative, but numerous stories told together in various conversations and formats. These include two creation narratives, the law presented in different versions, four gospel story traditions, and three accounts of Saul's conversion. Barnett suggested that since the Bible has numerous stories, it has room for our stories too. She invited the congregation to explore Genesis 1 and 2 using her "Twists and Turns" approach. This playful retelling offers an example of how the Bible tells two stories together and invites us to tell our story.

All-Age Story

> The Bible has stories,
>
> Some big some small,
>
> Stories tangled together
>
> With a thread through them all
>
> They don't all explain things
>
> In quite the same way
>
> So there's room for some questions
>
> And there's room for some play
>
> They're good to hear twice
>
> On the very same day
>
> And then come back for more
>
> After going away.
>
> I'd tell you one now

But that will not do

If I tell you one story

I will have to tell two

Because right at the start as the Bible gets going

We straight away see that its strange way of knowing

Declares God too great to be simply defined

In one quick sketch leaving questions behind

But in more than two stories, each with details specific

Told in songs, tales and poems — the Bible's prolific

You can't just take one bit and think you know all

The whole truth about God is a mighty big call

The First Story begins with some calendar days

And God's Voice speaks and makes things in wonderful ways

First the light, then the waters and seasons and land

Plants and animals sprout and then woman with man

So everything happens at the sound of God's speech

And it happens in order, with a neat place for each

But look, turn the page to see Story Two

And spot all the differences — there's quite a few

God's sleeves are rolled up and he's playing with mud

God makes first a garden and a man — flesh and blood

God makes animal friends for the man to name

But none of the animals are just quite the same

So God, with his own hands, still messy and muddy

Makes a woman, a sister, a life-long best buddy

What wonderful stories when taken in tandem

Show a God who can speak and whose ways are not random

> And that God is with us in muck and in mess
>
> And his purpose for us is to love, work and bless
>
> God's world works together in ways we can trust
>
> But he asks us to help and take care of the dust
>
> And the water and air and animals and plants
>
> And God's working with us, so it's not left to chance.
>
> Two stories together twisting round one another
>
> Show us more about God and more of each other
>
> Watch the twists of these stories as you follow along
>
> And see this is God's world, and it's where we belong.

In postmodernity the "metanarrative" has come under suspicion, but people still look for framing stories to describe where they belong. Barnett's approach, which AuburnLife is adopting, is one in which we can express unity and embrace through God's story, but not by having to make everyone's story sound the same. She suggests N.T. Wright's model of a one-act play still embraces this idea, as one "play" often weaves together plot and subplots that end up being just as much "the plot".

Another following Sunday (4 June 2014), when we discussed what biblical stories resonate with Auburn's story, gave opportunity for people to open their Bibles and explore which parts were most significant for them and the church, and fostered a conversation about what people most appreciate about Auburn. In small discussion groups and then with the congregation, people offered these passages as resonating strongly with Auburn:

- The Apostle Paul's story, who was persistent in ministry no matter what;
- Ruth who, like Israel, had her ups and downs, and who with Naomi had to leave her place, but who as a foreigner and alien came to a new place and belonged and was welcomed, like people who come to Auburn from all different sorts of backgrounds;
- The Psalms that speak of God offering a safe place and refuge in the wilderness (e.g., Psalms 46 and 91);
- Mary and Martha, who expressed warm welcome and hospitality, albeit in different ways (Luke 10:38–42);

- Noah's ark, which offered a home to different people and even animals (Genesis 6–8);
- Gospel stories of Jesus and his followers eating with different people (e.g., Luke 5:27–32);
- The early church's story in Acts sharing meals and Bible study (Acts 2:42), like AuburnHub's student community;
- The Prodigal Son and the father's non-judgmental welcome (Luke 15:11–32);
- The Mustard Tree and its creating hospitable space for the birds to nest (Matthew 13:31–32).

It was significant for the group to hear from one another that most people's stories resonated strongly with a theme of welcome and hospitality. For example, our Sunday Stuff co-coordinator Julia Rhyder had previously introduced the vision of the Mustard Tree to us. We were asking about our hopes as a church. Where would we most love to branch out? What would the kingdom of God look like in answer to our prayer, "Bring heaven to Hawthorn. Let your dream for our neighbourhood happen"? The parable of the Mustard Tree suggested not to hope to grow from a small seed into a huge tree, but to grow into a space that can be a safe place of inclusion and a hub of hospitality for all the stranded to find a place of belonging. It is not about impressive size or fancy structure, but the hospitality it offers.[25] Dreaming big when it comes to Mustard Tree hopes, therefore, is not to grow large, but to be generous with hospitality.

Jean Vanier's words resonated with us about his vision for church hospitality:

> In the midst of all the violence and corruption of the world God invites us today to create new places of belonging, places of sharing, of peace and of kindness, places were no-one needs to defend himself or herself; places where each one is loved and accepted with one's own fragility, abilities and disabilities. This is my vision for our churches: that they become places of belonging, places of sharing.[26]

Hospitality, especially to others who are different from us including international students, is an important way of improvising the life of Jesus in our neighbourhood.

One person added a non-biblical image of Auburn as like a "Clayton's church"; as the church you go to when you don't want to go to church (echoing the advertising slogan of the Clayton's drink — the drink you're having when you are not having a drink). We live in a post-Christian society where many people experience exclusion and loneliness. A dominant narrative is one of scarcity and self-sufficiency. Thus a community of generous inclusion is intrinsically a good news story to celebrate. It will be a worthwhile future exercise to invite AuburnLife to engage in deeper ways with the authority and example these Scripture stories offer for a countercultural witness of hospitality.

Open space questions

Discussing the narrative of Scripture and the narrative of our community also fed into a refreshed approach to Auburn's "Sunday Stuff"; our "AuburnWay" of fostering spirituality and worship. Over the last two years the church had become accustomed to an "Open Space" time of discussion after a "sermon" or interactive teaching time. Some Sundays we replace a teaching input, a "sermon" time, with invited congregational sharing. For example, one Sunday the preacher could not come because of family illness, and so we invited everyone to "bring-a-favourite-book" and share why we love it and how it engages with faith. That morning's discussion was profound and people are still talking about it (and comparing books). But we wanted to take all our gatherings, or "Sunday Stuff", to another level of encouraging one another in faith and mission, as well as to engage Scripture more deeply.

One change we adopted was to begin almost all our services with a "Connect" question. To connect afresh with God, one another, and the AuburnLife space, we have an open-ended question or two as people gather. For example:

- What is happening in your life and what is God doing in your life and neighbourhood that we can celebrate with you?
- Where have we seen signs of God's kingdom this week? Where have you longed to see signs of God's kingdom this week?
- What have you been learning about Jesus, faith, and life this last week? What are you curious about Jesus and what else would you like to be learning about and growing in?
- What has stuck with you about Jesus from last Sunday, or from reading John through this week?

These connecting questions and the conversation that flows from them at the beginning of our gatherings help us connect with the story of previous Sundays, the stories of people's lives, and the story of Scripture we want to improvise.

Moreover, after glimpsing the formative potential of Scripture's narrative, we decided to refocus our teaching times around reading and engaging the Bible. Woodward develops N.T. Wright's metaphor of reading Scripture as a five-act play that we improvise from and in, based on what God has done in the past and also where God is taking history in "making everything new" (Rev 21:5). He urges allowing what God has promised about the future to shape us:

> We can join God in writing a new future for the world by anticipating his future in the present. If God's future is the elimination of hunger and thirst, how are our economic practices at this moment anticipating the reality of abundance? If God's future is the elimination of weapons of war and having people live peacefully with each other, how should we treat our enemies at this moment? If God's future is renewed creation with clean air, fresh water and natural beauty, are we living sustainable lives in the present? Future-oriented living forces us to answer these questions in concrete ways.[27]

We wanted to regularly read and engage with Scripture and its narrative to see how we could continue to improvise that story, and to teach people to read and apply Scripture this way. Thus for several gatherings we have read the Bible and then asked two standard open-ended discussion questions:

a. What questions or response do you have about this part of our/God's story?

b. In what ways does this story connect with your/our story today, and how do we improvise and continue to live it?

We did this before any focused teaching time, so that we gave God and the people of God the first opportunity to speak into the gathering. The second question echoes the encouragement of N.T. Wright to see our church story as Act V of the five-act play that continues the biblical narrative. In asking that question, we want to create continuity with the opening invitation question of what God is doing in people's lives.

The following parts of the gathering would then structure around the text and its narrative, and respond to people's questions and discussion. A priority for worship leaders or "curators" has been to help people utilise their five senses and their eight intelligences.[28] We want AuburnLife to be a place for all cultures, all ages, all abilities, all stages of faith. Some people come with more doubts than faith, but we say that in a community of faith that is okay because we have faith and blessing to share.[29] As we pray, bring our offerings, discuss the passage further, sing in worship, and send each other out, the continuity of the gathering is the story of how we are continuing God's story.

Improvising a new future

It is important to understand the Bible and its narrative genre, rather than focusing on isolated verses. One of our leaders, Brad Jackel, who has a PhD in literature, has encouraged us to read the Bible as a literary text. When he preached recently he explained:

> I don't like thinking about Bible verses — there were no verse numbers originally — it is a pretty recent addition and like headings and red letters and all the other things we add to the Bible they change the way we read it. Among other things verse numbers encourage us to take things out of context and turn them into bumper stickers. I have just bought a Bible that doesn't have any verse numbers printed.[30]

The Bible is not so much a rulebook as a divine story about redemption. It is not an instruction manual for living life more comfortably, but a narrative that invites us to read ourselves into the ongoing story. It is "the story we find ourselves in", to borrow from the name of Brian McLaren's philosophical dialogue about the gospel.[31] Moreover, as McLaren says elsewhere, it engages with the most pressing crises of the story of our contemporary world. The Bible offers us resources to challenge. "Everything must change", since Jesus is better news than we had imagined and the Bible is potentially a more powerful story that models how God and people work together to transform society and avert self-destruction from the suicide machine of how the world is currently operating.[32] The beauty of this biblical story is that it invites us into a purpose greater than we had imagined. It invites us to live this story, not as isolated individuals but in solidarity and community with our sisters and brothers in the church universally, and also locally expressed in our congregation. The story calls us beyond ourselves as a church, which may not be as safe and reassuring as it sounds. N.T. Wright comments that the story is not supposed to have reassuring limits, but expansive growth for us and the kingdom:

God does not then want to put people into little boxes and keep them safe and sound. It is, after all, possible to be sound when you're sound asleep. I am not in favour of unsoundness; but soundness means health, and health means growth, and growth means life and vigour and new directions. The little boxes in which you put people and keep them under control are called coffins.[33]

Worship and Bible engagement, at their best, will breathe life into people and fire their imagination to change their world — by improvising and continuing the story of Jesus.

The ongoing renewal of our life and worship as a church comes from exploring what ways AuburnLife can continue to live into our biblical (and congregational and missional) narratives.

Darren Cronshaw is pastor of AuburnLife and Mission Catalyst-Researcher with Baptist Union of Victoria. He teaches as Professor of Missional Leadership and Head of Research with Australian Colleges of Ministries (SCD) and is an Honorary Research Fellow with Whitley College (University of Divinity) and Adjunct Professor with Swinburne Leadership Institute. Email: pastor@auburn.org.au

Conclusion

Darren Cronshaw and Darrell Jackson

In 2015, as we gathered this volume's contributions about Australian Baptist cultural diversity and worship, we both had the opportunity to travel and learn from some other contexts. Such opportunities continue to influence and shape our work as practical theologians and missiologists. The churches of Australia continue to be blessed by the presence of Christian sisters and brothers who have arrived in Australia to live, work, and worship alongside us. The culturally varied church life which emerges, not without its tensions, serves as a vital reminder that much remains to be done if our churches are to effectively minister and witness in the culturally diverse cities and towns of Australia.

Each of us has invested in this second volume of the *New Wineskins* series because we believe that the church is immeasurably stronger where it engages with the cultural riches of "every nation under the heavens".

During 2015, I (Darrell) travelled to Manila, Kuala Lumpur, Korea, and the UK. In each of these places I engaged with church and mission leaders from around the world. The range of local, regional, and global experiences that were shared in each of these venues was truly amazing.

In Korea I was privileged to lead the Bible Study for thirty Korean mission agency and church leaders and a further twenty-nine mission agency and church leaders from around the world. Together, sixty mission leaders reflected on the implications of the church growth that Luke reports in Acts 11: growth in a culturally diverse congregation. The Korean Global Mission Leaders' Forum (KGMLF) was intentional in its ethnic inclusivity: thirty Koreans and thirty non-Koreans from the USA, UK, Netherlands, Nigeria, Ghana, Brazil, and other Asians from Myanmar, India, and China. For such a small gathering this was a triumph of ethnic diversity and representation.

Korea has often been heralded as one of the more ethnically homogenous nations in the world with a cultural worldview that many in the West find challenging. My involvement with the KGMLF encouraged me to consider the rapidly changing nature of Korean society — increasingly open to the influence and impulses of the global church. As Koreans present at KGMLF became aware that I was on the faculty of Morling College, many approached me and expressed appreciation for the work of my colleague, Mike Frost, and his writings on missional theology. Nobody was more surprised than Mike to learn that he had such a wide readership in a land that many people might assume to be wedded irreversibly to the idea of the megachurch.

In Korea, it is Australian ideas (and those from elsewhere in the world) that introduce the element of cultural diversity and profoundly shape the worship experience of Korean Christians. This second volume of *New Wineskins* presents us with a more familiar set of portraits from our own backyard. However, it will be important for us to avoid letting their familiarity lull us into a sense that everything is therefore fine and that the Baptist churches of Australia have achieved the vision of a truly ethnically and culturally integrated life of worship and witness. Many of us will recognise that there is still a long way to go.

That could not have been better reinforced than with the presentation of the Director of the National Church Life Survey (NCLS) Dr Ruth Powell, at the 7th International Lausanne Researchers' Conference, meeting in Kuala Lumpur in 2015. Her presentation pointed to the cultural diversity of the wider family of churches in Australia and demonstrated that there is still work to be done in addressing misunderstanding, division, and a lack of cooperation. I'm personally grateful that elements of Ruth's presentation in Kuala Lumpur feature here in this volume, in an article co-authored with Ian Duncum.

As I've worked on editing each of the chapters in this volume, I've come to appreciate that there are many fine minds, open hearts, and willing hands which are engaging with the increasing cultural diversity of Australia and people who are working to ensure that this continues to be a source of enrichment for our shared life together in Christ as well as a resource for our Spirit-inspired ministry and mission to our culturally diverse neighbourhoods, workplaces, and families.

Also during 2015, I (Darren) travelled to Pretoria, South Africa, for a practical theology conference. The conference input was inspiring, but the country visit was especially insightful. In talking to local people, reading Archbishop Tutu's *No Future Without Forgiveness*, and as I learned about the country's history and its current political and social challenges, I realised that so much is related to cultural diversity and ethnic division. Sadly, this was reinforced by poor theology and the way churches worshipped, until a different story captured people's imaginations.

Conclusion

The Apartheid Museum had a special display on the life of Nelson Mandela. One of the displays celebrated how he had said: "I will pass through this world but once, and I do not want to divert from my task, which is to unite the nation". Of course Mandela's leadership was incredible in uniting the nation and bringing hope for a new day of reconciliation. The country made huge steps forward under his Presidency and the Truth and Liberation Commission. But most South Africans — black, white, and coloured — would say they have now taken a step backward, and that ethnic difference underlies many of the social challenges in the country.

I left South Africa with two strong convictions. Firstly, I was convinced that as Christians we need to offer prophetic leadership and compassionate service for the problems and dilemmas society faces. South Africa is in desperate need of that, it was obvious. But Australia also needs leaders from civil society and the church who will take an interest in issues that are challenging our neighbourhoods — not be preoccupied with what happens within the walls of the church.

Secondly, I realised that among the areas where we need more thoughtful theological reflection and practical action — whether in South Africa, Australia, or almost anywhere on the globe — are our approach to cultural diversity and how we relate interculturally, including how we shape the life of church and our worship together. That is why I enjoyed and appreciated reading the contributions in this volume.

There is still more work to be done — these topics demand our most careful theologising and best thinking. For example, another area we are convinced needs more attention is how our churches welcome and include the contributions of first generation migrants, and then how to best continue to connect with 1.5, second, and third generation young people in nurturing their faith and developing their leadership potential. That may be a key topic of our next National Baptist Symposium and the third *New Wineskins* volume.

The invitation to imagine and use new wineskins encourages us to be open to new forms and approaches of cooperating with what God is doing in our communities. In these *New Wineskins* volumes, we invite you to keep reflecting with us, as readers and contributors to future symposia or publications, what "new wineskins" are needed? And as the cultural diversity and disconnect from church increase in Australia, what are the needs and opportunities for transforming our churches and mission?

Endnotes

Australian Baptist Churches and the Marginalisation of Ethnicity

1. FaceBook post, 19th March 2014. I have chosen not to reveal the contributor's identity.
2. Oliver Buswell, *Slavery, Segregation, and Scripture* (Grand Rapids: Eerdmans, 1964).
3. See, for example, G.L. Byron, "Race, Ethnicity, and the Bible: Pedagogical Challenges and Curricular Opportunities", in *Teaching Theology and Religion*, 15, no.2, April (2012), 8.
4. Cited in Byron, *Teaching Theology and Religion*, 2012, 107.
5. D. Jacobs, "Ethnicity", in Moreau, S., ed. *Evangelical Dictionary of World Missions* (Grand Rapids: Baker, 2000), 323.
6. Ashby, 1998, cited in Prill, T., *Global Mission on Our Doorstep: Forced Migration and the Future of the Church* (Münster: MV Wissenschaft, 2008), 51.
7. Eric Barreto, "Theology and Ethnicity in the Acts of the Apostles", *Word and World*, 31, no.2, Spring (2011), 132.
8. Christopher J.H. Wright, *The Mission of God: Unlocking the Bible's Grand Narrative* (Leicester, UK: IVP, 2006), 455–456.
9. *Acta NGK*, 1857, 60, cited in Plaatjies-Van Huffel, M-A, and R. Vosloo, eds., *Reformed Churches in South Africa and the Struggle for Justice: Remembering 1960–1990* (Stellenbosch: African Sun Media, 2013), 334.
10. J.C. Pauw, *Anti-Apartheid Theology in the Dutch Reformed Family of Churches* (Amsterdam: Free University PhD, 2007), 232.
11. H. Richmond and M.D. Yang, eds. *Crossing Borders: Shaping Faith, Ministry and Identity in Multicultural Australia* (Sydney: UCA Assembly and Board of Mission, 2006), 313.
12. Darrell R. Jackson, "Europe and the Migrant Experience: Transforming Integration", in *Transformation*, 28, no.1, January (2011), 8–9.
13. Brian Edgar, *Christ and Multiculturalism* (Melbourne: Evangelical Alliance, 2007), 1.
14. Al Tizon, *Transformation after Lausanne: Radical Evangelical Mission in Global-Local Perspective* (Oxford: Regnum Press, 2008), 207.
15. Paul Freston, "Evangelicalism and Globalization", in Hutchinson, M. and Kalu, O., eds. *A Global Faith: Essays on Evangelicalism and Globalization* (Sydney: Centre for the Study of Australian Christianity, 1998), 72.
16. Dewi Hughes, "Following Jesus in a Broken World of Ethnic Identity", in *Evangelical Review of Theology*, 31, no.4 (2007), 331.
17. Lalsangkima Pachau, "Ethnic Identity and the Gospel of Reconciliation", in *Mission Studies* 26 (2009), 49.
18. J. Toews, "Paul on Ethnicity" in *Direction* 17, no.1, Spring (1988), 79.
19. Toews, "Paul on Ethnicity" in *Direction* 17, no.1, Spring (1988), 80.
20. Barreto, *Ethnic Negotiations: The Function of Race and Ethnicity in Acts 16* (Tübingen: Mohr Siebeck, 2010), 25.

21. Barreto, "Theology and Ethnicity", 2011, 131.
22. Barreto, "Theology and Ethnicity", 2011, 136–7.
23. Hughes, "Following Jesus…", 2007, 331–341.

Ministry in Urban Aboriginal Communities

1. This term is common place amongst Indigenous Australians as they refer to colonisation.
2. Rosalind Kidd, "The Biggest Broker of Them All: The State of Queensland and Aboriginal Labour" (paper presented at the Eighth Australian Labour History Conference, 3 October 2003, Queensland College of Art, South Bank, Brisbane, 2003).
3. Indigenous peoples operate under a system of associations. Therefore, since the Australian political system is seen as a non-Indigenous initiative, the association is then that Christianity is likewise a non-Indigenous initiative because the "same people" are involved in administering it, often in the same way historically (i.e. forced involvement and imposition: politicians make laws governing society and these must be adhered to; children on missions during 1960–70s were forced to go to Sunday School).
4. The landmark 1997 report, *Bringing Them Home*, told the stories of many Indigenous children and communities devastated by government policies and laws which allowed Indigenous children to be taken from their families. The report estimated that "between one in three and one in ten Indigenous children were forcibly removed from their families between 1910 and 1970". www.hreoc.gov.au/Social_Justice/info_sheet.html
5. Rowena MacDonald, *Between Two Worlds* (Alice Springs: IAD, 1995), 32.
6. John Harris, *One Blood. 200 Years of Aboriginal Encounter with Christianity: A Story of Hope* (Sutherland NSW: Albatross, 1990), 609.
7. Reconciliation and Social Justice Library, "National Report Volume 2-11.12 Aboriginal Identity", www.austlii.edu.au/au/special/rsjproject/rsjlibrary/rciadic/national/vol2/61.html. Accessed 6 November 2007.
8. The Aboriginal and Torres Strait Islander population predominantly lives in Australia's most populous areas, with about 60 percent living in major cities and inner regional areas, and just over 20 percent living in remote and very remote areas: http://www.abs.gov.au/ausstats/abs@.nsf/latestProducts/3238.0.55.001Media%20Release1June%202011
9. Ivan Jordan, *Their Way: Towards an Indigenous Warlpiri Christianity* (Darwin, NT: Charles Darwin University, 2003), 16.
10. Issa Diab, "The Christian Faith and Culture during the First Years of the Church. A Pattern for Making Theology for Other Cultures: Prospects and Retrospects of Theological Education in the Twenty-First Century", *International Congregational Journal* 6, no.1 (2006), 19.
11. Jordan, *Their Way*, 61.
12. www.tsra.gov.au/the-torres-strait/events/coming-of-the-light.aspx. The website also states that, "this is a significant day for Torres Strait Islanders, who are predominantly of Christian faith, and religious and cultural ceremonies across Torres Strait and mainland Australia are held on 1 July each year".
13. Examples include Pastor Sir Douglas Nicholls, (www.kooriweb.org/foley/heroes/nicholls.html,) and the church's role in aiding the establishment of what is now known as NAIDOC (National Aboriginal and Islander Days Observance Committee) Week celebrations, www.naidoc.org.au/history.

14. Charles H. Kraft, "Culture, Worldview and Contextualization", in *Perspectives on the World Christian Movement: A Reader*, ed. Ralph D. Winter and Steven C. Hawthorne (Pasadena: William Carey Library, 1999), 384.
15. Graham Paulson, "Towards an Aboriginal Theology", *Pacifica: Australasian Theological Studies* 19, no.3 (2006), 310–320.
16. See Billy Williams, "A Theology of Evangelism", (Malyon College, 2013).
17. A.H. Maslow, "A Theory of Human Motivation", *Psychological Review* 50(1943), 380–81.
18. Raymond F. Collins, *The Many Faces of the Church* (New York: Crossroad, 2003).
19. Kraft, "Culture, Worldview and Contextualization", 384.
20. Paulson, "Towards an Aboriginal Theology", 311.
21. Gil Cann, "Belonging or Believing?" John Mark Ministries, http://www.jmm.org.au/articles/8522.htm.
22. Steve Taylor, *The Out of Bounds Church?* (Grand Rapids: Zondervan, 2005), 116.
23. David J. Bosch, *Transforming Mission: Paradigm Shifts in Theology of Mission* (Maryknoll: Orbis Books, 1991), 23.
24. Michael Frost and Alan Hirsch, *The Shaping of Things To Come* (Peabody: Hendrickson, 2003), 74.
25. Kraft, "Culture, Worldview and Contextualization", 389.
26. Diab, "The Christian Faith and Culture during the First Years of the Church. A Pattern for Making Theology for Other Cultures: Prospects and Retrospects of Theological Education in the Twenty-First Century", 12.
27. Jordan, *Their Way*, 71.
28. Jordan, *Their Way*, 74.
29. Jordan, *Their Way*, 71.
30. Rodney Stark and William Sims Bainbridge, *The Future of Religion: Secularization, revival, and Cult Formation* (Berkley: University of California Press, 1985), 305–345.
31. Michael K. Roberts and James D. Davidson, "The Nature and Sources of Religious Involvement", *Review of Religious Research* 25(1984), 347.
32. John Bellamy et al., *Why People Don't Go to Church* (Adelaide: Openbook, 2002), 34–40.
33. John Bellamy et al., *Enriching Church Life* (Adelaide: Openbook, 2006), 52.
34. Frost and Hirsch, *The Shaping of Things To Come*, 27.
35. Bosch, "Evangelism: Theological Currents and Cross-Currents Today", in *The Study of Evangelism: Exploring a Missional Practice of the Church*, ed. Paul W. Chilcote and Lacye. C. Warner (Grand Rapids, MI: Eerdmans, 2008), loc. 423.
36. Peter Kaldor and John Bellamy, "Fresh through the Door: Newcomers to the Church Life in Australia", in *Joining and Leaving Religion: Research Perspectives*, ed. Leslie J. Francis and Y. J. Katz (Leominster, England: Gracewing, 2000).
37. Nichols in Peter Kaldor et al., *Shaping Our Future: Characteristics of Vital Congregations* (Adelaide: Openbook, 1997), 115.
38. Harris, *One Blood*, 71.
39. Mark Connor, "Evangelism for Non-Evangelists", in *A Passion for Evangelism: Turning Vision into Action*, ed. B. Hughes and J. Bellamy (Adelaide: Open Book., 2004), 161.
40. Quoted in Bosch, "Evangelism", loc.423.

41. T. Sarbin and N.J. Adler, "Self-Reconstitution Process: A Preliminary Report", *Psychoanalytic Review* 57(1970).
42. Bosch, "Evangelism", loc 423.
43. Kim Hammond, "Characteristics of a Missional Church", John Mark Ministries, http://www.jmm.org.au/articles/567.htm.
44. A song by Aboriginal singer Kev Carmody contains the lyrics, *"And race is a contradiction that is understood by none but mostly their left hand holds the Bible, the right hand holds the gun... Woah black woman thou shalt not steal; Hey black man thou shalt not steal. We're gonna civilize your black barbaric lives; And we'll teach you how to kneel. But your history couldn't hide the genocide; The hypocrisy that was real. For your Jesus said you're supposed to give the oppressed a better deal; We say to you: yes our land thou shalt not steal. Whoa, yeah our land you better heal."* "Through the lyrics of 'Thou shalt not steal' Carmody draws attention to the hypocrisy of British settlers who brought Christianity to Indigenous Australians, including the commandment prohibiting theft, and yet took the land that Indigenous people had inhabited for more than 60,000 years." <www.australianscreen.com.au/Otles/blood--brothers-- little--things/clip3/>
45. Michael Frost, *Exiles: Living Missionally in a Post-Christian Culture* (Massachusetts: Hendrickson, 2006), 315.
46. Laurence R. Iannaccone, "Rational Choice: Framework for the Social Scientific Study of Religion", in *Rational Choice Theory and Religion*, ed. L. A. Young (New York: Routledge, 1997).
47. Lewis R. Rambo, "The Psychology of Conversion", in *Handbook of Religious Conversion*, ed. H. N. Malony and S. Southard (Birmingham, AL: Religious Education Press, 1992).
48. Sarbin and Adler, "Self-Reconstitution Process".
49. Graham Cooke and Gary Goodell, *Permission Granted To Do Church Differently in the 21st Century* (Shippensburg, PA: Destiny Image, 2006), 90.
50. Bosch, *Transforming Mission*, 498.
51. Joon Sik Park, "Hospitality as Context for Evangelism", *Missiology: An International Review*, 30, no.3 (2002), 386.
52. Harris, *One Blood*, 890.
53. James Lawrence, *Growing Leaders: Reflections on Leadership, Life and Jesus* (Abingdon: Bible Reading Fellowship, 2004), 224.
54. Aubrey Malphurs and Will Mancini, *Building Leaders: Blueprints for Developing Leadership at Every Level of Your Church* (Grand Rapids: Baker, 2004), 31.
55. R. Foreman, J. Jones, and B. Miller, *The Leadership Baton: An Intentional Strategy for Developing Leaders in Your Church* (Grand Rapids: Zondervan, 2004), 24.
56. Paulson, "Towards an Aboriginal Theology", 311.
57. Harris, *One Blood*, 869.

Baptists Responding to Cultural Diversity

1. Australian Bureau of Statistics, *Australia, Census of Population and Housing Basic Community Profile*, Tables B09 and B11, Catalogue number 2001.0 (Canberra: ABS, 2011), http://www.censusdata.abs.gov.au/census_services/getproduct/census/2011/communityprofile/0?opendocument&navpos=220 ; Department of Immigration and Citizenship, *Australia's Migration Trends 2011–12 at a glance* (Belconnen, ACT: Department of Immigration and Citizenship, 2013), http://www.immi.gov.au/media/publications/statistics/immigration-update/australian-migration-trends-2011-12-glance.pdf

2. Australian Bureau of Statistics, *Reflecting a Nation: Stories from the 2011 Census, 2012–2013*, Catalogue number 2071.0 (Canberra: ABS, 21/6/2012), http://www.abs.gov.au/ausstats/abs@.nsf/Lookup/2071.0main+features902012-2013
3. Ruth Powell, *2011 NCLS Operations Survey* [computer file] (Sydney: NCLS Research, 2011); ABS, Tables B10a and B10b.
4. Powell, (2014) [computer file], 2011 NCLS Attender Sample Survey N v2. Sydney, Australia: NCLS Research.
5. Powell, (2011) [computer file], 2011 NCLS Operations Survey. Sydney, Australia: NCLS Research.
6. Miriam Pepper, Sam Sterland, and Ruth Powell, (2015), Methodological Overview of the Study of Wellbeing through the National Church Life Survey. *Mental Health, Religion & Culture* (in press).
7. Philip J. Hughes, "The Persistence of Religion: What the Census Tells Us", *Pointers*, Vol. 22, no. 3, September (2012); Philip Hughes, "The Impact of Recent Immigration on Religious Groups in Australia", *Pointers*. Vol. 22, no.4, December (2012)
8. Philip J. and Darren Cronshaw, *Baptists in Australia*, 72; ABS, *Reflecting a Nation*.
9. Affiliation is not a straightforward measure for Australian Baptists in terms of migration inflow. That is, migrants who are Baptists in their country of birth don't necessarily become Baptists in Australia. Some non-Baptist Christian migrants attend Baptist churches in Australia, and some migrants from non-Christian or non-religious backgrounds become Christians and attend Baptist churches. Accurate data in these various categories is difficult to source.
10. Hughes and Cronshaw, *Baptists in Australia: A Church with a Heritage and a Future* (Nunawading, Vic: Christian Research Association, 2013), 72.
11. Hughes and Cronshaw, *Baptists in Australia*, 75; ABS, *Australia, Census* 2001 and 2011.
12. Hughes and Cronshaw, *Baptists in Australia*, 76.
13. Andrew Markus, *Immigration*, (Melbourne: Monash University, 2014), http://monash.edu/mapping-population/public-opinion/fact-sheets/immigration-intake-fact-sheet.pdf
14. Elizabeth Vreugdenhil, *Becoming a Diverse Multicultural Church in Central Adelaide: A Case Study* (paper presented at Triennial Conference of the Australian Association for Mission Studies, Tabor Adelaide, Adelaide, 2–5 October, 2014), 4.
15. Gordon Stewart, *Welcoming the Stranger: Addressing Issues of Ethos and Praxis in Multi-Cultural Church Communities* (paper presented at Triennial Conference of the Australian Association for Mission Studies, Tabor Adelaide, Adelaide, 2–5 October, 2014), 2.
16. David Turnbull, *Clergy and Diasporic Voices in Australia: Deepening the Conversation through Cultural* Intelligence (paper presented at Triennial Conference of the Australian Association for Mission Studies, Tabor Adelaide, Adelaide, 2–5 October, 2014).
17. Ian Duncum, N. Hancock, Miriam Pepper, and Ruth Powell, Church Involvement in Migrant Ministry, NCLS Research Fact Sheet 14008. (Adelaide: Mirrabooka Press, 2014)
18. NCLS Research, "Overseas Migrants" http://www.ncls.org.au/default.aspx?sitemapid=2293
19. K. Castle, 2001 NCLS Operations Survey. Sydney, Australia: NCLS Research. Castle, K., (2006) [computer file], 2006 NCLS Operations Survey. Sydney, Australia: NCLS Research.
20. R. Miranti, B. Nepal, and J. McNamara, Income and Wealth Report Issue 27 — Calling Australia Home. (Bruce, ACT: AMP.NATSEM (The National Centre for Social and Economic Modelling), 2010), 3, http://www.natsem.canberra.edu.au/storage/AMP_NATSEM_27.pdf

21. Darren Cronshaw, Ner Dah, Si Khia, Arohn Kuung, Japheth Lian, Stacey Wilson and Meewon Yang, "God called us here for a reason" …Karen and Chin Baptist Churches in Victoria: Mission from the Margins of a Diaspora Community (An Australian Case Study in Diaspora Mission) (paper presented at Triennial Conference of the Australian Association for Mission Studies, Tabor Adelaide, Adelaide, 2–5 October, 2014), 4–5.
22. ABS, Australia, Census, Table B11.
23. Duncum, Hancock, and Powell, Local Church Engagement with Non-English-Speaking Churches, NCLS Research Fact Sheet 14009. (Adelaide: Mirrabooka Press, 2014)
24. M. Yang, "Ways of Being a Multicultural Church: An Evaluation of Multicultural Church Models in the Baptist Union of Victoria" (MTh Thesis, Parkville, Vic: Whitley College (Melbourne College of Divinity), 2012), 23–24. A deeper examination of models for multicultural ministry can be found in Duncum, I., Pepper, M., Hancock, N. and Powell, R. *A Comparison of the Vitality of Monocultural and Multicultural Churches*, Occasional Paper 24. (Sydney: NCLS Research, 2014).
25. Yang, "Ways", 30.
26. NCLS Research, "Overseas Migrants" http://www.ncls.org.au/default.aspx?sitemapid=2293; see for example Samuel Chan and Kim Chan, *A Mission of Second Generation (Australian Born Chinese (ABC)) in South Australian Migrant Churches: Dealing with Unintentional Marginalisation due to Confucian values* (paper presented at Triennial Conference of the Australian Association for Mission Studies, Tabor Adelaide, Adelaide, 2–5 October, 2014).
27. Noel Connolly, "Growing a Truly Multicultural Australia Catholic Church" (paper presented at Triennial Conference of the Australian Association for Mission Studies, Tabor Adelaide, Adelaide, 2–5 October, 2014).

Being the Church without Four Walls

1. Alister E. McGrath, *Christian Theology: An Introduction*. 5th ed. (West Sussex: Wiley-Blackwell, 2011), 375–399.
2. McGrath, 375.
3. McGrath, 375.
4. Joseph A. Komonchak, *Who Are the Church?* The Père Marquette Lecture in Theology. (Milwaukee: Marquette University Press, 2008), 31–32.
5. Aubrey Malphurs, *Planting Growing Churches for the 21st Century: A Comprehensive Guide for New Churches and Those Desiring Renewal*. (Grand Rapids: Baker Books, 2004), 24.
6. E. Swanson and R. Rusaw, *The Externally Focused Quest: Becoming the Best Church for the Community*. (San Francisco: Jossey-Bass, 2010), 39.
7. Gil-Soo Han, "Korean Christianity in Multicultural Australia", *Studies in World Christianity* 10, no. 1(2004), 114–135.
8. Elisabeth Gerle, "Multicultural Communities: Dilemmas and Prospects", *Swedish Missiological Themes* 90, no. 4 (2002), 485–500.
9. Gerle, 486.
10. Graham Kings, "Multicultural Communities: Identity and Diversity", *Swedish Missiological Themes* 9, no. 4 (2002), 501–10.

Strengthening Intercultural Ministry in Local Congregations

1. We are sympathetic to, and have experience of, the ministry challenges of pastors, mission agencies, and theological academies. We aim to write sympathetically but also with a challenge to all parties addressed in this chapter.
2. Whether or not ethnicity is a socially defined construct is an issue for another paper. For the sake of this argument, we choose to use a commonly understood definition of ethnicity which implies deeply rooted difference.
3. Peter C. Earley and Soon Ang, *Cultural Intelligence: Individual Interactions Across Cultures*, (Palo Alto, CA: Stanford University Press, 2003). See also Douglas K. Detterman and Robert J. Sternberg, eds., *What is Intelligence? Contemporary Viewpoints on its nature and Definition* (Norwood, NJ: Ablex, 1986).
4. David Livermore, *Cultural Intelligence: improving your CQ to engage our multicultural world* (Grand Rapids, IL: Baker Books, 2009)
5. The passages discussed are just some of many in the New Testament we could have selected. One could point to the entire ministry of Jesus as a ministry of inclusion; as well as passages such as Acts 10 and the dream of Peter, Galatians 3:28, or whole sections of some of the epistles. For our purposes, though, we have highlighted a few that particularly strike us as pertinent to good pastoral practice.
6. N.T. Wright, "Paul and the People of God: Whence and Whither Pauline Studies and the Life of the Church." http://feeds.feedburner.com/TheNTWrightPodcast.
7. The Greek word *ethne* used in Matthew 28:19 is sometimes translated "peoples" or "tribes" or "nations". It has the sense of an all-encompassing term incorporating both nations and smaller, linguistically and culturally unique groups. It is further added to in Revelation 7:9 with various parallel terms encompassing almost every possible variety of Greek word for people groups. It is this latter verse that calls us toward a future where each community has something culturally unique to bring to the throne in worship. This vision of the future ought to drive our present praxis. See for example, Philip Edgcumbe Hughes, *The Book of Revelation: A Commentary* (Grand Rapids, MI: Eerdmans, 1990), 95.
8. Miroslaf Volf, *Exclusion and Embrace: A Theological Exploration of Identity, Otherness, and Reconciliation* (Nashville: Abingdon Press, 1996), 51, 54, 67.
9. Kenneth Bailey, *Proclamation, Justice, Compassion: A Message to Strangers from the Valley* (Minneapolis, MN: Fortress Press, 1999), *Church & Society*, 90, no.1, 106.
10. Bailey, *Proclamation*, 106.
11. Kenneth Bailey, *Poet and Peasant and through Peasant Eyes: A Literary-Cultural Approach to the Parables of Luke* (Grand Rapids, MI: Eerdmans, 1983), 42.
12. A helpful text in this respect is the story of the Good Samaritan. This parable is played against a background ripe with ethnic and tribal tension. It presents to us the naked "everyman", free of his ethnic/tribal clothes (Bailey, *Through Peasant Eyes*, 42). It calls us to join with others "not like us" (the Samaritan), to care for the person without a passport or other identifiable features, broken and wounded and in our path. We often state that this parable is at the heart of Christian love, but we wonder if our congregations have fully grasped some of its cross-cultural implications. Is it possible that part of what Jesus is saying here is that we have to reach out to people we don't easily relate to and serve with people who are culturally different? Furthermore, the lawyer in the story is called to view the enemy Samaritan as someone on whom the grace of God is at work and who therefore has things to teach the Jewish people (Luke 10:27).

13. Ralph P. Martin, *The Epistle of Paul to the Philippians: An Introduction and Commentary* (Wheaton: Tyndale 1969), 95.
14. Craig Van Gelder, "The Future of the Discipline of Missiology: A Brief Overview of Current Realities and Future Possibilities", *International Bulletin of Missionary Research*, 38, no.1 (Jan 2014).

Drinking New Wine Together

1. Sugirtharajah writes: "There has been a marked hesitancy to critically evaluate the impact of the empire among systematic theologians, both during and after the European expansion". He goes on: "While other disciplines have grappled with the wider cultural implications of the empire, European colonialism has never been a popular subject for theological enquiry in Western discourse". Rasiah S. Sugirtharajah, *Postcolonial Reconfigurations: An Alternative Way of Reading the Bible and Doing Theology* (London: SCM, 2003), 143. This chapter is a modest attempt to offer little more than a starting point for a new conversation amongst Baptists, especially in Australia.
2. There are a number of Australian Baptist scholars who have explored this vexed question of Baptist identity in recent years. For example, see the series of three papers prepared by David Parker for the Baptist World Alliance, David Parker, "Mapping a 21st-Century Global Baptist Identity" (2013). http://www.dparker.net.au/parkerbapident.pdf and Ken Manley, "A Survey of Baptist World Alliance Conversations with Other Churches and Some Implications for Baptist Identity" (2002). My discussion of identity here is not aiming to provide a definitive answer to the question "What is Baptist identity?" but to contribute to the conversation by bringing the postcolonial context to the question. As should become clear from this chapter, to ask the question about Baptist identity with an assumption that the answer can be found relies on an objectivist, positivist methodology and a fixed ontology — none of which I support.
3. The field of postcolonial studies — which I take to include the broad range of postcolonial fields such as postcolonial literary criticism, postcolonial biblical criticism, postcolonial theory etc. — is complex, diverse, and the writing often turgid. In a chapter such as this, there are two immediate risks. Firstly, the treatment of postcolonialism and its application may be overly simplistic and superficial. Secondly, in an attempt to traverse the tricky terrain, the writing may mirror some of the more difficult theorising and become almost unintelligible to the uninformed reader. I will do my best to avoid both of these risks, but fear I will, at times, become victim to both.
4. Of course, after Foucault, it is difficult to grasp for some kind of fixed and uncomplicated origin. See, Michel Foucault, "Nietzsche, Genealogy, History", in *Language, Counter-Memory, Practice: Selected Essays and Interviews*, ed. D.F. Bouchard (Ithaca, NY: Cornell University Press, 1977).
5. The rise in Public Theology is an example of this. See footnote 3 in Doug Hynd, "Public Theology after Christ and Culture: Post-Christendom Trajectories", in *Christian Mission in the Public Square* (Canberra: Australian Centre for Christianity and Culture, 2008), 3. Other evidence can be gleaned from books such as Stuart Murray, *Church after Christendom* (Milton Keynes, UK: Paternoster, 2004). So to the "Fresh Expressions" movement in the Anglican Church, see for example, Graham Cray, *Mission-Shaped Church: Church Planting and Fresh Expressions of Church in a Changing Context* (London, UK: Church House, 2004).
6. This is not to say that the church today does not enjoy privilege or is floundering on the margins. The church still holds more power in the West and in many of the former colonies than other religions and belief systems.

7. As one might expect, there exists a wide variety of opinions as to how one might understand these texts. My point here is not to provide an exegesis; I do not have the expertise to do so nor is it my particular task here. A synopsis of many of the varying positions can be found in Joseph F. Mali, "Two Sayings on the 'New' and the 'Old': Mark 2:21–22 in Context" (PhD, Fordham University, 2009).
8. Matthew 9:14–17; Mark 2:18–22; Luke 5:36–39.
9. Suzanne Watts Henderson, "What Is Old? What Is New? A Reconsideration of Garments and Wineskins", *Horizons in Biblical Theology* 34, no. 2 (2012), 118.
10. Indeed Jeffrey, in reflecting on Jesus' comment that the old wine is more palatable, writes, "A question thus remains about how to understand Jesus' saying at this point. Perhaps he is just saying that he understands their [the Pharisees'] resistance to change". David L. Jeffrey, *Luke* (Grand Rapids, MI: Brazos, 2012), 84.
11. Indeed, many scholars cite the critique of fixed representations in *Orientalism* (London: Penguin, 2003) as a key moment in the development of postcolonial studies.
12. Ania Loomba, *Colonialism/Postcolonialism* (London, UK: Routledge, 2005), 12.
13. Leela Gandhi, *Postcolonial Theory: A Critical Introduction* (Delhi, India: Oxford University Press, 1999), 3.
14. For an example, see Kwasi Wiredu, "Toward Decolonizing African Philosophy and Religion", in *Society and Politics in Africa, Volume 14: Inculturation and Postcolonial Discourse in African Theology*, ed. Edward P. Antonio (New York: Peter Lang, 2006).
15. Gandhi, *Postcolonial Theory*, 122.
16. Frantz Fanon, *The Wretched of the Earth* (London, UK: Penguin, 2001). See especially chapters 3 and 4.
17. Luis Galanes Valldejuli, "Are We There Yet? The Tension between Nativism and Humanism in Fanon's Writings", *Human Architecture: Journal of the Sociology of Self-Knowledge* 5 (2007), 63.
18. Edward W. Said, *Culture and Imperialism* (New York: Knopf, 1993), 277.
19. Sugirtharajah, *Postcolonial Reconfigurations*, 123.
20. Homi K. Bhabha, *The Location of Culture* (London, UK: Routledge, 1994), 4.
21. Rasiah S. Sugirtharajah, *The Bible and Empire: Postcolonial Explorations* (Cambridge: Cambridge University Press, 2005), 3. Kang also argues that postcolonial theology must include hypersensitivity as a characteristic of its endeavour. See Namsoon Kang, "Theology from a Space Where Postcolonialism and Theology Intersect", *Concilium* 2013, no. 2 (2013), 67.
22. Pui-lan Kwok, *Postcolonial Imagination and Feminist Theology* (Louisville, KY: Westminster John Knox Press, 2005), 63: "There are several characteristics of postcolonial criticism: (1) it challenges the totalizing forms of Western interpretation, exposing its co-optation by imperial interests and destabilizing its frame of meaning; (2) it is a counterhegemonic discourse, paying special attention to the hidden and neglected voices in the Bible; (3) it places the Bible within the multifaith context of many Third World situations; (4) it encourages and welcomes contributions from marginalized groups that have not been fully heard: the Dalits, the indigenous peoples, the migrants, people in diaspora and in borderland, and especially women in these communities; and (5) it debates with and draws insights from other hermeneutical frameworks, such as postmodernism."
23. Sugirtharajah writes that postcolonialism adopts "a combination of clashing and contradictory voices from literary theory, philology, psychology, anthropology, political science, and feminist studies, with a view to exposing the collusive nature of Western historiography and its hidden

support for imperialism". R. S. Sugirtharajah, *Exploring Postcolonial Biblical Criticism: History, Method, Practice* (Chichester, West Sussex, UK; Malden, MA: Wiley-Blackwell, 2012), 13.

24. Kwok, *Postcolonial Imagination and Feminist Theology*, 2–3.
25. Amos Yong, "Many Tongues, Many Practices: Pentecost and Theology of Mission at 2010", in *Mission after Christendom: Emergent Themes in Contemporary Mission*, ed. Ogbu Kalu, Peter Vethanayagamony, and Edmund Chia (Louisville, KY: Westminster John Knox Press, 2010), 44.
26. Bruce T. Gourley, "Baptists and Theology — Broad, Deep, and Diverse", *Baptist History & Heritage* 47, no. 2 (2012), 2.
27. C. D. Tew, "A Varied Theology", *Baptist History & Heritage* 47, no. 2 (2012), 4.
28. Derek Christopher Hatch, "E.Y. Mullins, George W. Truett, and a Baptist Theology of Nature and Grace", (University of Dayton, 2011).
29. Paul S. Fiddes, *Tracks and Traces: Baptist Identity in Church and Theology* (Milton Keynes, UK: Paternoster, 2003), 3.
30. Furthermore, I would suggest that "diversity" is not a position which Baptists seek to hold philosophically or doctrinally like they may do with, say, baptism. Rather, I take Baptist diversity to be a historical "reality" resulting from other more philosophically held positions such as the autonomy of the local church.
31. H. Leon McBeth, *The Baptist Heritage* (Nashville, TN: Broadman, 1987), 19.
32. McBeth, *Baptist Heritage*, 20.
33. It is interesting to note that Edward Said has been criticised for essentialising the Occident or "Europe" in his seminal work *Orientalism*, despite the fact that this book mounts a critique of the essentialising of the Orient. However, the very fact of the critique is evidence of the way in which postcolonial scholarship invites the constant critique of essentialisations – whether of "Europe", "Africa", "Islam" or anything else. Indeed, it is one of the tensions in an essay such as this that is seeking to argue for the difference which constitutes Baptists from within which, in turn, risks essentialising difference itself. A critical attentiveness to the movements of difference is required in an attempt to avoid such essentialisations. Said's response to this criticism can be read in the 'Afterword' of the revised edition, Edward Said, *Orientalism* (London, UK: Penguin, 2003), pp.329ff.
34. McBeth, *Baptist Heritage*, 21.
35. Robert E. Johnson, *A Global Introduction to Baptist Churches* (Cambridge, UK: Cambridge University Press, 2010), 428.
36. Kwok writes, "The colonial process, as Stuart Hall has pointed out, is doubly inscribed, affecting both the metropolis [the coloniser] and the colonies, and the decolonizing process also restructures both, though in different ways". Kwok, *Postcolonial Imagination and Feminist Theology*, 3.
37. Brian Haymes, cited in Fiddes, *Tracks and Traces*, 17.
38. Johnson, *Global Introduction to Baptist Churches*, 389.
39. While this is certainly the case in the USA, it is also true in Australia. Indeed, highlighting the diversity within the Baptist tradition is core to this chapter's argument.
40. Ken Manley, *From Woolloomooloo to Eternity: A History of Australian Baptists, Vol. 2. A National Church in a Global Community (1914–2005)*, vol. 16 (Milton Keynes, UK: Paternoster, 2006), 160–65.
41. See R. Stanton Norman, *The Baptist Way: Distinctives of a Baptist Church* (Nashville, TN: Broadman & Holman Publishers, 2005).

42. Sugirtharajah, *Postcolonial Reconfigurations*, 100.
43. Sugirtharajah, *Exploring Postcolonial Biblical Criticism*, 13.
44. For a discussion on reading the Bible in community for the purpose of formation as opposed to gaining information, see Frank D. Rees, "Enabling Congregations To Become Theological Communities", *Evangelical Review of Theology* 30, no. 1 (2006).
45. Brian J. Walsh, "Transformation: Dynamic Worldview or Repressive Ideology?" *Journal of Education and Christian Belief* 4, no. 2 (2000), 107–108.
46. Paul Fiddes writes, "It seems to be a mark of Baptist life to adapt to the present and constantly seek to reinvent itself, which at best can be seen as openness to the Spirit of God, and at worst, as a neglect of the lessons which the Spirit has wanted to teach the church during its history". Cited in Manley, "A Survey of Baptist World Alliance Conversations with Other Churches."
47. Yong, "Many Tongues, Many Practices", 57.
48. Of course, concern for the marginalised is prominent in the biblical narrative.

Welcoming the Stranger

1. http://www.teara.govt.nz/en/maori-pakeha-relations/page-5.
2. NZ census statistics, 2013: Quickstats-culture-identity.pdf.
3. http://www.stats.govt.nz/Census/2013-census/profile-and-summary-reports/qstats-culture-identity-auck-mr.aspx
4. It is acknowledged that the statistics derived from censuses relating to religious adherence, and in particular with affiliation with the "Christian religion", need often to be evaluated carefully. Such data are useful for the way they indicate trends within our community contexts to which missional responses can be made.
5. http://www.stats.govt.nz/Census/2013-census/profile-and-summary-reports/quickstats-culture-identity/religion.aspx
6. Over the 12-year period the number of adherents of non-Christian religions increased from 144,360 to 357,000, an increase of almost 250 percent.
7. In our major cities, it is often easy to name suburbs that have a predominance of people of a certain ethnicity.
8. Leviticus 19:34.
9. Numbers 15:15, and see also Exodus 22:21; Leviticus 25:35; Deuteronomy 24:19.
10. Matthew 5:46.
11. 1 Corinthians 9:20–22.
12. Galatians 3:26–28.
13. Ephesians 2:14–15 within the wider context of 2:11–22.
14. Paul, for example, repeatedly encourages both Jewish and Gentile believers in the community in Rome to acknowledge their need of the other, recognise their interdependence, and value the mutuality of their relationship.
15. Romans 11; 13:8–10; 14–15.
16. Alan Hirsch, *The Forgotten Ways* (Grand Rapids, MI: Brazos Press, 2006), 34–35.
17. Michael Frost and Alan Hirsch, *The Shaping of Things To Come* (Peabody, MA: Hendrickson, 2003), 17.
18. Ibid.10.

19. Hirsch, *Forgotten Ways*, 128.
20. Frost and Hirsch, *Shaping*, 12. "Messianic" and "apostolic" are two further descriptors of the missional church provided by the authors. "Messianic" connotes the worldview of Jesus the Messiah who did not see the world in dualistic terms (sacred/secular) but as "holistic and integrated". "Apostolic" describes a leadership style that is not hierarchical but rather a "flat-leadership community" releasing the diverse giftings mentioned in Ephesians 4:11–12.
21. David Bosch, *Transforming Mission* (Maryknoll, NY: Orbis, 2011), 400.
22. Paul Hiebert, "The Category 'Christian' in the Mission Task", in *Anthropological Reflections on Missiological Issues*; Bruce Bradshaw, in *Bridging the Gap*; Frost and Hirsch in *The Shaping of Things To Come*; Dave Andrews in *Christi-Anarchy*.
23. Dave Andrews, "Paradigms of Salvation", *Stimulus*, 7, no.4 (Nov 1999), 20.
24. Dave Andrews, *Christi-Anarchy: Discovering a Radical Spirituality of Compassion* (Armidale: Tafina Press, 1999), 67.
25. Matthew 16:24, Luke 14:27.
26. Andrews, *Christi-Anarchy*, 67–68.
27. Gene Daniels, "Event-speech as a Form of Missionary Education", *Evangelical Missions Quarterly*, 44, no. 1 (2008) 80–87.
28. Andrew Walls, *The Missionary Movement in Christian History: Studies in the Transmission of the Faith*, (Maryknoll, NY: Orbis, 1996), 3–15.
29. See James Engel and Wilbert Norton *What's Gone Wrong with the Harvest?* (Grand Rapids, MI: Zondervan, 1975).
30. See Hirsch for a more recent formulation of the scale of cultural distance, *Forgotten Ways*, 56–57.

New Parishes for Anglicans and Baptists?

1. Thomas Picketty, *Capital in the Twenty-First Century* (Cambridge MA: Belknap/Harvard, 2014). See pp. 174, 178 for graphs showing Australia following the standard western U shape of rising inequality rates. My review essay on Piketty's *Capital* is in *Zadok Perspectives* 128, Spring 2015, 15–20.
2. In a report released for the Davos forum by Oxfam 20/1/15. http://www.abc.net.au/news/2015-01-20/oxfam-say-wealth-inequality-joblessness-on-the-rise/6027744
3. www.nytimes.com/2015/10/19/business/international/chinas-Growth-Slows-to-6.9.htm
4. Mike Steketee, "How John Howard's tax cuts undid his protégé Tony Abbott", Dec 20, 2014. https://www.thesaturdaypaper.com.au/...john-howards-tax.../14189940001389
5. See Gordon Preece, "Don't Lean on Us, We Won't Be Your Friend", *Zadok Perspectives* 125, Summer 2014
6. http://www.bsl.org.au/fileadmin/user_upload/files/media_releases/MyChanceOurFuture%20Media%20Release2014.pdf
7. Used with kind permission of the Brotherhood of St Laurence, Fitzroy, Vic. 2016, *Australia's Youth Unemployment Hotspots: Snapshot March 2016* http://library.bsl.org.au/jspui/bitstream/1/9004/1/BSL_Aust_youth_unemployment_hotspots_Mar2016.pdf on pages 3 and 4. Regional unemployment rates figures estimated using 12-month averages (i.e. Feb 2015 to Jan 2016). Source: ABS 2016, Labour force status by region (ASGS SA4), sex and age, datacube RM1.Many of these young people will be cast on the mercy of their parents, friends, or the

streets, for the first month of unemployment, then consigned to long-term adult-escence, making the 2014 Treasurer Joe Hockey's labelling self-fulfilling. Some of the Productivity Commission's proposals will also only exacerbate the situation of the casual youth precariat through reduced penalty rates for Sunday work.

8. The International Labour Organisation's *Global Employment Trends for Youth 2015* gives a comprehensive overview and in Ch. 4 "Youth transitions and labour market" provides a helpful paradigm of transitions. http://www.ilo.org/wcmsp5/groups/public/---dgreports/---dcomm/---publ/documents/publication/wcms_412015.pdf

9. http://library.bsl.org.au/jspui/bitstream/1/7151/1/BSL_Paying_a_price_young_joblessness_2015.pdf

10. *Working Faithfully?* Report summary www.eauk.org/snapshot. Accessed Jan 19, 2015.

11. Michael Greene, *A Way Out of No Way*, Eugene OR: Cascade, 2014, vii and back cover. Cf. pp. 22–23.

12. Greene, *A Way Out of No Way*, 27, 29.

13. *The Economist*, 18th January 2014, 23–26.

14. See Robert J. Samuelson, "Automation, Robotization, Computerization and Permanent Job Loss", http://paxonbothhouses.blogspot.com/2013/07/automation-robotization-software.html

15. For example, Don Thompson in a personal email suggests churches could stimulate interest in reform by acknowledging that many of their assets are exempt from municipal rates, and volunteering to contribute an amount equal to the exempted rate to a mutual enterprise established for reconciliation and community rebuilding purposes. This challenges churches to contribute more to the community and also pre-empts attacks on church tax exemptions. But it ignores the enormous amounts of social capital already contributed by churches as shown by Deloittes/Access Economics and being explored further by a religious coalition including Christian Research Association, Australian Catholic University, and other religious groups.

16. Gordon Preece, "Sewage Problems in Sydney", in 1990 Anglican Social Justice Statement on the Environment.

17. For more on WorkVentures and Malabar Anglican Parish see Gordon Preece, *Changing Work Values*, (Brunswick: Acorn, 1995), especially ch. 2.

18. "A transition town is a grassroots community project . . . to build resilience in response to peak oil, climate destruction, and economic instability". Founded in 2006 at Totnes UK, it exemplifies "fiscal localism" in a time of glocalisation, or local alternatives to global problems including many in Australia. http://en.wikipedia.org/wiki/Transition_town. See Rob Hopkins, *The Transition Handbook: From Oil Dependency to Local Resilience* (Green Books: 2008). Former Zadok editor Janet Down is President of Maroondah Transition Town http://ttm.org.au/contact-us/ . Francis Schaeffer's prophetic 1970 book *Pollution and the Death of Man* (Wheaton: Crossway, 1992) encourages us to be co-belligerents with those holding different presuppositions. Theologian Tim Gorringe of Exeter University is heading a research project examining the values and assumptions of the Transition movement and the extent of compatibility and potential partnership with Christianity. http://humanities.exeter.ac.uk/theology/news/title_129056_en.html

19. My forthcoming *Moth and Rust Consume: Christ, Wealth and Chronic Financial Crises* tackles this.

20. Gordon Preece, "Parish or Perish: The Church as a Community in the Community", *Southern Cross*, July 1987, 8–10.

21. The great Swedish Lutheran theologian Gustav Wingren notes that a parish "is a combination

22. Lesslie Newbigin, *The Good Shepherd: Meditations on Christian Ministry in Today's World* (Oxford: Mowbray, 1977), "The Role of the Parish in Society", 85–87.

23. Newbigin, "Parish", 88–89. Cf. L. Newbigin, "On Being the Church for the World" in Giles Ecclestone ed. *The Parish Church?* (Oxford: Mowbray, 1988), 25–42 especially p. 42 where he describes a kind of local ecumenical accepting of one another despite divisions and misunderstandings which "is the Catholic Church in that place trying to erect the sign of the Kingdom for that place. These two things are mutually involved . . . I do not think we shall recover the true form of the parish until we recover a truly missionary approach to our culture" nor "a truly missionary encounter with our culture without recovering the true form of the parish" as being from and for its local community. He opposes this locational, parish model to the associational model based on shared interests.
Distinguished sociologist David Martin's "A Cross-Bench View of Associational Religion" is sharply critical of Newbigin and other defenders of the "communitarian" parish model versus the associational one. But he actually prefers the parish (p.51). "Although there are so many social trends moving against 'the parish'" it has strengths such as networks of charity and the arts, including a non-utilitarian, aesthetic architecture, linking in with the social networks of the parish. Some of his comments now sound outdated but he is right in saying: "People are still in some ways *located*; whatever social and geographical mobility does to them, many people retain a sense of place . . . of origin . . . of continuity . . . social and geographical mobility is not so peculiar to our time as we think it is; [it] goes back several hundred years. So it is in 'place' the continuities are sought and still maintained".

24. Glen Hohnberg, "Rethinking Reaching Australia, Part I", *Essentials*, Autumn, 2014. http://www.efac.org.au/index.php?option=com_content&view=article&id=462&Itemid=509. For Hohnberg "Our working life dictates relationships" and we are "Busy and more disconnected from where we live than ever before".

25. I'm on the Theology of Work board (www.theologyofwork.org) and theologian for the Lausanne Congress of World Evangelisation Marketplace Ministry stream and main author of its book *Marketplace Ministry* (www.lausanne.org).

26. Andrew Davidson and Alison Milbank, *For the Parish: A Critique of Fresh Expressions* (London: SCM, 2010). A helpful summary by Alison Milbank is on http://www.abc.net.au/religion/articles/2011/03/22/3170655.htm. Accessed Jan 21, 2015.

27. Locally I have seen both these things happening: first at Mt Evelyn Christian School where kids on their last chance in the school system, who had left in year 11 for TAFE, were brought back at graduation to be celebrated along with their cohort. The school helped found a Christian TAFE called Rangers in the Lilydale-Croydon high youth unemployment area. Second, at SouthPort Uniting Care, one of four only remaining parish partnerships or missions in Victoria, the Bolt Project for repairing bikes at school pairs mentors with socially and educationally challenged young people at risk of dropping out. Attendance and behaviour have benefitted.

28. John Milbank, "The Big Society Depends on the Big Parish", ABC Religion and Ethics Online, 30 Nov 2010, http://www.abc.net.au/religion/articles/2010/11/30/3080680.htm

29. Paul Sparks, Tim Soerens and Dwight J. Friesen, *The New Parish: How Neighborhood Churches Are Transforming Mission, Discipleship and Community* (Downers Grove, IL: IVP, 2014), 47.

30. http://journalofmissionalpractice.com/index.php/d-cronshaw

31. See Michael Frost and Alan Hirsch's seminal *The Shaping of Things To Come: Innovation and Mission for the 21st Century Church* (Peabody MA, Hendrickson, 2003), 41–42. While rightly stressing incarnational mission it leaves out a mediating missing piece in their binary opposition of incarnational and attractional models. That is commitment to a shared place or parish where people can share each other's stories. Frost's *Small Boat, Big Sea* church community seems to practise this commitment to place in a way that nuances their stark contrast of the two approaches. So does ch. 7 "The Risk of Neighbourliness" of their *The Faith of Leap*, (Grand Rapids: Baker, 2011) where they kindly cite my "Parish or Perish" and Marcus Curnow's helpful "Missionary Grow Home!" *Zadok Papers*, S167, Autumn 2009. Further, the example of Ruth that Frost and Hirsch use in *The Shaping* is profoundly attractional (in both a broader sense than Hirsch and Frost's critique of programmatic, come-to-us churches and in an erotic sense). The widow Ruth finds in Israel and Boaz a community and a kinsman-Redeemer who practises the grace of the gleaning laws (a biblical basis for the commons) and takes her under its and his wing. See Gordon Preece, "How Not To Be Ruthless at Work", *Zadok Perspectives* 90, Autumn, 2006; *Faith in Business Quarterly*, Dec. 2006.
32. http://journalofmissionalpractice.com/index.php/d-cronshaw.
33. Kosuke Koyama, *Three Mile an Hour God (Marymount, NY: Orbis), 1980.*
34. See my "Vocation in a Vocation-less World: The Meaning, De-Meaning and Re-Meaning of Work", in Gordon Preece and Simon Holt ed., *The Bible and the Business of Life* (Hindmarsh SA: ATF Press, 2004), 192–215 citing Simone Weil, *The Need for Roots: Prelude to a Declaration of Duties Towards Mankind* (London: Routledge Classics, 2001).
35. *Facing Leviathan,* (Chicago: Moody, 2014), 216.
36. Joseph Schumpeter's concept from *Capitalism, Socialism and Democracy* (1942), developed from reading Marx.
37. *Facing Leviathan,* 217–18.
38. See on various church actions http://www.pbs.org/wnet/religionandethics/2005/09/02/september-2-2005-hurricane-katrina-faith-based-relief-efforts/12722/ . For broader evidence in other places in the US, particularly Philadelphia see R.A. Cnaan, (2009) "Valuing the Contribution of Urban Religious Congregations", *Public Management Review* 11(5): 641–62.
39. John Millbank, *After Virtue: A Study in Moral Theory*, 2nd ed. (Notre Dame, IN: University of Notre Dame Press, 1984), 263. For a discerning critique see Samuel Goldman, http://www.theamericanconservative.com/articles/what-would-jeremiah-do/ subtitled "What Jewish History Can Teach Christians Today about Avoiding Cultural Secession", August 13, 2014. Cf. former UK Chief Rabbi Jonathon Sacks' 2013 Erasmus Lecture. http://www.firstthings.com/article/2014/01/on-creative-minorities.
40. http://www.geraldschlabach.net/the-vow-of-stability/.
41. Stanley Hauerwas, *In Good Company: The Church as Polis* (Notre Dame, IN: 1995), 26, 73.
42. Cf. J.K.A. Smith, *Desiring the Kingdom, Worship, Worldview, and Cultural Formation* (Cultural Liturgies) (Grand Rapids: Baker Academic, 2009), 211.
43. See Dietrich Bonhoeffer, *Life Together* (London: SCM, 1954), "Community". Bonhoeffer's own fleeing to the US, for apparently good reasons, nonetheless perhaps came to be seen by him as a violation of his own vow of stability, a violation he quickly reversed.
44. Stanley Hauerwas, *The Peaceable Kingdom: A Primer in Christian Ethics* (Notre Dame, IND: 1983), 99.
45. Stanley Hauerwas, *After Christendom: How the Church Is To Behave if Freedom, Justice, and a Christian Nation Are Bad Ideas* (Nashville, TN: Abingdon, 1991).

46. See John Perkins, *Let Justice Roll Down* (Grand Rapids MI: Baker, 2012) for his 3Rs model based on Jesus' encounter with the Samaritan woman. Jesus *relocated*, going through Samaria; he *reconciled* Jews and Samaritans, males and females; and he *redistributed* resources of God's self-revelation and the Spirit's "living water" to the Samaritans in John 4.
47. See summary at http://www.jimcollins.com/article_topics/articles/building-companies.html.
48. "The Shaking of the House: Being the Household of God in the Midst of Dangerous Climate Change". 'E(Oi)konomics and E(Oi)cology Part I, *Zadok Papers,* Summer 2014. Cornford's movement Manna Gum has useful resources like the Household Covenant to help Christians be economically and ecologically transparent. See too Ian Barns, "E(Oi)conomics and E(Oi)cology Part III. Climate Change and the New Economy Movement: A Timely Opportunity for Christian Renewal", *Zadok Papers*, Autumn 2015. Cf. Lesslie Newbigin, *The Household of God* (London: SCM, 1953), 141.
49. http://www.christian-ecology.org.uk/cit-leaflet.pdf. See also Australian eco-missiologist and Yarraville Anglican member Dr Mick Pope, coordinator of Ethos Environment http://www.ethos.org.au/Online-Articles/Engage-Mail/Preaching-to-the-Birds.aspx and his and Claire Dawson's, *A Climate of Hope* (Dandenong: UNOH), 2014. Also go to http://hopeforcreation.com.au/ that Ethos partners in. It provides resources for churches and a pledge for personal and political action.
50. Zygmunt Bauman's *Liquid Modernity* (Cambridge UK: Polity, 2000) is the first in a stimulating series of "Liquid" books exploring the fluid social software of today's global postmodern, post-industrial capitalism compared with the hardware of modern, factory, place-based capitalism

Contemporary Spirituality and Mission

1. The data is from A. Evans, *The Australian Survey of Social Attitudes* (Canberra: Australian Social Science Data Archives, 2009).
2. David Tacey, *The Spiritual Revolution: The Emergence of Contemporary Spirituality* (Sydney: Harper Collins, 2003).
3. David Voas and Steve Bruce, "The Spiritual Revolution: Another False Dawn for the Sacred", in *A Sociology of Spirituality*, ed. Kieran Flanagan and Peter C. Jupp (Aldershot, UK: Ashgate, 2007).
4. Voas and Bruce, "The Spiritual Revolution", 57.
5. J. Carrette and R. King, *Selling Spirituality: The Silent Takeover of Religion* (London: Routledge, Taylor and Francis, 2005), 41.
6. Carrette and King, *Selling Spirituality*, 15.
7. Paul Heelas and Linda Woodhead, *The Spiritual Revolution: Why Religion Is Giving Way to Spirituality* (Oxford, UK: Blackwell Publishing, 2005).
8. Anthony Giddens, *Modernity and Self-Identity: Self and Society in the Late Modern Age* (Stanford, CA: Stanford University Press, 1991).
9. Peter Berger, Brigette Berger, and Hansfried Kellner, *The Homeless Mind* (London, UK: Pelican, 1974).
10. Philip J. Hughes, Stephen Reid, and Margaret Fraser, *Australia's Religious Communities: Facts and Figures* (Melbourne: Christian Research Association 2012), 74.
11. Antoon Geels, "Glocal Spirituality for a Brave New World", in *Postmodern Spirituality*, ed. Tore Ahlback and Bjorn Dahla (Abo, Finland: Donner Institute for Research in Religious and Cultural History, 2009).

12. Peter Kaldor, Philip J. Hughes, and Alan Black, *Spirit Matters: How Making Sense of Life Affects Wellbeing* (Melbourne: Mosaic, 2010).
13. Heelas and Woodhead, *A Spiritual Revolution*, loc. 474.
14. Heelas and Woodhead, *A Spiritual Revolution*, loc. 927.
15. Karen Armstrong, *A History of God* (London, UK: Random House, 1993).
16. See, for example, Harvey Cox, *Fire from Heaven: The Rise of Pentecostal Spirituality and the Reshaping of Religion in the Twenty-First Century* (Cambridge, MA: Da Capo, 1995); and Sam Hey, *Australian Megachurches: Origins, Ministry and Prospects* (Melbourne: Mosaic, 2013).
17. Philip J. Hughes, *Putting Life Together: Findings from Australian Youth Spirituality Research* (Melbourne: Fairfield, 2007) 75–88.
18. Philip J. Hughes, *Spiritual Capital: An Important Asset of Workplace and Community?* Occasional Research Papers 8 (Melbourne: Christian Research Association 2008).
19. Philip J. Hughes, "Opening the Doors: Teenage Participation in Local Churches", *Pointers* 23, no. 3 (2013), 1–4.

Two Streams Converging

1. Robert Raikes (1736–1811), an Anglican layman, pioneered the Sunday School Movement as an aspect of the ministry of the church during the late eighteenth century. It helped establish the idea of universal, free education in England, and set a pattern for Sunday School focused around basic Christian instruction in the biblical text.

Transforming Expectations

1. Graham Hill, *Salt, Light and a City: Introducing Missional Ecclesiology*, (Eugene, OR: Wipf & Stock, 2012) 199–200. The term "eschatological community of salvation" is drawn from Hans Küng, *The Church* (London: Search, 1968), especially pages 96–103.
2. John V. Taylor, *The Go-Between God: The Holy Spirit and the Christian Mission* (London: SCM, 1972), 72–81.
3. Findley B. Edge, *The Greening of the Church* (Waco, TX: Word Books, 1971), 37.
4. Timothy George, *Theology of the Reformers* (Nashville, TN: Broadman Press, 1988), 95.
5. Jürgen Moltmann, *Theology of Hope: On the Ground and Implications of a Christian Eschatology* (London, UK: SCM, 1967), 330.
6. George, *Theology of the Reformers*, 95–98.
7. George, *Theology of the Reformers*, 95 and 96.
8. The argument that follows is explored in various aspects in Frank D. Rees, "The Worship of All Believers", *Baptist Quarterly*, 41 (July 2005), 175–89, and Frank D. Rees, "A Conversational Theology for a Conversational Church", *Asia Journal of Theology*, 21, no.1 (April 2007), 32–49.
9. Philip J. Rosato, "The Mission of the Spirit within and beyond the Church", *Ecumenical Review*, 41, no.3 (1989), 388–97; and Bradford Hinze, (ed.) *The Spirit in the Church and the World*, Catholic Theological Society Annual Volume 49 (Maryknoll, NY: Orbis, 2004).
10. Rosato, "The Mission of the Spirit within and beyond the Church".
11. Rees, "A Conversational Theology for a Conversational Church", 44 and 45.
12. Rees, "New Perspectives in Australian Spirituality: Sabbath beyond the Church", *Colloquium*, 47, no.1 (May 2015) 75-88.

Re: Baptism

1. "Baptism and Church Membership", BUNSW, accessed June 11, 2009, http://baptistnsw.asn. au/_Media/baptism_and_church_membersh.pdf., 1.
2. John Hammett, *Biblical Foundations for Baptist Churches: A Contemporary Ecclesiology* (Grand Rapids, MI: Kregel Publications, 2005), 57.
3. BUNSW generally practised open membership in its earliest days, followed by a closed membership, until 1995 when local churches were given the opportunity to decide for themselves. It must also be acknowledged that there are some churches within the BUNSW who have already changed to a more open membership.
4. "Church Constitution Template", BUNSW, accessed May 28, 2009, http://admin.baptistnsw.asn. au/church_constitution/constitution_template_05-de.doc., 4.
5. "What Do Baptists Believe?" BUNSW, accessed May 22, 2009, http://www.baptistnsw.asn.au/ what_do_baptists_believe.html. It is also declared in the statement of beliefs in *Schedule A* (no.8) of the *Baptist Union Incorporation Act* (1919) that one of the doctrines of the Baptist church in NSW is "The baptism of believers only by immersion". This may also have legal implications for open membership, particularly in a church meeting on property affected by the *Baptist Churches of NSW Property Trust Act* (1984) which includes the same *Schedule A*. cf. Geoffrey Moore, "Baptist Church Membership: Reports Presented to the 1994 and 1995 Baptist Union Annual Assemblies". http://baptistnsw.asn.au/_Media/church_membership.pdf., 11.
6. John Tyler, *Baptism: We've Got It Right and Wrong: What Baptists Must Keep, What We Must Change, and Why* (Macon, GA: Smyth & Helwys, 2003), 81.
7. H. Leon McBeth, *The Baptist Heritage* (Nashville, TN: Broadman, 1987) 64.
8. McBeth, *The Baptist Heritage*, 64.
9. William Lumpkin, *Baptist Confessions of Faith* (Valley Forge, PN: Judson Press, 1974), 297.
10. Tyler, *Baptism*, 79.
11. Thorwald Lorenzen, "Baptists and Ecumenicity", *The Ecumenical Review* (1980), 269.
12. Ken Manley, *From Woolloomooloo to 'Eternity': A History of Australian Baptists. Volume 1 "Studies in Baptist History and Thought"*, (Milton Keynes, UK: Paternoster, 2006), 11.
13. Manley, *From Woolloomooloo to 'Eternity'*, 10.
14. "NCLS Occasional Paper 8 — Inflow and Outflow between Denominations: 1991 to 2001", *National Church Life Survey*, Sam Sterland, Ruth Powell, and Keith Castle, accessed May 23, 2009, http://www.ncls.org.au/download/doc3869/NCLS%20Occasional%20Paper%208%20 -%20Inflow%20and%20Outflow%20between%20denominations.pdf.
15. Sharon Bond, "Now and Then: Finding a New Spirituality", *Christian Research Association* (n.d.), accessed May 23, 2009, http://www.cra.org.au/pages/00000070.cgi.
16. "NCLS Occasional Paper", 8.
17. Tyler, *Baptism*, 3.
18. Lorenzen, "Baptists and Ecumenicity", 269.
19. Tyler recounts an "observer reporting that he [Smyth] baptised himself by pouring, one observer reporting that Smyth 'cast water upon himself'; he then baptised Helwys and about forty others". Tyler continues to note: "Immersion would not become the mode of baptism among Baptists for another generation". Tyler, *Baptism*, 79–80.
20. G. Todd Wilson, "Why Baptists Should Not Rebaptize Christians", in *Proclaiming the Baptist Vision: Baptism and the Lord's Supper*, ed. Walter B. Shurden, (Macon, GA: Smyth and Helwys, 1999), 42.

21. John Briggs, "A Historical Introduction", in *Believing and Being Baptized: Baptism, So Called Re-Baptism, and Children in the Church* (Didcot, UK: Baptist Union of Great Britain, 1996), 4.
22. David Wright, "Christian Baptism: Where Do We Go from Here?" *Evangelical Quarterly* 78, no. 2 (2006), 166–67. Luther makes a similar complaint regarding Anabaptists. He challenges them "to say whether they accepted that there had been no Christian baptism for some 1500 years and consequently no Christian church" (Wright, *What Has Infant Baptism Done to Baptism?* 11).
23. Wayne Stacey, "A Baptist Theology of Baptism", in *Proclaiming the Baptist Vision: Baptism and the Lord's Supper*, ed. Walter Shurden, (Macon, GA: Smyth & Helwys, 1999), 104. This appears to have been the motivation from the beginnings of the Baptist churches as "Smyth's most basic concern may not have been for baptism but for a pure church" — Susan Woods, *One Baptism: Ecumenical Dimensions of the Doctrine of Baptism* (Collegeville, MN: Liturgical Press, 2009), 82.
24. Tyler, *Baptism*, 81.
25. David Wright, *What Has Infant Baptism Done to Baptism? An Enquiry at the End of Christendom* (Milton Keynes, UK: Paternoster, 2005), 83ff.
26. Stacey, "A Baptist Theology of Baptism", 93.
27. Stacey, "A Baptist Theology of Baptism", 105.
28. Stacey, "A Baptist Theology of Baptism", 107.
29. Anthony Cross, *Baptism and the Baptists* (Carlisle, UK: Paternoster Press, 2000), 30.
30. Lorenzen, *"Baptists and Ecumenicity"*, 269.
31. George Beasley-Murray, *Baptism in the New Testament*, (London, UK: Macmillan, 1973), 387–88.
32. "What Do Baptists Believe?"
33. Cf. Beasley-Murray, *Baptism in the New Testament*, 279.
34. Wilson, "Why Baptists Should not Rebaptize Christians", 42.
35. Wright, "Christian Baptism", 165.
36. Ben Witherington III, *Troubled Waters: Rethinking the Theology of Baptism* (Waco, TX: Baylor University Press, 2007), 128.
37. Wright, "Christian Baptism", 163.
38. Douglas Wilson, *To a Thousand Generations: Infant Baptism — Covenant Mercy to the Children of God* (Moscow, ID: Canon Press, 1996), 101–108.
39. Lumpkin, *Baptist Confessions of Faith*, 167.
40. Christopher Ellis, *Believing and Being Baptised: Baptism, So-Called Re-Baptism, and the Children of the Church* (Didcot, UK: Baptist Union of Great Britain, 1996), 11.
41. Witherington, *Troubled Waters*, 34.
42. Leon Morris, *The Gospel According to Matthew* (Grand Rapids, MI: Eerdmans, 1992), 65.
43. Wilson, *To a Thousand Generations*, 109.
44. Wright, "Christian Baptism", 163–64.
45. Wilson, *To a Thousand Generations*, 101.
46. Roy Henson, "Baptist Beginnings". *Belconnen Baptist Church* accessed June 9, 2009, http://www.belconnenbaptist.org.au/resources/images/Baptist%20Beginnings.pdf.
47. For the purpose of this argument, the restrictions referred to here are in regard to baptism. The term "open" can be deceiving, as it would be rare for a church to have no conditions for

membership. Open membership in this case refers to a church that does not require baptism or any other rite or ritual as a requirement for membership.
48. Cross, *Baptism and the Baptists*, 38.
49. Wilson, *Why Baptists Should not Rebaptize Christians*, 45.
50. Errol Hulse, "Where I Buried the Old Errol Hulse: A Journey in Believer's Baptism", in *Why I Am a Baptist*, ed. Tom Nettles and Russell Moore, (Nashville, TN: Broadman and Holman, 2001), 83.
51. "How is Church Organised?" BUNSW, accessed June 9, 2009, http://www.baptistnsw.asn.au/how_is_church_organised.html.
52. Wilson, "Why Baptists Should not Rebaptize Christians", 45.
53. Wright, "What Has Infant Baptism Done to Baptism?" 83–84.
54. W. Payne, *The Fellowship of Believers* (London, UK: Carey Kingsgate: 1952), 82.
55. Wilson, "Why Baptists Should not Rebaptize Christians", 46.
56. Stacey, "A Baptist Theology of Baptism", 104.

The Lord's Supper as Meaning-Full Sacrament

1. Philip J. Hughes and Darren Cronshaw, *Baptists in Australia: A Church with a Heritage and a Future* (Nunawading, Vic: Christian Research Association, 2013), 39.
2. Hughes and Cronshaw, *Baptists in Australia*, 39.
3. Hughes and Cronshaw, *Baptists in Australia*, 39.
4. For example, The Baptist Union of NSW and ACT, "Statement of Beliefs", http://www.nswactbaptists.org.au/about-us/beliefs, accessed 25 Feb, 2014.
5. For example, Queensland Baptists, "Queensland Baptists Guidelines for Belief and Practice", http://www.qb.com.au/wp-content/uploads/2010/09/QB-Guidelines-for-belief-and-practice.pdf, accessed 23 Nov, 2011.
6. Qld Baptists, "Queensland Baptists Guidelines for Belief and Practice".
7. Baptist Churches of Western Australia, "Statement of Faith", http://www.baptistwa.asn.au/view/about/statement-faith, accessed 1 Nov, 2011.
8. J. N. D. Kelly, *Early Christian Doctrines* (London: Adam & Charles Black, 5th edition, 1977), 423, 424. Alister E. McGrath, *Reformation Thought* (Chichester, UK: Wiley-Blackwell, 2012), 163.
9. Alistair McGrath, *Reformation Thought*, 174.
10. Stanley K. Fowler, *More Than a Symbol: The British Baptist Recovery of Baptismal Sacramentalism* (Carlisle: Paternoster, 2002), 19.
11. "The Second London Confession of Faith," in *Baptist Confessions of Faith*, ed. William L. Lumpkin (Valley Forge: Judson, 1969), 293.
12. "The Orthodox Creed", in *Baptist Confessions of Faith*, ed. William L. Lumpkin (Valley Forge: Judson, 1969), 321.
13. E.P. Winter, "Calvinist and Zwinglian Views of the Lord's Supper among the Baptists of the Seventeenth Century", *Baptist Quarterly* 15, no. 7 (1954), 324.
14. David W. Bebbington, *Baptists through the Centuries: A History of a Global People* (Waco, TX: Baylor University Press, 2010), 185.
15. Bebbington, *Baptists through the Centuries*, 186.

16. Bebbington, *Baptists through the Centuries*, 186–87.
17. David W. Bebbington, *Evangelicalism in Modern Briitain: A History from the 1730s to the 1980s* (London: Routledge, 1989), 80, 81.
18. Bebbington, *Baptists through the Centuries*, 188. See also Ken Manley, *From Woolloomooloo to "Eternity": A History of Australian Baptists. Volume 1. Growing an Australian Church (1831–1914)* (Milton Keynes : Paternoster, 2006), 200, 204, 423ff.
19. See, for example, C.H. Spurgeon, "Another Word Concerning the Downgrade", in *A Sourcebook for Bapitst Heritage*, ed. H. Leon McBeth (Nashville, TN: Broadman & Holman, 1990), 200.
20. Fowler, *More Than a Symbol*, 87, emphases in original. This idea was particularly promulgated by William Whitley (1861–1947), first principal of the Victorian Baptist College, who, regarding the Lord's Supper, went as far as to criticise *The Second London Confession* for its "sacramentarian heresy". Manley, *Woolloomooloo to "Eternity"*, 1:249, 285.
21. James Wm. McClendon, *Ethics*, Systematic Theology Vol. 1 (Nashville, TE: Abingdon, 1994), 30, 33, emphasis in original. In fact McClendon actually practises a significant degree of engagement with the Baptist tradition.
22. Martin Sutherland, "Gathering, Sacrament and Baptist Theological Method", *Pacific Journal of Baptist Research* 3, no. 2 (2007), 55–56.
23. Sutherland, "Gathering", 55, 56.
24. Sutherland, "Gathering", 56; Paul S. Fiddes, *Tracks and Traces: Baptist Identity in Church and Theology*, (Carlisle: Paternoster, 2003).
25. Fiddes, *Tracks and Traces*, 1.
26. Fiddes, *Tracks and Traces*, 1.
27. Sutherland, "Gathering", 41.
28. Paul S. Fiddes, "'Walking Together': The Place of Covenant Theology in Baptist Life Yesterday and Today", in *Pilgrim Pathways: Essays in Baptist History in Honour of B.R. White*, ed. William H. Brackney and Paul S. Fiddes (Macon, Georgia: Mercer University Press, 1999), 47.
29. See Stanley K. Fowler, "Is 'Baptist Sacramentalism' an Oxymoron?: Reactions in Britain to *Christian Baptism* (1959)", in *Baptist Sacramentalism*, ed. Anthony R. Cross and Philip E. Thompson (Milton Keynes: Paternoster, 2003), 129–150.
30. John Colwell, *Promise and Presence: An Exploration in Sacramental Theology* (Eugene, OR: Wipf & Stock, 2005), 28.
31. Colwell, *Promise and Presence*, 72.
32. Colwell, *Promise and Presence*, 56
33. Sutherland, "Gathering", 51.
34. See, for example, Fiddes, *Tracks and Traces*, 122–24. Sutherland, "Gathering", 46.
35. James Wm. McClendon, *Doctrine*, Systematic Theology Vol. 2 (Nashville: Abingdon, 1994), 403.
36. McClendon, *Doctrine*, 402.
37. Nigel G. Wright, *Disavowing Constantine: Mission, Church and the Social Order in the Theologies of John Howard Yoder and Jurgen Moltmann*, Paternoster Theological Monographs (Eugene, OR: Wipf & Stock, 2000), 12.

38. If the peace is shared before the Lord's Supper it might recognise the imperative of coming to the Table as a reconciled people. If the peace is shared after the Supper, it might recognise the indicative "given" of the reconciliation which is gifted in that Supper.
39. McClendon, *Doctrine*, 390.
40. Paul S. Fiddes, *Participating in God: A Pastoral Doctrine of the Trinity* (London: Darton, Longman and Todd, 2000), 281.
41. Brian Haymes, "The Moral Miracle of Faith", in *Dimensions of Baptism: Biblical and Theological Studies*, ed. Stanley E. Porter and Anthony R. Cross, *Journal for the Study of the New Testament Supplement Series* (Sheffield, UK: Sheffield Academic Press, 2002), 328. Haymes' original statement is made in relation to baptism, but is, as his allusion to the cross indicates, equally applicable to the Lord's Supper.
42. Haymes, "The Moral Miracle of Faith", 330.
43. Robert Banks, *Paul's Idea of Community: The Early House Churches in Their Historical Setting* (Peabody: Hendrickson, 1994), 83.
44. James D.G. Dunn, *Beginning from Jerusalem*, Christianity in the Making Vol. 2 (Grand Rapids, MI: Eerdmans, 2009), 816.
45. Ben Witherington, *Making a Meal of It: Rethinking the Theology of the Lord's Supper* (Waco, TX: Baylor University Press, 2007), 58, 59.
46. Carole Bailey Stoneking, "Receiving Communion: Euthanasia, Suicide, and Letting Die", in *The Blackwell Companion to Christian Ethics*, ed. Stanley Hauerwas and Samuel Wells (Malden, MA: Blackwell, 2004), 375–86.
47. Stoneking, "Receiving Communion", 376.
48. Stoneking, "Receiving Communion", 379.
49. Stoneking, "Receiving Communion", 379–80.
50. Stoneking writes of Christian hope in a general way but does not make this eschatological connection explicit.
51. The phrase comes from Hauerwas' seminal work. Stanley Hauerwas, *A Community of Character: Toward a Constructive Christian Social Ethic* (Notre Dame, IN: Notre Dame Press, 1981).
52. Brian Haymes, "Baptism as a Political Act", in *Reflections on the Water: Understanding God and the World through the Baptism of Believers*, ed. Paul S. Fiddes (Oxford: Regent's Park College, 1996), 80.
53. Suzanne McDonald, *Re-Imaging Election: Divine Election as Representing God to Others and Others to God* (Grand Rapids, MI: Eerdmans, 2010), 152.
54. McClendon, *Doctrine*, 403.
55. Anthony R. Cross, *Recovering the Evangelical Sacrament: Baptisma Semper Reformandum* (Eugene, OR: Pickwick, 2013).
56. Anthony Clarke, "A Feast for All? Reflecting on Open Communion for the Contemporary Church", in *Baptist Sacramentalism 2*, ed. Anthony R. Cross and Philip E. Thompson (Eugene: Paternoster, 2008), 99.
57. Fiddes, *Tracks and Traces*, 272.
58. Fiddes, *Tracks and Traces*, 272.
59. John Howard Yoder, *Body Politics: Five Practices of the Christian Community before the Watching World* (Scottdale: Herald, 2001), ix.

The Liturgical Participation of Children in Small Churches

1. For an excellent discussion of Christian education, see Joyce Ann Mercer, *Welcoming Children* (St Louis, MO: Chalice, 2005).
2. Scottie May et al., *Children Matter: Celebrating Their Place in the Church, Family and Community* (Grand Rapids, MI: Eerdmans, 2005).
3. David Ng and Virginia Thomas, *Children in the Worshiping Community* (Atlanta, GA: John Knox, 1981), 30.
4. See, e.g., John H. Westerhoff III, *Will Our Children Have Faith?* (New York: Seabury, 1976).
5. Barbara Rogoff, *Apprenticeship in Thinking: Cognitive Development in Social Context* (New York, Oxford: Oxford University Press, 1990).
6. Westerhoff III, *Will Our Children Have Faith?*
7. Lawrence O. Richards, *Theology of Children's Ministry* (Grand Rapids, MI: Zondervan, 1983), 76.
8. Mercer, *Welcoming Children*, 205.
9. The term "facilitators" comes from May et al., *Children Matter*.
10. Joyce Ann Mercer and Deborah L. Matthews, "Liturgical Practices with Children in Congregations", *Liturgy* 18, no. 4 (2003), 27-33.
11. Mercer, *Welcoming Children*, 171.
12. Richard A. Jensen, *Thinking in Story. Preaching in a Post-Literate Age* (Lima, OH: CSS, 1993).
13. This is, of course, the best case. For a discussion of the potentially negative formation provided by some congregations, see Mercer, *Welcoming Children*, 172ff.
14. Ivy Beckwith, *Postmodern Children's Ministry: Ministry to Children in the 21st Century Church* (Grand Rapids, MI: Zondervan, 2004), 142–43.
15. Mercer, *Welcoming Children*, 171.
16. Jerome W. Berryman, *Godly Play: A Way of Religious Education* (San Francisco: Harper San Francisco, 1991); Sonja M. Stewart and Jerome W. Berryman, *Young Children and Worship* (Louisville, KY: Westminster/John Knox, 1989).
17. Rogoff, *Apprenticeship in Thinking*.
18. Mercer, *Welcoming Children*, 171.
19. Beckwith tells a lovely story of a mother who realised her children were listening, in Beckwith, *Postmodern Children's Ministry*, 160.
20. Mercer, *Welcoming Children*, 171.
21. Beckwith, *Postmodern Children's Ministry*, 144.
22. Alison Sampson, "The Priesthood of All Believers: An Exploration of the Ministry of Children to the Church and Its Implications for Congregations", (Melbourne: Zadok, 2011).
23. Elise Boulding, "Children and the Politics of Culture", *Contemporary Sociology* 25, no. 5 (1996).
24. Richards, *Theology of Children's Ministry*.
25. Rogoff, *Apprenticeship in Thinking*.
26. So Karen-Marie Yust, *Real Kids, Real Faith* (San Francisco, CA: John Wiley, 2004), 24.

* Sections of this paper have appeared in 'Welcome the Children' in Equip no. 24 (2015) pp 4-5.and in "The Liturgical Participation of Children in Small Churches: The Theology Behind it, and How it Can be Done", in Eron Henry (ed), *Baptist Faith & Witness, Book 5: Papers of the Commission on Mission, Evangelism and Theological Reflection of the Baptist World Alliance* (Falls Church: Baptist World Alliance, 2015) p.247-256

Growing the Seeds of Emergence

1. This research was initiated as a denominational project of the Baptist Union of Victoria and was originally presented as "Training Emerging Leaders for a Life Worth Living", at ANZATS Conference, SCD, Sydney, Tuesday 30 June 2015, and to the Emerging Leaders Dreaming Group, Tuesday 14 July 2015. The larger report including interview questions and denominational recommendations is accessible at www.buv.com.au.
2. Cf. Philip J. Hughes and Darren Cronshaw, *Baptists in Australia: A Church with a Heritage and a Future* (Melbourne: Christian Research Association, 2013), 82.
3. BUV database, 2015. 309 out of 503 pastors, or 61%, have birth date recorded.
4. Mark McCrindle, *The ABC of XYZ: Understanding the Global Generations* (Bella Vista: McCrindle Research, 2013), 2; cf. http://www.buv.com.au/docman/doc_download/2254-abc-of-xyz-for-buv-and-cald-churches
5. Ruth Powell and Nicole Hancock, "Giving Newcomers a Voice: What Newcomers Reveal about Their Experience of Joining a Church", NCLS Research Report (Sydney: NCLS Research, 2014).
6. Darren Cronshaw, Ruth Powell, Glen Powell, Nicole Hancock and Stacey Wilson, "Churches that Inspire and Empower: A Case Study Survey of the Baptist Union of Victoria", *Australian eJournal of Theology* 21, no. 3 (Dec 2014), 229–30 (212–233), http://aejt.com.au/2014/volume_21/vol_21_no_3_2014/?article=695189.
7. Sam Hearn, Director Surrender, Interview 22 April 2015.
8. Andreana Reale, Urban Seed, "Urban Studies Centre" manager, Interview, 20 April 2015.
9. Beth Barnett, Coordinator, Victorian Council of Christian Education, Interview, 21 April 2015.
10. Gemma Bell, Fusion International trainer and mentor, Interview, 20 April 2015.
11. Hearn, Interview.
12. Simon Burnett, Pastor Kyneton Baptist, Interview, 5 May 2015.
13. Benjamin Watson, G3 Key Leader Crossway Baptist Church, Interview, 12 May 2015.
14. Robert Banks, *Re-envisioning Theological Education: Exploring a Missional Alternative to Current Models* (Grand Rapids, MI: Eerdmans, 1999); discussed in Darren Cronshaw, "Re-envisioning Theological Education, Mission and the Local Church", *Mission Studies* 28, no. 1 (June 2011), 92–99, 104–110 (91–115).
15. Mang Hre, Associate Pastor, Victorian Chin Baptist Church, Interview, 17 June 2015.
16. Burnett, Interview.
17. Andy Mitchell, Youth and Young Adult Pastor, Beaumaris Baptist Church, Interview, 22 April 2015.
18. Reale, Interview.
19. Tim Devlin, G3 leader Crossway Baptist Church, Interview, 12 May 2015.
20. Rowan Lewis, Coordinator Next, Interview, 29 April 2015.
21. Barnett, Interview.
22. Gavin Brown, Lead Youth Pastor, Crossway Baptist Church, Interview, 12 May 2015.
23. Watson, Interview.
24. Bell, Interview.
25. Mia Kafieris, Next Coordinator, Interview, 29 April 2015.
26. Mitchell, Interview.

27. Simon Burnett, Pastor, Kyneton Baptist Church, Interview, 5 May 2015.
28. Watson, Interview.
29. Lewis, Interview.
30. Steve Echols, "Transformational/Servant Leadership: A Potential Synergism for an Inclusive Leadership Style", *Journal of Religious Leadership* 8, no.2, Fall (2009), 85–116.
31. "Bridging the Gap: An Employer's Guide to Managing and Retaining the New Generation of Employees" (McCrindle Research), 18, http://www.mccrindle.com.au/resources/whitepapers/Bridging-the-Gap_EMPLOYERS.pdf
32. Previously discussed in Cronshaw *et al*, "Churches that Inspire and Empower (BUV)", 213–14.
33. Steve Echols, "Transformational/Servant Leadership", 85–116.
34. James Penner, Rachael Harder, Erika Anderson, Bruno Désorcy, and Rick Hiemstra, *Haemorrhaging Faith: Why & When Canadian Young Adults Are Leaving, Staying & Returning to Church* (Research Document, Commissioned by The EFC Youth and Young Adult Ministry Roundtable, 2011), 72. This report can be obtained from http://hemorrhagingfaith.com/ [accessed 22 April 2016].
35. Baptist Union of Victoria Leader Contact Database, 2015.
36. On two occasions, at different churches, Stacey has been asked not to accept a diaconate nomination. On the first occasion it was because she was a mother of primary-school-aged children, and on the second because she would put the leadership team on an unbalanced ratio of 3:1 women to men, despite the fact that the previous team had the same 3:1 ratio but male to female. On both occasions it was made clear that it wasn't Stacey's leadership skills that were the issue.
37. Private conversation used with permission.
38. Kafieris, Interview.
39. Steve Rabey, *In Search of Authentic Faith: How Emerging Generations Are Transforming Church* (Colorado: Waterbrook, 2001), 29–30.
40. Barnett, Interview.
41. Hre, Interview.
42. Meewong Yang, BUV Multicultural Minister, Interview, 15 June 2015; cf. Darren Cronshaw, Stacey Wilson and Meewon Yang, with Ner Dah, Si Khia, Arohn Kuung, and Japheth Lian. "'God Called Us Here for a Reason' … Karen and Chin Baptist Churches in Victoria: Mission from the Margins of a Diaspora Community." In *We Are Pilgrims: Mission from, in and with the Margins of Our Diverse World*, edited by Darren Cronshaw and Rosemary Dewerse (Melbourne: UNOH, 2015), 263–78.
43. Seung Taek Lee, Pastoral team member, City Baptist Church, Interview, 16 June 2015.
44. Soong-Chan Rah, *The Next Evangelicalism: Freeing the Church from Western Cultural Captivity* (Downers Grove, IL: IVP, 2009), 162; reviewed by Robyn Song and Darren Cronshaw in *International Journal of Practical Theology*, 16, no.1 (2012), 169–70.
45. Bell, Interview.
46. Leanne Hill, Lead Youth Pastor Crossway Baptist Church, Interview, 12 May 2015.
47. Mitchell, Interview.
48. Merryn James, Children and Families Pastor, Crossway Baptist Church, Interview, 12 May 2015.
49. Lewis, Interview.
50. Hearn, Interview.

51. Mitchell, Interview.
52. Bell, Interview.
53. Julian Dunham, Director, Emerging Leaders, Arrow Australia, Interview, 1 June 2015.
54. Reale, Interview.
55. Reale, Interview.
56. Hearn, Interview.
57. Janet Woodlock, Federal Coordinator, Churches of Christ Australia, Interview, 29 May 2015.

The Trinity and the Ontology of Worship

1. No better analysis of these trends can be found than in the incisive critiques of contemporary worship culture by Marva Dawn in *Royal Waste of Time: The Splendor of Worshipping God and Being Church for the World*, (Grand Rapids, MI: Eerdmans, 1999) and *Reaching Out without Dumbing Down*, (Grand Rapids, MI: Eerdmans, 1995) — whose comments continue to disturb and divide US pragmatists today though mostly directed at seeker sensitive or attractional churches.
2. Some argue this streak stems from the influence of the widely circulated writings of English Calvinist Whitfield who embraced the new technology of mass media and the mood of the times. Keeping current with technological shifts became a deep drive within both US culture and simultaneously evangelicalism from early times in the New World. P.C. Hoffer, *When Benjamin Franklin Met the Reverend Whitfield: Enlightenment, Revival and the Printed Word*, Witness to History Series, (Baltimore, MD: John Hopkins University Press, 2011).
3. See Charles Grandison Finney, *Lectures on Revivals of Religion*, (Alethia in the Heart Publications, 2005) (reprint of 1834-35 editions). Here in striking Pelagian fashion Finney promotes what his experience had proven that the conditions of exceptional revival can be constructed by human participants in a manner analogous to any human science and at any time.
4. John Jefferson Davis, *Worship and the Reality of God: An Evangelical Theology of the Real Presence* (Downers Grove, IL: IVP, 2010), 237f.
5. Kathleen Tanner, *Christ the Key* (Cambridge, UK: Cambridge University Press,, 2010), 207–246.
6. In fact from patristic times Trinitarian theologians such as Athanasius apportion the paucity of human awareness and appreciation of the divine to *both* the problem of sin aligning itself with our own 'ontological poverty' as finite creatures. Sin misdirects our worship so that, being mutable creatures, the inevitable and perpetual drift toward 'non-being' is irreversible without the interruption of salvation. Creatures are given the worship deserved only by the Creator and the result is the degradation of the worshipper. G. Hiestand "Not Just Forgiven: How Athanasius Overcomes the Under-Realised Eschatology of Evangelicalism" *Evangelical Quarterly* 84, no.1 (2012), 47–66.
7. In fact this prompted Barth to believe that worship was actually that place where sinners came to hold out against God's rule in a last ditch stand!
8. P. Roenfeldt, *The Impact of Church Growth and Emerging Missional Church on Evangelical Ecclesiology in Australia*, Doctor of Ministry thesis, Australian College of Theology, 2014.
9. Karl Barth, *Church Dogmatics* 1/1, Edinburgh, 1936, 98.
10. There are clear parallels with modernist disregard for and the postmodernist disavowal of preaching. The desacralising of worship parallels the misunderstanding and devaluation of the preaching event in worship in the contemporary suburban setting, called the shift toward the

audience that was recognised by Fred Craddock and others in the 1980s. In the emergent setting of the 2000s this disregard shifts to a disavowal as this act is simply undemocratic and for that it should be suspended or radically restructured to involve more voices than the clerical (See J. Mclure, *Otherwise Preaching: A Postmodern Ethic for Homiletics* (St Louis: Chalice 2001), and L. Atkinson Rose, *Sharing the Word: Preaching in the Roundtable Church* (Louisville: WJKP, 1997). It is becoming more important to speak than to hear. While there is some merit to a shift away from clericalism it is also true to say that contemporary views of preaching within either species of church are simply the outworking of the ontological reduction of level 1 activity into level 3 experience. As the sacraments are appreciated just for their educative potential or as tangible gospel illustrations, so the preaching event is appreciated through the tools of trade from level 5. Sermons are appraised as more or less adequate due to their inspirational qualities like their memorability or the provision of "jaw-dropping" moments. It is no accident that the more the once-evangelical-church adopts such an ontological low horizon that appreciation of the Scriptures and the crucial nature of the preached word diminish. This reductionism has parallels in many a seminary where the purpose of pastoral training parallels secular management training. In many places homiletics has already vanished from the curriculum in favour of its secular level 3 cousin, communication theory. These attitudes reflect a two-story view of the cosmos and a one-dimensional view of history. The Word becomes spectator, spoken about in his "un-realised" absence, rather than the real and present speaker. The Spirit is separated from his book. It will take a thoroughgoing re-education program to teach evangelicals to worship the present Christ through the arts of humble listening when the presumption is that all that is happening behind the pulpit is a Ted Talk for secularized saints.

11. Likewise Paul can exert apostolic discipline though physically absent from the Corinthian worship gathering (1Cor 5:3–5) and "refrain from boasting" of eavesdropping on level 1 while in the flesh (2Cor:12.1–6) and especially pertinent to this discussion, why those who do not discern this intersection of time or the real nature of this body are liable to experience the forfeiture of health or life in this level no less (1 Cor 11:27–32) through the discipline of the present Lord (cf. Acts 5:3ff). This judgement would not be possible if God's involvement was unrealisable in the present but reserved only post Christ's parousia.

12. T S Elliot, "Little Gidding" from *Collected Poems 1909–1962* (London: Faber and Faber), 202.

Improvising a Renewed Story at AuburnLife

1. This material was originally presented at AuburnLife, 11 May 2014, 18 May 2014 (Beth Barnett), and 4 June 2014; at a Uniting Church Presbytery of Yarra Yarra conference, 12 September 2014; and co-presented with AuburnLife Sunday Stuff co-coordinator Beth Barnett at the "This is My / Our Story: Narrative and Mission in Contemporary Contexts", British and Irish Association of Practical Theology conference, Edinburgh, 15–17 July 2014. Conference travel was supported with a University of Divinity grant, and the research is part of a broader Baptist Union of Victoria project on church revitalisation supported by a Collier Charitable Grant.

2. J. R. Woodward, *Creating a Missional Culture: Equipping the Church for the Sake of the World* (Downers Grove: IVP, 2012), 37–38.

3. Woodward, *Creating a Missional Culture.*

4. Darren Cronshaw, "Imagining a Renewed Story at Auburnlife: Utilising Congregational Timelines for Congregational Transformation", in *Congregational Transformation in Australian Baptist Church Life*, ed. Darren Cronshaw and Darrell Jackson, *New Wineskins Vol.1* (Sydney: Morling Press, 2015), 135–51.

5. Woodward, *Creating a Missional Culture*, 161.

6. Woodward, *Creating a Missional Culture*, 122.
7. N. T. Wright, "How Can the Bible Be Authoritative?", (Laing Lecture 1989 and Griffith Thomas Lecture 1989) *Vox Evangelica* 21(1991); discussed in Woodward, *Creating a Missional Culture*, 163–64.
8. Wright, "How Can the Bible Be Authoritative?"; also *The New Testament and the People of God*, vol. 1, Christian Origins and the Question of God (Minneapolis: Fortress, 1992), 140–43. An understanding of the narrative of Scripture as applied to ethics is explored in Samuel Wells, *Improvisation: The Drama of Christian Ethics* (London: SPCK, 2004), 52–53. Other helpful proposals of using narrative for interpreting and imaginatively applying or performing Scripture include Francesca Aran Murphy, *The Comedy of Revelation: Paradise Lost and Regained in Biblical Narrative* (Edinburgh: T & T Clark, 2000); Kevin J. Vanhoozer, *The Drama of Doctrine: A Canonical Linguistic Approach to Christian Theology* (Louisville: Westminster John Knox, 2005).
9. Wright, "How Can the Bible Be Authoritative?"
10. Christopher J. H. Wright, *The Mission of God: Unlocking the Bible's Grand Narrative* (Nottingham: Inter-Varsity Press, 2006), 534.
11. James William McClendon Jr, *Biography as Theology: How Life Stories Can Remake Today's Theology* (Philadelphia: Trinity Press International, 1990).
12. John Millbank, *Theology and Social Theory: Beyond Secular Reason* (Oxford: Blackwell, 1991), 330; in Jonathan Chaplin, "Politics", in *Living Witness: Explorations in Missional Ethics*, ed. Amdy Draycott and Jonathan Rowe (Norton Street, Nottingham: InterVarsity Press, 2012), 205.
13. Paul S. Fiddes, "Telling the Christian Story in a Postmodern Culture", in *BWA Church and Culture Commission* (Dresden: BWA 1999), 8; cf. Paul S. Fiddes, "The Story and the Stories: Revelation and the Challenge of Postmodern Culture", in *Faith in the Centre: Christianity and Culture*, ed. Paul S. Fiddes (Oxford: Regent's Park College, 2001), 75–96.
14. Lesslie Newbigin, *The Gospel in a Pluralist Society* (Grand Rapids: Eerdmans, 1989), 47, 51. Newbigin used Michael Polyanyi's language of "dwelling in" or "indwelling" in order to "break out of" existing frameworks of thinking. Michael Polanyi, *Personal Knowledge: Towards a Post-Critical Philosophy* (London: Routledge & Kegan Paul, 1962), 194–202, 79.
15. Newbigin, *Gospel in a Pluralist Society*, 97.
16. *Gospel in a Pluralist Society*, 227; cf. Darren Cronshaw and Steve Taylor, "The Congregation in a Pluralist Society: Rereading Newbigin for Missional Churches Today", *Pacifica* 27, no. 2 (2014): 206–28.
17. Martin Sutherland, "Gathering, Sacrament and Baptist Theological Method", *Pacifica Journal of Baptist Research* 3, no. 2, October (2007): 43–44, 51–53. Taylor builds on Sutherland to reflect on the story of a local church in New Zealand and their contextualised worship: Steve Taylor, "Baptist Worshp and Contemporary Culture: A New Zealand Case Study", in *Interfaces, Baptists and Others: International Baptist Studies*, ed. David Bebbington and Martin Sutherland, *Studies in Baptist History and Thought* (Milton Keynes: Paternoster, 2013), 294–307.
18. Sutherland, "Gathering, Sacrament and Baptist Theological Method", 54.
19. "Gathering, Sacrament and Baptist Theological Method", 55.
20. One American-originated church-planting network identifies as "The Acts 29 Network", see http://www.acts29network.org/about/. I am not involved with their network, but we share similar motivations to continue and multiply the work of the church we see first recorded in Acts 1–28.

21. Adapted from Gil Rendle, *The Multigenerational Congregation: Meeting the Leadership Challenge* (Bethesda, Md: Alban Institute, 2002), 51–54, 75–76, 97–100; in Gil Rendle and Alice Mann, *Holy Conversations: Strategic Planning as a Spiritual Practice for Congregations* (Bethesda, MD: Alban Institute, 2003), 211–16.
22. Ron Martoia, *The Bible as Improv: Seeing and Living the Script in New Ways* (Grand Rapids: Zondervan, 2010).
23. Dave Male, *Pioneering Leadership: Disturbing the Status Quo?* Grove Leadership Booklet S14 (Ridley Hall, Cambridge: Grove Books, 2013), 8–9, 15, 20.
24. Beth Barnett, "Twists and Turns"; Email to Author (10 July 2014); Beth Barnett, *Twists and Turns* (Melbourne: Scripture Union, 2012).
25. Julia Rhyder and Darren Cronshaw, "Mustard Tree Aspirations (Luke 13:18–19)", *W!tness* (2014), http://www.buv.com.au/buvblog/entry/mustard-tree-aspirations-luke-13-18-19.
26. Jean Vanier, *Befriending the Stranger* (Mahwaj, NJ: Paulist, 2010), 12.
27. Woodward, *Creating a Missional Culture*, 196.
28. Sue Wallace, *Multisensory Worship* (Queensway: Scripture Union, 2002); Howard Gardner, *Multiple Intelligences: The Theory in Practice* (New York: Basic, 1993). AuburnLife often uses Beth Barnett's intergenerational resources; e.g., Beth Barnett and Keith Dyer, *Party on Together: Multi-Age Worship Resources & Bible Studies* (Melbourne: Scripture Union, 2010).
29. Inspired by Keith Dyer.
30. Brad Jackel, AuburnLife sermon, 18 January 2015.
31. Brian D. McLaren, *The Story We Find Ourselves In: Further Adventures of a New Kind of Christian* (San Francisco: Jossey-Bass, 2003).
32. Brian D. McLaren, *Everything Must Change: Jesus, Global Crises and a Revolution of Hope* (Nashville: Thomas Nelson, 2007).
33. Wright, "How Can the Bible Be Authoritative?", *Vox Evangelica* 21(1991), 22.

Printed by Libri Plureos GmbH in Hamburg, Germany